Fodor's

E X P L O R I N G

HAWAII

FODOR'S TRAVEL PUBLICATIONS, INC.

NEW YORK • TORONTO • LONDON • SYDNEY • AUCKLAND

HTTP://WWW.FODORS.COM/

Copyright © The Automobile Association 1997
Maps copyright © The Automobile Association 1997

Published in the United States by Fodor's Travel Publications, Inc.
Published in the United Kingdom by AA Publishing.

Fodor's and Fodor's Exploring Guides are registered trademarks of Fodor's Travel Publications, Inc.

ISBN 0-679-03209-6
First Edition

Fodor's Exploring Hawaii

Author: **Emma Stanford**
Joint Series Editor: **Josephine Perry**
Copy Editor: **Susan Whimster**
Original Photography: **Kirk Lee Aeder**
Cartography: **The Automobile Association**
Cover Design: **Louise Fili, Fabrizio La Rocca**
Cover photograph: **Jack Hollingsworth**

Special Sales
Fodor's Travel Publications are available at special discounts for bulk purchases (100 copies or more) for sales promotions or premiums. Special editions, including personalized covers, excerpts of existing guides, and corporate imprints, can be created in large quantities for special needs. For more information, contact your local bookseller or write to Special Markets, Fodor's Travel Publications, 201 East 50th Street, New York, NY 10022.

MANUFACTURED IN ITALY
10 9 8 7 6 5 4 3 2 1

How to use this book

This book is divided into five main sections:

❏ Section 1: *Hawaii Is*
discusses aspects of life and living today, from cultural diversity to the *hula*

❏ Section 2: *Hawaii Was*
places the Islands in their historical context and explores those past events whose influences are felt to this day

❏ Section 3: *A to Z Section*
covers places to visit, arranged by island, with suggested walks and drives. Within this section fall the Focus-on articles, which consider a variety of topics in greater detail

❏ Section 4: *Travel Facts*
contains the strictly practical information that is vital for a successful trip

❏ Section 5:
Hotels and Restaurants
lists recommended accommodations in Hawaii, giving a brief resume of what they offer

How to use the star rating
Most places described in this book have been given a separate rating:

▶▶▶ **Do not miss**

▶▶ **Highly recommended**

▶ **Worth seeing**

Not essential viewing

Map references
To make the location of a particular place easier to find, every main entry in this book is given a map reference, such as 54A2. The first number (54) indicates the page on which the map can be found; the letter (A) and the second number (2) pinpoint the square in which the main entry is located. The maps on the inside front cover and inside back cover are referred to as IFC and IBC respectively.

Contents

Quick reference	6–7
My Hawaii by Emma Stanford	8
Hawaii Is	**9–28**
Hawaii Was	**29–49**
A to Z	
Oahu	50–89
Honolulu and Waikiki	53–79
Kauai	90–108
Niihau	109
Molokai	110–121
Maui	122–145
Lahaina	126–131
Lanai	146–150
Hawaii	152–177
Hilo	156–159
Travel Facts	**179–192**

Hotels and Restaurants	**193–203**
Index	204–207
Picture credits and Acknowledgments	208

5

Quick reference

This quick-reference guide highlights the elements of the book you will use most often: the maps; the introductory features; the Focus-on articles; the walks and the drives.

Maps

The Hawaiian Islands: three-star sights	IFC
Oahu	50–51
Honolulu and Waikiki	54–55
Walk: Historic Honolulu	60
Kauai	90–91
Molokai	110–111
Maui	122–123
Walk: Around Old Lahaina	130
Lanai	146
Hawaii	152–153
The Hawaiian Islands: relief	IBC

Hawaii Is

Aloha	10–11
Cultural diversity	12–13
The *hula*	14–15
Luaus and lychees	16–17
Spectacular scenery	18–19
Plants and trees	20–21
For the birds	22–23
For golfers	24–25
Festivals and events	26–27
Hawaiian and Pidgin	28

Hawaii Was

Fire and brimstone	30–31
The Polynesians	32–33
Created by the Gods	34–35
Captain Cook	36–37

United by Kamehameha I	38–39
The whalers	40–41
The missionaries	42–43
Plantations and migrants	44–45
Reciprocity and revolution	46–47
Annexation and statehood	48–49

Focus on

Weddings in Paradise	65
Surfing	84–85
Language of the *lei*	97
The underwater world	106–107
Father Damien	116–117
Whale-watching	134–135
Hawaii's *paniolo* cowboys	144–145
Pineapples	151
Mauna Kea and the Saddle	159
Coffee and chocolate	166
Petroglyphs	170
Sport fishing	178

Walks

Historic Honolulu	60–61
Two walks around Honolulu	69
Na Pali Coast Kalalau Trail	101
Around Old Lahaina	130–131

Drives

Southern Oahu	80–81
Molokai: From Kaunakakai to the East End	120–121

Maui: The road to Hana	138–139
Hawaii: North Kohala	174–175

Travel Facts

Arriving	180–181
Essential facts	182–183
Getting around	184–185
Communications	186
Emergencies	187
Other information	188–191
Tourist offices	192

My Hawaii by Emma Stanford

The headlights bore into the darkness and an enormous halogen-bright moon rose over the massive, sleeping shoulder of Mauna Loa. Despite the illuminations, the landscape remained featureless, an enigma all but forgotten in the comfort of a luxurious oceanfront hotel complete with golden beach and emerald green gardens. The next morning I drove back down the road to Kailua-Kona, on the Big Island's leeward side, and the full drama of blackened and barren lava fields was revealed.

Hawaii is full of surprises and abrupt contrasts. These extraordinary islands far out in the mid-Pacific are as idiosyncratic as they are beautiful. A few hours after a freezing, yet spectacular, dawn on the lip of Maui's Haleakala crater, I found myself quite alone and deep in rainforest jungle positively reeling from an intoxicating cocktail of clambering up a rocky stream bed in the heat of the day and the scent of crushed, fermenting mangoes and guavas on the path. Sodden and mud-splattered from a day's hike in Kauai's Kokee State Park, I soaked in the claw-foot bath of an old plantation cottage at Waimea, and then found an obliging gardener to lop the top off a coconut which had landed on my car (bit of a dent there) so I could slurp the juice on the *lanai*, watching sunset over the Forbidden Island of Niihau.

If you come here looking for a straightforward beach holiday served up with a round of golf and several rounds of *mai-tais*, Hawaii is, as ever, happy to oblige. But look beyond your beachfront *lanai* (and I urge you to do so), and you'll find even more staggeringly beautiful vistas and, of course, the Hawaiian people, who remain the embodiment of *aloha*. The endless patience of the Molokai Visitors Bureau, and Mike the golf buggy rally driver; the laconic *paniolo* cowboy riding out one crisp, blue, upcountry morning; Mr. Kamaka, the ukelele-maker; and Debbie, the wedding specialist, all spring to mind. And the charming waitress who rugged me up with napkins when a mix-up left me luggage-less and sartorially challenged for a dinner date at the exclusive Lodge at Koele on Lanai. At 1,200 feet on a cool May evening, open fires notwithstanding, shorts and a T-shirt did little to conceal the goose bumps...

Emma Stanford.

■ **Ask the man in the street to describe Hawaii, and his response will probably feature coconut palms and idyllic beaches, beautiful grass-skirted girls garlanded with fragrant flowers, the lazy notes of the slack-key guitar, and maybe even Elvis crooning away in front of an impossibly lurid Technicolor sunset.** ■

Aloha Replace Elvis with a trio of talented local musicians, and every word of it is true. Hawaii really is Everyman's tropical paradise. All the necessary ingredients are in place, plus one vital addition: the spirit of *aloha*, the warmth and generosity of the islands and the welcome of their people, which is what makes the Hawaiian experience so memorable.

10

Setting the scene The Hawaiian archipelago numbers 132 islands, shoals and reefs spread across 1,523 miles of the mid-Pacific. You will not hit a mainland city for almost 2,400 miles to the east, or 3,800 miles to the west. Just eight main islands – Oahu, Kauai, Maui, Molokai, Lanai, Hawaii, Niihau and Kahoolawe – account for 99 per cent of the total 6,450-sq-mile Hawaiian land mass. Of these, Kahoolawe was a military installation, used for bombing practice, and family-owned Niihau is accessible only by private invitation or by authorized helicopter tours.

Hula heaven

Island round-up Thus the visitor is left with a choice of six Hawaiian islands. There is, however, no need to feel short-changed. Each island has its own individual style, and almost all can boast an astonishing range of physical beauties, from lush rain forest to blistering beaches, and from misty volcanic peaks to rolling upcountry pasture, all within a short drive of the main resort areas.

Oahu, home to the state capital, Honolulu, is usually the first stop for visitors to Hawaii. Nicknamed the "Gathering Place," it is the most developed island, but still preserves quiet corners where life proceeds at a leisurely pace that is far removed from the frenetic action of Honolulu and Waikiki.

To the north, beautiful **Kauai** is the "Garden Isle." Mount Waialeale, the wettest spot on earth, ensures that Kauai's streams and waterfalls never run dry, and it is a haven for nature lovers, offering dozens of hiking trails, gardens, horse-riding, canoeing, diving, snorkeling, and other outdoor pursuits.

South of Oahu, across the Kiawi Channel, rural **Molokai** hides behind a wall of vertiginous sea cliffs, amongst the tallest in the world. However, this natural barrier belies the easygoing nature of the "Friendly Isle," where native Hawaiians comprise over 50 percent of the population, and farming and fishing still take precedence over tourism. Molokai has only one low-key resort and is just the place for some quiet fishing, sailing, or golf, and the chance to really unwind.

It is a 9-mile hop across the Pailolo Channel from Molokai to **Maui**,

11

number two in the visitor stakes after Oahu. The "Valley Island" combines sophisticated resorts with cowboy country, white-sand beaches with spectacular Haleakala, the 10,023-foot volcano, which dominates the southern half of the island. A jet-set destination with a difference, Maui is more than big enough to cope with the crowds of vacationers who flock there.

A football team would constitute a crowd on **Lanai**. The "Private Island" was once

Perfect for a dip

famous for its pineapples, but now boasts two exclusive resort hotels, a small inn, and a campsite. Snorkeling, golf, hiking, and off-road jeep trails are the order of the day; great cuisine and utter quiet feature at night.

And so to **Hawaii**, the "Big Island" at the southern end of the main island group. Hawaii is by far the largest and most diverse of the *Hawaii nei* (local dialect for the entire island group). Its sunny beaches and snow-capped volcanoes, wide open spaces and rain forests provide a wealth of natural beauties and excursions for enterprising visitors.

■ "The meeting place of East and West," a multiracial "melting pot"—Hawaii and its people have been described as both of these and more. Inter-racial marriages account for some 50 percent of all Hawaiian weddings, and the children of these unions may combine half a dozen ancestral nationalities. ■

Racial mix Of a total population of 1.1 million, the three main racial groups are the Hawaiians or part-Hawaiians (31 percent), the *haoles*—whites—(25 percent), and the Japanese (24 percent). Minority groups include Filipinos (12 percent), Chinese (5 percent), and small numbers of other Asian peoples such as Koreans, Vietnamese, and Samoans.

Much is made of Hawaii's "golden" (mixed-race) children and the relative lack of racism experienced in the islands, but that is not to say racial tension does not exist. Despite their often exotic pedigree, Hawaiian people of all backgrounds tend to identify with one or other of the various ethnic groups. It is between these larger divisions that resentments arise, particularly if one ethnic group is seen to have prospered to the detriment of another.

The Hawaiians The fastest-growing ethnic group is the Hawaiians or, more accurately, people of Hawaiian blood. (Less than 4 percent of

Modern replicas of ancient idols

Hawaiians can claim to be pure-blooded descendants of the first Polynesian settlers.) A drop of Hawaiian blood guarantees entry into the Hawaiian community with its extended families, but the Hawaiians are also the most disenfranchised sector of society. Proportionately, they receive more welfare and are convicted of more crimes than any other group.

The resurgence of Hawaiian culture since the 1970s has spawned a number of successful rallying points for the community, from Hawaiian-language and traditional craft programs to schools teaching *hula*, the Hawaiian dance form and chants. Hawaiian-ness is now seen as something to be proud of. This new sense of empowerment has in turn fueled pressure groups, notably the Hawaiian sovereignty movement. The movement's agenda addresses valid political points such as the need for official recognition of the Hawaiian race, as well as several issues viewed with exasperation by non-Hawaiians. Examples are the suggestion of recompense to full- and part-blood Hawaiians for U.S. annexation of the Islands in 1898; and the demand that the U.S. withdraw, to be replaced by a Hawaiian kingdom. These issues hamper the movement's credibility in the view of outsiders, and betray resentment of other ethnic groups. However, the Hawaiians have found an identity and a voice which they are now not afraid to use.

Haole heaven After the Hawaiians came the *haoles,* a catch-all term embracing the original white-skinned New England missionaries and West

Coast whalers, Scandinavian, German and British traders and plantation owners. In recent years, these ruling-class *kamaaina haoles* (old-timers) have been joined by a stream of immigrants of all social backgrounds from the U.S. mainland. The ties between the various *haole* classes are loose, and many of them have intermarried with the Islands' other ethnic groups.

Eastern promise The close-knit Japanese community makes the fewest inter-racial marriages and has maintained strong peer-group and family bonds. Americans of Japanese Ancestry (AJAs) hold some 50 percent of government positions at all levels and represent Hawaii's

Conch shell concerto

most powerful political lobby. Japanese success in business is matched only by that of the long-standing Chinese community, which can count amongst its numbers some of Hawaii's top merchants, financiers and philanthropists, as well as the first Asian-American member of the U.S. congress, Hiram Fong.

The Filipinos and Portuguese add their Catholic heritage and colorful fiestas to the Hawaiian scene. Filipinos are particularly noticeable on public holidays, when the women sport elaborate formal dress and the men preen in the manner of their beloved cockerels, which are bred for popular but illegal cockfights.

■ *"Hula* is the language of the heart, and therefore the heartbeat of the Hawaiian people," wrote King David Kalakaua. But when the "Merrie Monarch," as Kalakaua was affectionately known, ascended to the Hawaiian throne in 1874, the *hula* was a dying art. ■

Origins of the *hula* Before the written word existed in Hawaii, the time-honored traditions of the *mele oli* (poetic chants) and *mele hula* (chants with movements) were the chief means of passing information from one generation to the next. Legend traces the origins of *hula* to the goddess Laka, and *hula halau* (hula schools) were established near *heiaus* (temples) constructed in her honor. Here, students were taught the sacred music and dance forms of the *kahiko*, or classical *hula*. The training was rigorous and the stylized delivery of the chants and dances had to be strictly observed. Far from being the "exhibitions of unrivaled licentiousness" that the missionaries claimed, the *mele hula* was performed at religious and ceremonial occasions and recorded historical events, ancestor genealogies, customs, and legends.

The art of story-telling

The Hawaiians believed that by evoking physical events through words and gestures they could control them. A broad repertoire of chants was created to extoll every aspect of Hawaiian life and legend. Dozens of individual movements were added to accompany the *mele hula*, each telling a story in itself. A flutter of the hand, a particular sway of the hips or a footstep can be used to signify a bird, blossom, rainstorm, or canoe ride. However, by the time Kalakaua ascended the throne many of these movements, and the ancient *mele* (chants) themselves, had been lost and forgotten. In less than half a century, zealous missionaries had virtually expunged the mainstay of Hawaiian history and culture by suppressing the native dance form and replacing the traditional *mele* with Christian hymns.

***Hula* revived** In keeping with his dual passions for entertainment and

things Hawaiian, Kalakaua set up a royal *hula* troupe to revive old dances and introduce new ones. He wrote much-admired *mele*, including the state anthem *Hawaii Ponoi*, and had them set to music by the Prussian bandmaster Henri Berger, director of the Royal Hawaiian Band.

During the 19th century, Hawaiian music underwent a sea change. In the old days, the *hula* had been accompanied by rhythmic chants and rudimentary native instruments such as drums, simple flutes, wooden sticks, and rattles. The hymn-singing missionaries and the whalers with their sea shanties introduced harmonies which the musical Hawaiians embraced with gusto. They also adopted a four-stringed guitar, known as the *braguinha* to the Portuguese migrants who brought it from Madeira in 1879, which they renamed the ukelele, or "jumping flea." From this fusion of styles and influences a definitive Hawaiian sound began to emerge.

Hula hits Hollywood A Hawaiian *hula* troupe brought the house down at the 1915 Panama-Pacific Exposition in San Francisco. Before long every reputable music hall and vaudeville theater worth its salt fielded a "Hawaiian revue," though most of the latter bore little relation

Hula *for all*

to the real thing. English lyrics and phony Hawaiian words were thrown together, and the good-humored Hawaiians adapted the *hula* in a way which confirmed all the missionaries' worst fears. Popular demand was so great that Hollywood initiated a series of Hawaiian films with stars such as Bing Crosby and Elvis Presley.

Today, *hula* is back on course. The revival of interest in Hawaiian culture over the last 20 years has turned it from a picaresque tourist sideshow into a respected cultural art form. The ersatz tourist revue is still going strong, but for a glimpse of real *hula* look in the newspapers for details of competitions. The most prestigious is the annual springtime Merrie Monarch Festival held on the Big Island (see page 26).

Chanting the mele hula

Luaus and lychees

■ **First, take a fertile volcanic island or six and place in a bountiful ocean. Add balmy temperatures, sunshine and rain, and leave to set. Then sprinkle liberally with Polynesians and food staples such as coconuts, bananas, yams, chickens and pigs, top with exotic fruits and spices—*et voilà*! A recipe for culinary success. ■**

Culinary mix From the staples introduced by the early Polynesian settlers, the Hawaiian larder has burgeoned. Captain Cook donated onions, pumpkins and melons. Citrus, mangoes, guavas, papayas and pineapples followed, and Chinese immigrants brought rice, spices, Chinese vegetables, lychees, and persimmons.

Hawaii's range of cuisines provides some of the most diverse culinary experiences imaginable. Portuguese chicken *adobo*, Chinese *chop suey*, Japanese *sushi* and Korean *kim chee* are familiar favorites, alongside Uncle Sam's hamburgers and pizza parlors. Meanwhile, the talented chefs of Hawaii's top restaurants are going back to their multicultural roots to develop an innovative new style they call Hawaiian Regional cuisine, which features fresh local produce and ingredients prepared with a distinctive Asian influence.

Long live the *luau* We can only guess what the well-rounded Hawaiians of old would make of the delicious but dainty dishes of modern-day Hawaiian Regional cooking. It is said that the Hawaiian does not stop eating when he is full but will carry on until he is tired, and there is no better place to experience the generosity of Hawaiian portion control than at that most traditional of local culinary and social events, the *luau*.

In ancient times, the Hawaiians would arrange feasts to thank the gods for a good harvest or victory in battle. Today, holidays and festivities from the birth of a child to a wedding are all good excuses for a *luau*. Preparations begin with the *imu*, a cooking-pit dug into the earth and lined with lava stones. A fire is lit to heat the stones, then the ashes

The unveiling of the imu

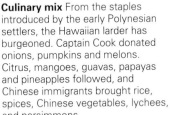

Traditional luau *foods*

is the Kona Village Luau on the Big Island (see page 171), where the groaning buffet provides all the usual *kalau* (cooked in an *imu*) favorites, plus other traditional foods such as mauve *poi* paste and *lomi* (a salmon salad with onions and tomatoes).

Poi-fection? Beloved of the Hawaiians, *poi* is definitely an acquired taste. Made from the root of the taro plant, which is rather like a purple potato and makes good fries, *poi* is served up in several consistencies measured by how many fingers are needed to eat it: "one-finger" *poi* is thick; "three-finger" runny. *Poi* is highly nutritious, but it is almost tasteless even with the addition of sugar or salt.

are swept away and the food is added, wrapped in a protective layer of banana or *ti*-leaves. The center-piece is generally a whole pig, and there are plenty of *lau-lau*, little packages of other meats, vegetables or fish wrapped in taro leaves. The pit is then covered with more leaves, layers of earth and damp burlap sacks. For the next four or five hours the *imu* bakes and steams away until the coverings are ready to be stripped off amid clouds of steam.

Few visitors are lucky enough to attend a real Hawaiian *luau*, and most of the commercial *luau* ventures are a pale imitation of the real thing. However, one of the best

First-class fish Hawaiian menus are long on excellent, locally caught seafood. Fish fans should look for *ono* (wahoo, a member of the tuna family), *opakapaka* (pink snapper), *onaga* (red snapper), *uku* (gray snapper), *ulua* (jack fish), and the ever-popular *mahimahi* (dolphin fish—a fish, not a dolphin). Other local favorites include *ahi* (yellowfin tuna) and *au* (swordfish), as well as *opae* (baby shrimp), *opihi* (limpets) and little *aloalo* (lobsters).

Kalau *pork is the main event*

■ **Mark Twain described Hawaii as "the loveliest fleet of islands anchored in any ocean." Like the galleons of the past, the Hawaiian "fleet" is laden with treasures, including some of the world's most spectacular scenery. Hawaii's extraordinary diversity of landscapes and outstanding natural habitats are some of its most arresting features.** ■

The seeds of change The early Polynesian settlers changed the face of Hawaii forever by introducing non-native food plants and clearing land for farming. Later, vast tracts of forest and native vegetation were destroyed by logging, clearance for sugar-cane and pineapple plantations during the 19th century, and by 20th-century development.

However, all has not been lost. Hawaii's rugged topography has confounded the most tenacious developers, and an impressive number of national, state and country parks ensures that many of Hawaii's most precious landscapes will be preserved for future generations.

Waterfalls in the pali *on the island of Hawaii*

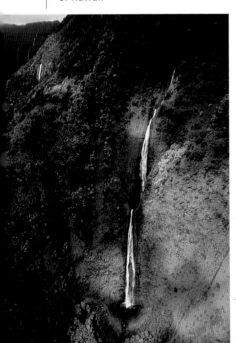

The coast The six main islands of Oahu, Kauai, Molokai, Maui, Lanai, and Hawaii boast almost 1,000 miles of tidal shoreline between them. The palm-fringed strands of golden sand, such as Oahu's Waikiki, are just one side of a range of coastal scenery which includes the undulating dunes of Polihale State Park on Kauai, and the jewel-like bays of Hanauma on Oahu and Kealakekua on the Big Island, which shelter Hawaii's two underwater parks.

For towering cliffs, head for Kauai's beautiful Na Pali Coast, or dramatic Palaau State Park on Molokai. Maui's Waianapanapa State Park features windswept headlands of black volcanic rock battered and carved into bizarre shapes by wave action. Meanwhile, the Puu Oo vent in the Hawaii Volcanoes National Park has spent the last few years creating a stunning new jet-black beach of volcanic sand on the Big Island's southern shore.

Volcano watch Sulphurous Hawaii Volcanoes National Park is a must for any visitor to the Big Island. The 229,000-acre park covers parts of Kilauea and Mauna Loa, two of the five volcanoes comprising the Big Island. Both are still active and offer more than a dozen special ecological areas. The dormant Haleakala crater on Maui is another tourist favorite, and although volcanic activity is a thing of the past in Oahu, the cinder cones of Diamond Head, and the Koko and Punchbowl craters are still impressive.

In a class of its own Carved by the Waimea River and dozens of lesser

18

streams and waterfalls, Kauai's Waimea Canyon is arguably the single most spectacular natural feature in the state. The red- and purple-faced gorge, 10 miles long and over 3,000 feet deep, is more than a match for its nickname, the "Grand Canyon of the Pacific."

Water, water everywhere Hawaii offers waterfalls aplenty, often surrounded by luxuriant rain-forest jungle. The 420-foot-high Akaka Falls on the Big Island are an example, as are the waterfalls cascading past giant breadfruit, mango, *kukui* (candlenut) and *hau* trees on the winding coast road to Hana on Maui's windward coast. Helicopter rides along Kauai's Na Pali Coast reveal dozens of waterfalls coursing down from Mount Waialeale, which also feeds the Opaekaa and Wailua Falls, popular beauty spots on the

Rainbows add to the spectacle

island's windward coast. Oahu has the Manoa Falls above Honolulu, and a 30-minute hike from the windward coast road near Kaaawa brings you to the Sacred Falls.

Forests and swamps Hawaii's lush native forests are an endangered ecosystem. The precious Kamakou Preserve on Molokai boasts 219 uniquely Hawaiian plants amongst its towering woodlands, densely massed ferns and the eerie Pepeopae Bog on the mountain top. Both Kamakou and the upland forest and Alakai Swamp areas of Kauai's Kokee State Park are important havens for Hawaiian birdlife, as are the rain-forested windward coasts of Maui and the Big Island.

Maui moonscape: Haleakala crater

Plants and trees

■ Hawaii's flora is as diverse and eclectic as its people. Thousands of plants from all over the globe have flourished in the Islands' friendly environment, but their very success has threatened, or even vanquished entirely, some of the world's rarest plants, endemic species which occur only on these isolated islands. ■

A closed world The first plant seeds' washed up on Hawaiian shores found an inhospitable world of barren lava. Only the adaptable survived, but with no competitors and only a few birds and insects representing the animal kingdom, these plants never developed the ability to compete with vigorous non-native species when they were introduced.

Nowhere is the adaptability of the Islands' endemic plants better shown than in the *ohia*. A member of the myrtle family, the *ohia* is one of the first plants to colonize new lava flows; there is a miniaturized

Red ginger

❑ **Endemic** Hawaiian plants are those that exist nowhere else in the world. These are distinct from **native** plants whose sea-, wind- or animal-borne seeds arrived without human intervention. **Non-native** plants are those introduced deliberately by humans. ❑

variety that grows in swamps and bogs, and it can grow to heights of 80 feet or more in forest areas. The size, color and texture of the *ohia*'s leaves change from tree to tree, and its distinctive red pompom blooms, *lehua*, are said to be the property of the fire goddess, Pele.

Coconuts and candlenuts The Polynesians came well prepared to colonize new lands. They brought the coconut palms, which shade the beaches, breadfruit, bananas, yams, and taro. The light-green-leaved *kukui*, or candlenut tree was also an import, named for its nuts, which could be burned for light. The timber of the magnificent native *koa* tree was highly prized for canoe-building and surfboards.

Culture clash Since Captain George Vancouver presented several hundred orange tree saplings to the Big Island chieftains in 1792, almost 2,000 non-native plant species have been introduced to the Islands. Exotic foreign fruits such as mangoes, papayas, guavas and Java plums now grow in the wild. Ornamental bamboos, orchids, gingers and heliconias have joined them. Ironwood trees and weeds

Fragrant plumeria blossoms

also colonized Hawaiian shores, and beware the *noni*, or Indian mulberry, with its vile-smelling fruit.

Glorious gardens To get to grips with the best of Hawaii's endemic, native and non-native flora, buy one of the specialist plant guides on sale in good bookshops. Plant lovers will find that the Islands' botanical gardens can also provide a colorful on-site introduction to what to look for. The Foster Botanical Garden and Lyon Arboretum in Honolulu are two of Oahu's finest gardens. On the other islands, try Kauai's National Tropical Botanical Garden (see page 104) ; Kula Botanical Gardens, Maui (see page 141); and the Hawaii Tropical Botanical Garden, north of Hilo, Hawaii (see page 176).

Deep in the jungle: Hawaii Tropical Botanical Garden, Hilo

21

such as lantana and the parasitic strangler fig have taken a firm grip on the environment, ousting less forceful native species. But even though the botanical mixture may alarm the conservationists, Hawaii's wealth of native and introduced flowers and trees is a real treat.

Many of Hawaii's endemic plants survive only in high and inaccessible areas, so the majority of the plants and trees enjoyed by the visitor are non-natives. The *lei*-makers' favorite fragrant plumeria, scarlet-bloomed poincianas from Madagascar, monkeypod trees from South America, banyans and the aptly named yellow-flowering "golden shower" from India are a common sight, as are the spreading thorny branches of non-native *kiawe* (mesquite) in dry areas.

Native plants that have survived in coastal regions include the distinctive *hala* (screw pine, *Pandanus*), balanced on a tepee of aerial roots, and creeping plants such as *pohinahina* (vitex), *ilima*, *Pau-o-Hiaka* (convolvulus, or Morning Glory), and beach *naupaka* with its half-formed white flowers (see panel, page 165). Non-native sea-grape trees, Indian almonds and tree heliotropes have

■ **Just 15 or so species of land birds found their way to the Hawaiian Islands before the arrival of the early Polynesians. Left to their own devices, these birds performed a small miracle, evolving into more than 70 different varieties endemic to the islands.** ■

Honeycreepers By far the most intriguing family of Hawaiian birds, the honeycreeper finches (*Drepanidadae*), diversified into at least 40 different types. The most common today is the crimson *apapane* with its black beak and tail feathers. It lives high up in the forest tree-tops and feeds off red *lehua* flowers, which makes it difficult to spot. One of the rarest is the crested honeycreeper (*akohekohe*), found only on the windward slopes of Haleakala on the island of Maui. It can be distinguished by the splash of orange plumage at the neck of its otherwise black and gray coloring.

Fashion accessories Two native Hawaiian birds were particularly

Top: the nene *goose*
Below: the tiny iiwi *honeycreeper*

❏ Since the arrival of humans, more than half of Hawaii's endemic birds have gone, hunted to extinction for food or feathers, or deprived of their natural habitats. Most of the survivors are confined to upland areas of native forest and swamp, where they delight ornithologists and scientists, providing an unrivaled opportunity for the study of evolution. ❏

prized for their plumage. The *iiwi*, with its brilliantly colored orange-red body feathers and matching curved beak, escaped from extinction when the bottom dropped out of the royal feathered-cape market. The "king of Hawaiian plumage birds," the *ooaa*, which supplied the all-important yellow feathers (80,000 of them for a full-length cape) may still survive in Kauai's Alakai Swamp, but has not been seen for years.

Hawaii has a native owl, the *pueo*, which hunts by day. Recognized as a benign ancestor spirit by some Hawaiians, the brown and white owl grows to between 15 and 18 inches high, and has huge yellow eyes. Another hunter, the Hawaiian hawk (*io*), is similarly revered, and soars above the forests of the Big Island on the lookout for its prey.

Goosey, goosey gander Hawaii's state bird, the *nene*, rescued from extinction by captive breeding programs, is a conservation success story. Gaggles of these brown and white geese (their name means "to sit together and talk") can be seen waddling about the Hawaii

For the birds

Volcanoes National Park and at Haleakala on Maui, and they have recently been introduced to Kauai's Na Pali Coast.

Here to stay Many of the most common birds seen around the islands have been introduced. Cardinals, bulbuls, finches and mynah birds have all been released over the years. Sparrows and pigeons have made their home here, too, though they are outnumbered by flocks of zebra doves imported from Asia.

In upland regions, gamebirds include several types of pheasant, francolin, and quail. There are chukar (a red-legged partridge), grouse and wild turkey, too, and in the Kokee State Park on Kauai, jungle fowl (*moa*), descended from domestic birds imported by the Polynesians, forage around in the undergrowth.

Common natives The yellow-green *amakihi*, a small honeycreeper, is the most widely seen native bird, and the plumage of the Pacific golden plover makes it an easy bird to identify. Ponds and marshy regions make valuable nesting and feeding places for a variety of waterfowl, from gallinules and ducks to the increasingly rare Hawaiian coot (*alae keokeo*) and the Hawaiian stilt (*aeo*) with its long pink legs. At cliff sites such as Kilauea Point on Kauai,

Red-crested cardinals are residents of the Islands

brown boobies, Newell's shearwaters (*ao*) and great frigate-birds roost and rear their young on the rocky headlands. Laysan albatross also breed here, as do the red-footed boobies with their unmistakable red galoshes, blue beaks, and blacktipped, 40-inch wings.

A well-balanced red-footed booby

23

■ **Hawaii is a golfer's paradise. Scattered over the six main islands, more than seven dozen challenging and attractive courses cater to golfers of every ability. Several times a year top golfers flock to the Islands for championship tournaments, and there is a busy calendar of local professional and amateur events.** ■

Golfing Mecca There are few places on earth where golfers can enjoy themselves as much as they do in Hawaii. Golf can be played 365 days of the year, and the game has boomed on the Islands in the last decade with the addition of more than two dozen new courses carved out of ancient lava flows, laid out on magnificent cliff-top sites and tucked into rain-forested mountain valleys.

Spoiled for choice It is possible to play a different course a day for five weeks on Oahu without a repeat. In addition to municipal and public courses, such as the spectacular mountainside Koolau Golf Course, Oahu has superb resort courses. The Links at Kuilima is the new Arnold Palmer and Ed Seay creation at the Turtle Bay Hilton and Country Club; the same duo was responsible for the Hawaii Prince Golf Club at Ewa. The Ko Olina Golf Club in the south-west is a Ted Robinson design, and the Sheraton Makaha Resort and Country Club, on the west coast, offers great sea views as well as challenging golf.

The Neighbor Islands Kauai is a favorite with the professional tour circuit and amateurs alike. Robert Trent Jones Jr.'s Prince Course at Princeville is considered one of the hardest 18 holes of golf in the Islands. Also well known are his Princeville Makai Course, the Poipu Bay Resort Golf Course, and the Kiele Course, one of two Jack Niklaus-designed courses at Kauai Lagoons.

Molokai's Kaluakoi Resort and Country Club, designed by Ted Robinson, occupies a stunning oceanfront site where axis deer and wild turkeys strut about the greens. Whale-watching is an additional attraction at the Challenge at Manele, Jack Niklaus's award-laden *tour de force* on Lanai.

Each of Maui's three top resort areas offers a choice of fine golf courses. Around the Kapalua Bay resort are the oceanfront Bay Course, Ben Crenshaw and Bill Coore's Plantation Course, and Arnold Palmer's Village Course. Just down the road are another two 18-hole layouts at Kaanapali. On East

---

❏
Oahu
Hawaii Prince Golf Club
(tel: 808/944-4567)
Koolau Golf Course
(tel: 808/235-3886)
Ko Olina Golf Club
(tel: 808/676-5309)
Links at Kuilima
(tel: 808/293-8574)
Sheraton Makaha Resort &
Country Club (tel: 808/695-9544)
Kauai
Kauai Lagoons Resort
(tel: 808/246-5061)
Makai Course
(tel: 808/826-3580)
Poipu Bay Resort Golf Course
(tel: 808/742-9489)
Prince Course
(tel: 808/826-5000)
Molokai
Kaluakoi Resort & Country Club
(tel: 808/552-2739)
Lanai
Challenge at Manele
(tel: 808/565-2222)
Experience at Koele
(tel: 808/565-4653) ❏

For golfers

Maui's leeward coast, Wailea's Blue, Gold and Emerald courses and the two neighboring Makena courses each provide an entirely different golfing experience in the lee of Mount Haleakala.

❏
Maui
Kaanapali Golf Courses
(tel: 808/661-3691)
Kapalua Bay Course
(tel: 808/669-8820)
Kapalua Plantation Course
(tel: 808/669-8877)
Kapalua Village Course
(tel: 808/669-8835)
Makena Golf Club
(tel: 808/879-3344)
Wailea Blue Course
(tel: 808/879-2966)
Wailea Gold & Emerald Course
(tel: 808/879-2966)
Hawaii
Hapuna Golf Course
(tel: 808/882-1035)
Makalei Hawaii Country Club
(tel: 808/325-6625)
Mauna Kea Beach Golf Club
(tel: 808/882-7222)
Mauna Lani Resort
(tel: 808/885-6655)
Waikoloa Beach Course
(tel: 808/885-6060)
Waikoloa Kings' Course
(tel: 808/885-4647)
Waikoloa Village Golf Club
(tel: 808/883-9621)   ❏

The Challenge at Manele Bay, Lanai

On Hawaii are the emerald-green Mauna Lani Resort courses etched against the black lava fields, Robert Trent Jones Sr.'s much-acclaimed Mauna Kea Golf Course, and the Palmer/Seay Hapuna Course. There are three very individual courses at the Waikoloa Resort, and the nearby Makalei Hawaii Country Club is a fine upcountry course between 2,100 and 2,800 feet above sea level.

Teeing off at Poipu, Kauai

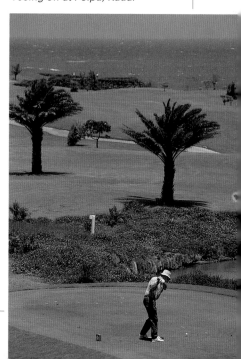

■ **The Hawaiian calendar is packed with festivals and events: international surfing competitions, children's *hula* contests, ukelele festivals, long-distance outrigger races... Some are state-wide celebrations, while others are low-key local or island activities. There is something for everyone—the events listed below are just a sample of what's offered.** ■

26

January
Molokai Makahiki, Molokai. New Year's celebrations with Hawaiian games, sports, ceremonies, and popular local entertainers.
Hawaiian Open PGA Golf Tournament, Oahu.

February
Hilo Mardi Gras, Hawaii. Costumed revels in the Big Island's capital.
Narcissus Festival, Oahu. Chinese New Year is celebrated in Honolulu's Chinatown.
Cherry Blossom Festival, Oahu. Japanese cultural celebrations with music, dancing and food in Kapiolani Park, Waikiki. (Also in March.)
Mahaka World Surfing Championships, Oahu. Spectacular surfing plus cultural events on the Waianae Coast.

On parade in Kaiwa-Kona

March
Hawaiian Song Festival and Composing Contest, Oahu. Music and *hula* competitions in Kapiolani Park, Waikiki.
Prince Kuhio Festival, Kauai. Music, *hula*, canoe races, pageants, and a royal ball feature in the week's festivities.

April
Merrie Monarch Festival, Hawaii. Advance reservations are a must for this Festival, the most prestigious *hula* competition in the Islands (tel: 808/935-9168).
Pineapple Festival, Lanai. Entertainments, fishing and tennis tournaments, craft fair, and lots of pineapples. (Also in May.)

May
Lei Day, State-wide flower festival and *lei*-making competitions on May 1. Concerts in Oahu's Kapiolani Park.

Many traditional Hawaiian festivals have been revived

Molokai Ka Hula Piko, Molokai. *Hula* demonstrations, music, crafts, cultural lectures, and "talking story."

June
King Kamehameha Day, State-wide celebrations on June 11. Parades, bands, and *hula* competitions in Honolulu.

July
Fourth of July, State-wide events and celebrations. Rodeos at Parker Ranch, Hawaii, and Makawao, Maui.
Hawaiian International Billfish Tournament, Hawaii (into August).
International Festival of the Pacific, Hawaii (mid-July). Celebrates the Islands' multiracial background with dances performed in native costumes.
Prince Lot *Hula* Festival, Oahu. Ancient and modern *hula,* arts and crafts in Moanalua Gardens, Honolulu (third Saturday).
Ukelele Festival, Kapiolani Park, Waikiki, Oahu (last Sunday).

August
Hawaii Pahinui Slack-Key Guitar Festival, Oahu.
Hawaiian Professional Champion-ship Rodeo, Waimanalo, Oahu.

September
Mokihana Festival, Kauai. Ten days of *hula,* concert, and arts and crafts exhibitions.
Aloha festivals, State-wide cultural events and entertainment lasting through October.

October
Bankoh Molokai Hoe outrigger canoe championships, Oahu.
Talking Island Festival, State-wide Hawaiian and Polynesian storytelling program.
Hula O Na Keiki, Maui. Children's *hula* event (third weekend).
Hilo Macadamia Nut Festival, Hawaii. It's nuts.

November
Kona Coffee Festival, Hawaii. A week-long party of coffee-tastings, pageants, craft fairs, and beauty contests.
Hawaii Pro Surfing Classic and Triple Crown of Surfing, North Shore, Oahu.

December
Na Mele O Maui, Maui. Traditional song competition, plus *hula,* arts and crafts exhibits.
Honolulu Marathon, Oahu. Attracts top runners from around the world.
First Night Honolulu, Oahu. Street entertainment leads up to fireworks at midnight for the New Year.

Festive Kona coffee bean leis

■ The language of the first Polynesians to reach Hawaii (see page 32) has become Hawaiian but is closely related to that of other Polynesian peoples. It is a melodic language with many vowels and repeated syllables. Several Hawaiian words are now common currency amongst the English speakers in the islands, such as *mahalo* (thank you), *kapu* (forbidden) and *aloha*, used as both a greeting and farewell. ■

Hawaiian The missionaries were the first people to write Hawaiian and they kept it simple, giving the alphabet just 12 letters. In Hawaiian, a consonant (h, k, l, m, n, p, w) is always followed by a vowel (a, e, i, o, u), forming two-letter syllables. Vowels also come in pairs, and sometimes threes, but a glottal stop will break them up as in Kawaa'a. A *w* in the middle of a word is often sounded as *v*, hence Kawaaa is pronounced "ka-vah-ah."

Pidgin While Hawaiian is an official state language alongside English, Pidgin is the language of the streets. Considered by some to be nothing more than slang, it derives from the plantation days when the *haole* (white owners) and Portuguese *lunas* (overseers) needed to communicate with their mainly Asian labor force. Pidgin is an organic mishmash of words and phrases drawn from half a dozen languages and is constantly changing. Although it is the preferred tongue of many islanders, they do not necessarily

Mix and match languages

Mahalo For keeping off the grass.

appreciate tourists and *malihini* (newcomers) attempting to use it.

❏ **Common Hawaiian words**

alii	ancient Hawaiian royalty
hale	house or building
haole	originally any foreigner; now, white people
heiau	place of worship, temple
hula	Hawaiian dance form accompanied by chants
kahili	royal standard made of feathers
kahuna	priest, minister or expert
kamaaina	native-born Hawaiian, old-timer
kane	man
keiki	child
lanai	veranda, porch
lei	garland of flowers
luau	Hawaiian feast
makai	toward the sea (directions)
mauka	toward the mountains
mele	song or chant
muumuu	loose-fitting gown
ono	delicious, tasty
pali	cliff
pupu	hors-d'oeuvres
shaka	hand signal made with closed fist, raised thumb and little finger used as greeting or to mean "hang loose"
wahine	woman ❏

HAWAII WAS

■ **Hawaii is a geological infant formed by volcanic activity in the middle of the Pacific Ocean over 2,000 miles from the nearest continent. Some 25 to 40 million years ago, when other corners of the planet were already inhabited by a wide variety of plants and animals and the dinosaurs had come and gone, Hawaii was just a bubble of magma on the ocean floor.** ■

Hot spots and volcanoes The 1,500-mile chain of Hawaiian islands did not appear all at once. The partly submerged mountain range arrived peak by peak, starting in the north with the Kure Atoll and Midway Islands. These northernmost Hawaiian islands once occupied a position near the modern location of Hawaii, the most southerly island in the chain. Here, a fixed hot spot some 18,000 feet beneath the ocean's surface pumps molten lava up through a group of vents at a weak spot in the earth's crust.

Countless eruptions over millions of years formed shield volcanoes (see box) which eventually rose from the sea and were carried gradually north by the movement of the Pacific Plate. As each volcano and its vent was carried inexorably northward away from the hot spot, there was a decreasing likelihood of eruption and

Steam rises from a cinder cone

it became extinct. The hot spot would then begin all over again, creating a new volcano.

Nowadays, there are two active volcanoes in the islands: Mauna Loa

❑ Shield volcanoes are named for their gently sloping shape, which resembles a warrior's long, convex, shield. The comparatively young volcanoes of the Big Island, Mauna Loa and Kilauea, still retain this appearance. However, the extinct volcanoes of the more senior Hawaiian Islands have been dramatically eroded by wind, rain and waves. As a result, the oldest in the island chain have been reduced to little more than shoals and reefs, though beneath the waves they are still substantial mountains rising from the sea bed. ❑

and Kilauea, both on Hawaii. There are also three dormant volcanoes: Mauna Kea and Hualalai on Hawaii, and Haleakala on Maui. Some 30 miles southeast of the Big Island, the Loihi Sea Mount has another 3,300 feet, and probably several thousand years, to go before it breaks the surface to become the latest link in the chain.

Hawaii's active volcanoes produce two different types of lava with the same chemical composition. Fast-flowing, smooth *pahoehoe* ("pa-hoy-hoy") courses down the mountain-side at a considerable rate. As the lava's surface cools and sets into a crust, it insulates the molten lava beneath, which can travel on for miles. Slow-moving *aa* ('ah-ah') lava is partially solidified and laced with jagged chunks of rock.

Water, winds and erosion The towering peaks of these volcanoes snag moisture-laden clouds carried on the northeastern trade winds, releasing hundreds of inches of rain every year. Rainwater and winds have eroded deep clefts and gullies into the mountainsides and created the fluted knife-edge ridges and folds of the *pali* (cliffs). The effects of erosion are most visible on the Islands' windward coasts, such as the north face of Molokai, where forbidding cliffs slashed by plunging valleys rise 3,300 feet sheer out of the ocean. Kauai's serrated Na Pali Coast and magnificent Waimea

A molten lava tube

Canyon were carved with the help of torrents of rain gushing down Mount Waialeale, "the wettest spot on earth," which can receive more than 50 feet of rain a year.

Signs of life In whatever manner the first living organisms arrived in Hawaii, it is fairly safe to assume it was by chance. Seeds, spores and insects were washed up by the ocean, blown in on the wind or came attached to lost birds. The volcanic islands offered fresh rainwater and fertile soil, and with no competitors the estimated 250 original plant varieties and an equal number of insect species, plus approximately 15 species of land birds, flourished. They gradually evolved into thousands of new species found nowhere else in the world.

Lava building a new coastline

31

The Polynesians

■ Around AD 500, a small group of Polynesians reached Hawaii. Probably fewer than 100 men and women disembarked from their double-hulled voyaging canoes onto the beach. They had brought provisions which would allow them to settle the land, but exactly why they had sailed across 2,000 miles of uncharted ocean remains a mystery. ■

First inhabitants The first settlers are thought to have journeyed from the Marquesas Islands, the most easterly group of islands in the Polynesian South Pacific. They were warlike people, and perhaps the early migrations were a result of internecine fighting. Alternatively, over-population might have caused migration, or perhaps the Polynesians just decided to put to use the navigational skills they had honed over several thousand years. Legends spoke of a "heavenly home-land" in the north, and navigating by the stars and prevailing winds, the sailors fetched up in Hawaii. Here they stayed, undisturbed for more than five centuries.

Hawaiians built koa-*wood canoes*

These early Hawaiians introduced pigs, chickens, dogs, and perhaps two dozen species of plants for food, medicine and fiber. Unintentional additions probably included rats, mice, lice, fleas, small lizards, and weeds. The Hawaiians cleared forests with fire, built terraces in the hills and irrigated them by diverting mountain streams and waterfalls. Taro fields, coconut, *kukui* (candlenut), banana and breadfruit groves were planted. Fishermen harvested the ocean with nets, spears, hooks and traps, and stone-walled fishponds were constructed along the shore.

Paradise lost This peaceable lifestyle was brought to an end by the arrival of Tahitian immigrants in

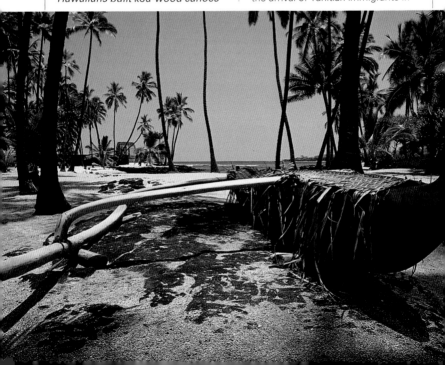

the 12th or 13th century. The Tahitians were led by the powerful figure of Paao, and they initiated a century of two-way traffic between Tahiti and Hawaii which resulted in eight of the Hawaiian islands being inhabited. Unimpressed by the laid-back lifestyle of the early Hawaiians, Paao launched a rigorous shake-up of religious and social practices. He introduced warlike gods, human sacrifice and a rigid social hierarchy which he enforced with the *kapu* (taboo) system which ruled every aspect of daily life.

Kapu Under *kapu*, society was broken down into four main classes. The *alii* were chiefs and royalty, one step removed from the gods, and were invested with considerable spiritual powers, or *mana*. Priests, professionals and craftsmen were *kahuna*; ordinary citizens were *makaainana*; and there was an underclass known as the *kauwa*. Commoners were forbidden to eat certain foods reserved for the *alii*, and had to prostrate themselves on the ground in the presence of these superior beings. Women could not eat with men, or touch foods such as pork, bananas or coconut. Certain fish were *kapu* during certain seasons, while others, along with many of the best fishing and hunting

Terraces were cut into the hillsides and irrigated to grow taro

areas, were reserved exclusively for the *alii*.

To break *kapu* was to insult the gods, who could retaliate by arranging natural disasters—from tempests and tidal waves to fire and famine. The punishment for breaking *kapu* was death; there were no mitigating circumstances. The only hope for a *kapu*-breaker was to reach sanctuary in a sacred *puuhonua* refuge, where the priests could perform a purification ceremony. Only one of these refuges remains, Puuhonua O Honaunua, on the Big Island of Hawaii.

To appease the gods and ask their assistance with new ventures, huge open-air temples, or *heiaus*, were constructed from black volcanic boulders arranged in a series of stone terraces. More demanding gods, such as Ku, the god of war, were worshipped at *luakini*, sacrificial temples. Religious ceremonies played a large part in Hawaiian life, and with them developed the *hula* (dance form) and *mele oli* (poetic chants), which described important events, traced the *aliis'* genealogies back to the gods, and told the *Kumulipo,* the Hawaiian version of the Creation (see pages 34–5).

■ **In the beginning, there was darkness, *po*, until the gods descended to earth and created light, *ao*. Kane, the life-giving god of sunlight and fresh water, fashioned Man (who takes his name) from sand or clay, and made Woman from his shadow. He breathed life into them, and all Mankind is descended from him.** ■

34

Polynesian pantheon The Polynesians brought their gods and animist beliefs with them to Hawaii. There were four main gods: Kane; Kanaloa, the god of the sea, trade winds and healing; Ku, the god of war, also responsible for rain, fishing and sorcery; and peaceable Lono, whose jurisdiction included clouds, agriculture and fertility. Beneath these major figures were numerous lesser deities, and protective spirits known as *aumakua*, which guarded individuals and families. Many natural things were also believed to be invested with some degree of *mana*, or spiritual power, from trees and waterfalls to rocks and mountains.

Sky Father, Earth Mother The gods and the earth were given life by Wakea, the Sky Father, and Papa, the Earth Mother. Wakea and Papa's first Hawaiian island children were Hawaii, Maui, and Kahoolawe.

Needing a rest, Papa went home to Tahiti, but while she was away, Wakea decided to continue without her, producing Lanai with his second wife, and Molokai with his third. Papa, in a fury, ran off with a dashing young god called Lua, and gave birth to Oahu. Reconciled, Wakea and Papa produced Kauai, Niihau, Kaula, and Nihoa.

The only island named for a god is Maui, a favorite subject for the Hawaiian storytellers. Maui was a son of the goddess Hina, and shortly after his birth he was cast into the ocean to die, but survived and grew into a strapping young demi-god with a knack for mischief and useful feats of strength. He stole, he tricked, he womanized, but all in a good cause as he lifted the sky so Man could walk erect, fished up new islands

The ancient Hawaiians built heiau *(temples) throughout the Islands*

with a magic hook, and discovered the secret of fire. Maui's most useful and celebrated good deed was to trap the sun in a lasso made from his sister's hair and force it to slow down its passage through the sky, thereby giving more daylight hours for fishing and farming.

Madame Pele Today, long after many more important deities have been forgotten, the legendary powers of Madame Pele, the goddess of fire and volcanoes, still command respect. As a young and beautiful goddess, Pele fell in love with a handsome *alii* chief from Kauai, but fought over him with her sister Namakaokahai, the sea goddess. After Namakaokahai dashed Pele into fragments on the rocky coast of Maui, she pieced herself together and took up residence in the firepit of the Kilauea volcano on the Big Island. Here Madame Pele lives today, able to manifest herself in numerous disguises and giving vent to explosive bursts of temper. The red *lehua* is Pele's flower, and she is partial to *ohelo* berries, which are often left as offerings.

Mistaken identity When the god Lono left Hawaii on a voyage he promised to return on a floating

Madame Pele's firepit home

island. During his absence, the Hawaiian people continued to honor him in the winter Makahiki season, when they celebrated the end of harvest. The absentee god's image, perched on top of a long pole draped with white *tapa* cloth, was carried around by representatives of the *alii* as they collected tithes.

On January 18, 1778, near the end of the Makahiki season, a floating island moved by white sails hove into view off the Islands. When Captain James Cook dropped anchor in Waimea Bay on Kauai, the Hawaiians believed Lono had returned.

35

Ferocious carved Kii *idols protected sacred sites*

■ **Captain James Cook, one of the world's greatest explorers, first sighted the Hawaiian Islands in January 1778. Although Ferdinand Magellan had made the first circumnavigation of the globe in 1519, and Spanish galleons had sailed from Mexico to the Philippines for over 200 years, the isolated Hawaiian archipelago had thus far remained uncharted territory. ■**

The Sandwich Islands Captain James Cook had visited the South Pacific twice before in search of the mythical Great Southern Continent. On this voyage, his goal was to discover the equally elusive (and of course non-existent) Northwest Passage linking the Pacific and the Atlantic across the top of the North American continent. He set sail from England in 1776, and came around Africa to Polynesia, then struck north from the Society Islands for the west coast of America and Alaska.

On January 18, 1778, his two ships, HMS *Resolution* and HMS *Discovery*, sighted Oahu. They landed at Waimea on Kauai two days later during the Makahiki festival when the god Lono (see pages 34–5) is fêted with feasts, sports and entertainment. Cook's expedition spent two weeks reprovisioning, cleaning their ships and being royally entertained by their Hawaiian hosts.

Captain James Cook (1728–79)

Cook named his finds the Sandwich Islands for his patron, the Earl of Sandwich, First Lord of the Admiralty. The captain was pleased to note similarities in the language and culture of the Hawaiians with the already familiar Polynesian people of Tahiti. He was impressed by the Hawaiians' friendliness, generosity, and swimming and surfing skills, and made presents of goats, pigs and vegetables, as well as iron, which was highly prized by the Hawaiians. Then, after a brief stop in Niihau, the expedition sailed north.

Lono returns The news of Cook's visit to Kauai probably reached Hawaii during the ten months which he spent in a fruitless search for the Northwest Passage. The expedition abandoned the task in the fall, and returned to winter in the Hawaiian Islands, sighting Maui on November 25-26. The ships then spent almost two months sailing around the archipelago before putting in to Kealakekua Bay on the Kona Coast of Hawaii on January 17, 1779. In a rerun of the previous year, Cook and his men arrived during the Makahiki festival, and were welcomed as gods. His auspicious arrival during the Makahiki season was further augmented by his chosen landing place: *kealakekua* means "path of the gods."

Cook entertained the Hawaiian chieftain, Kalaniopuu, and his retinue on board and introduced them to all manner of Western gadgets and weapons. Yet despite the cordial atmosphere, several small incidents occurred over the following weeks which may have had a bearing on

what was to come.

The curious Hawaiians were attracted like magnets to anything made of iron and freely pilfered any such object that was not nailed down. Cook's men chased them off in a most inhospitable and, to the offended Hawaiians, un-godlike manner. A ship's boat was stolen and a member of the *alii* (royal or chieftain class) was treated roughly as it was recovered.

Trouble in Paradise Reprovisioned, Cook's ships upped anchor and sailed northwards once more on February 4, but were forced to return

The crews of Cook's ships were welcomed at first

a week later after a storm damaged the mast of HMS *Resolution*. This time there was no welcome as Cook set about repairs. Another boat was stolen, and Cook went ashore with a party of marines to take Kalaniopuu hostage until the craft was returned. A scuffle broke out, and Cook and four of his men were hacked to death, close to the point where a white obelisk now stands overlooking Kealakekua Bay.

Death of Cook at Kealakekua Bay

■ **After Cook's ships sailed away from Kealakekua Bay, the Hawaiians saw no more visitors until 1786. Chief Kalaniopuu fought with his great rival Kahekili of Maui, and his nephew Kamehameha acquitted himself well on the battlefield. When Kalaniopuu died, he bequeathed his lands to his son, Kiwalao, but the guardianship of the family war god, Kukailimoku, he left to Kamehameha.** ■

Kukailimoku, the Land Snatcher

Following Kalaniopuu's death in 1782, a power struggle developed between Kiwalao, his brother Keoua, and Kamehameha. After Kiwalao was killed in battle, Keoua controlled the Puna area of Hawaii in the south, while Kamehameha held sway in the north. In 1790, Kamehameha launched an offensive against Kahekili on Maui, and began the construction of a vast *luakini heiau* (sacrificial temple) to Kukailimoku on the northwest coast at Kawaihae. It was prophesied that Kamehameha would conquer all the islands if he honored the war god in this fashion.

As the building work was under way, Kamehameha successfully repelled a combined warring party of warriors from the other islands. It was a good omen. The gods also appeared to be on his side when Madame Pele's firepit dispatched a contingent of Keoua's troops as they

Kamehameha I (c.1758–1819)

crossed the Kilauea crater. The Puuokohala *heiau* was completed in 1791, and Keoua was summoned to the dedication ceremony. Bravely he appeared, resplendent in his finest robes, and was slaughtered on the beach. His body was the inaugural human sacrifice to Kukailimoku, the Land Snatcher.

The red-mouthed weapon

Cook was a man ahead of his time in his concern that contact with the West would change the Hawaiian way of life forever. Captain George Vancouver, who had sailed with Cook and who became a trusted adviser to Kamehameha, refused to trade guns with the Hawaiians, but other visitors were less high-minded. After 1785, ships *en route* to China from the American northwest found the islands a convenient stopping-point for provisions. Kamehameha acquired guns and small cannons, and used them to great effect as he conquered first Maui, then Molokai, Lanai and, finally, Oahu.

In 1794, Kamehameha sailed for Maui with 16,000 warriors and easily defeated the opposition. Faced with a flotilla of war canoes 4 miles long, Molokai, too, was subdued in short order. Kahekili died the same year and in February 1795 Kamehameha landed with his army at Waikiki, and cornered and massacred the defenders in the Nuuanu Valley.

Kamehameha was now the power in the land, though Kauai still eluded him. Two attempts to lead a seaborne invasion were defeated by the weather, but the island was finally brought under his control in 1810

when the Kauai chief, Kaumaualii, agreed to act as the governor of his own island under the ultimate rule of King Kamehameha.

Kamehameha the Great

Kamehameha consolidated his position by adhering strictly to the old religion and enacting laws that forbade Hawaiians from trading directly with Western ships. Visiting captains had to seek the king's assent to trade. The safe anchorage of Honolulu harbor was the center of the action, and Kamehameha moved his court here in 1804. He appointed loyal governors to oversee the other islands, including the

Kamehameha the Great, Hawaii's warrior-king

Englishman John Young in Hawaii, who also acted as the king's business agent.

In 1812 Kamehameha returned to Hawaii and died there in 1819. The succession was secured by the sons borne for him by Keopuolani, his "Sacred Wife," whom he had married in 1795. Though the king had perhaps 20 other wives, Keopuolani was *naiupio*, the highest possible caste, the daughter of a Molokai chieftainess and her brother in a prescribed marriage ordained to produce just such a *naiupio* child.

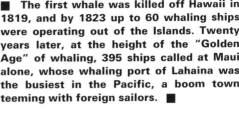

■ **The first whale was killed off Hawaii in 1819, and by 1823 up to 60 whaling ships were operating out of the Islands. Twenty years later, at the height of the "Golden Age" of whaling, 395 ships called at Maui alone, whose whaling port of Lahaina was the busiest in the Pacific, a boom town teeming with foreign sailors.** ■

40

Press-ganged into service It has been estimated that over 100,000 men sailed from New England aboard ships for the rich whaling grounds of the Pacific. However, unlike their contemporaries, the strait-laced, well-intentioned and zealous missionaries, morality was not the whalers' strong suit and a good many were not volunteers. To fill their crew lists, captains frequently relied on the services of ruthless press-gangs, so careless drunks and down-and-outs were in very real danger of waking up one morning to an unplanned life sailing the seven seas.

Life on the ocean wave Life on board a whaling ship was surely one of the most unpleasant experiences imaginable. It was dirty, dangerous, lonely and badly paid. Men were signed up for three- or four-year voyages which took them to the Arctic whaling grounds in summer, and the waters off Japan in winter. Wages were a mere pittance, and after deductions for food and grog many men ended up in debt to the ship. They lived in cramped, filthy quarters, spent months on end at sea, and risked their lives to provide the whale oils which greased the cogs of America's industrial age, provided the fuel to light homes and streets, and were transformed into soap, candles, and cosmetics.

Catching the whales Boredom and danger were two constants in the life of a whaler. The initial journey from New England around Cape Horn could be a terrifying experience, but it paled into insignificance alongside the realities of 19th-century whale

Whaling ships at anchor in Lahaina

Harpooning whales off Hawaii

hunting. When a whale was spotted, the whaling ship drew near to it and cast off her boats. These six-man vessels were about half the size of the whale and only a fraction of its weight. Hand-launched harpoons were plunged into the whale, which could then tow the puny craft for miles before tiring enough to allow the crew to come alongside and pierce the giant beast through its lungs to kill it.

Harvesting the whale oil was almost as dangerous as capturing its source. As the oil-rich blubber was cut away, the ship's decks turned into a treacherous slick of blood and oil. Most of the carcass and flesh was then thrown overboard, except for the baleen found in the mouths of toothless whales. Known quite erroneously as "whalebone," these hair plates are used by the whale to filter its food, and are made of keratin, as are human nails and hair. "Whalebone"-baleen, which was both strong and flexible, was the forerunner of modern plastics and was widely used for making buggy whips, fishing rods, corset stays, and hoops for crinolines.

Shore excesses At the end of the season, the whalers sailed for Lahaina and Honolulu to off-load their cargoes and set about an orgy of drinking and whoring. Missionaries tried to curb the whalers' wild behavior by imposing curfews and forbidding native women on the ships. The sailors for their part took pot-shots at the missionary house in Lahaina, and continued to bestow their legacy of venereal diseases, influenza and smallpox on a native population with no natural defenses.

By the late 1860s the whaling boom was over. The introduction of petroleum reduced the market for whale oil, and the sheer hardship of the whaling lifestyle took its toll. Equally, between 1835 and 1872 the American whaling fleet slaughtered 292,714 whales; they were no longer abundant in Hawaiian waters, and the whaling fleets moved on.

■ **Within six months of the death of Kamehameha in May 1819, the ancient *kapu* (taboo) system, which underpinned both Hawaiian society and religion, had been destroyed. Chiefly responsible were Kamehameha's queens, Keopuolani and Kaahumanu, who persuaded the young king Kamehameha II to break *kapu* by dining with them at a public feast.** ■

***Kapu* collapses** After the arrival of Captain Cook, some Hawaiians began to question the alleged power of the gods as Westerners appeared to be able to break *kapu* without any retribution. Kamehameha I had managed to keep the old religion afloat, but Kamehameha II was no match for the royal womenfolk who were determined to dispense with the restrictive *kapu* regime. When the public flouting of the *kapus* against men eating with women, and women eating taboo foods such as pork, bananas and coconut provoked no response from the gods, *heiaus* (temples) were desecrated, idols smashed, and the Hawaiians were left in a spiritual vacuum.

Cue the brig *Thaddeus* In October 1819, 14 Protestant missionaries bound for Hawaii sailed from Boston, New England, aboard the brig *Thaddeus*. They arrived in Kailua, on the Big Island, in April 1820, and then went on to Honolulu on Oahu, where on April 25 the Reverend Hiram

Missionary church in Halawa Valley

❑ The original mission buildings in Honolulu now contain the fascinating Mission Houses Museum (see page 64). Other fine mission house museums include the Waioli Mission at Hanalei, Kauai (see page 100); the Baldwin House at Lahaina, Maui (see page 127); and Lyman House in Hilo, Hawaii (see page 157). ❑

Bingham took his first service on Hawaiian soil. Several of the mission brothers and their wives were reported to have been moved to tears at the sight of the Hawaiian "naked savages," but they soon pulled themselves together and got down to their work.

The headquarters of the Sandwich Islands Mission was founded in Honolulu, and by the 1840s there were 17 mission outposts spread throughout the Islands. The missionaries built churches, schools and printing houses, and in their first few years achieved several important conversions. Both Keopuolani and Kaahumanu were converts, as was the powerful chieftainess of Hawaii, Kapiolani, who made a dramatic declaration of faith at the Kilaeau crater, home of Madame Pele. There she ate sacred *ohelo* berries, flung stones into the firepit and declared the Christian God, not Pele, responsible for the volcano's actions.

The missionaries provided the Hawaiians with an alphabet, the means of written communication for their native tongue, but they were also responsible for all but expunging the ancient oral and visual traditions of the *hula* (dance form). Deemed licentious and depraved, the *hula* was swiftly banned. Its female practitioners were trussed up in sack-like *muumuus* (loose-fitting gowns), and taught more socially acceptable pastimes such as hymn-singing and quilting. Games and entertainments were forbidden on the Sabbath, and considerable energy was expended in preaching against alcohol, adultery, and gambling to the initial bemusement of the easy-going Hawaiians.

Merchants and ministers Never had a contingent of missionaries turned up at a more propitious moment in a host country's history. With Hawaiian society in disarray and organized religion conveniently dismantled by the Hawaiian people themselves, the missionaries were extraordinarily successful in their efforts. By the 1850s around a third of the population had been converted and the New Englanders were able to entrust the continuance of their work to the Hawaiians. Catholic missions followed the Protestants, and after them came the Mormons.

Missionary influence extended far beyond the introduction and spread of Christianity in the Hawaiian Islands. They started commercial and trading ventures and were increasingly drawn into the political arena. By the time Kamehameha III had ascended the throne in 1827, Hawaii was in political turmoil; foreign newcomers tried to achieve a political toehold, challenging the legitimacy of Hawaiian rule by claiming the Islands for their European countries (see page 44). Kamehameha III turned to the missionaries for advice, and William Richards was released from his religious duties to help the king.

Other distinguished missionaries were Geraint Judd, who served as chief government minister, and Samuel Alexander and Henry Baldwin, who met as mission children in Lahaina and went on to found together one of Hawaii's most important trading companies. Wilcoxes, Thurstons, and Cooks also flourished, their influence playing a vital part in securing close ties between Hawaii and the U.S.

A legendary figure, missionary Father Damien tended the lepers at their colony on Molokai

■ **When Kamehameha II died in 1824, and was succeeded by his 9-year-old brother, Kamehameha III, control of the kingdom passed to the dowager queen, Kaahumanu, and, later, to the king's sister, Kinau. Following advice from the missionaries, the basic framework of government and legal systems began to take shape.** ■

Libertine turned law-maker Even after he had achieved his majority, Kamehameha III showed very little interest in the workings of state. The fun-loving king declared "war" on missionary morality; he drank, gambled, danced the forbidden *hula*, surfed, and conducted a passionate love affair with his younger sister, Nahienaena, to the horror of the Christian brothers. But after Nahienaena's death in 1836, Kamehameha reformed. Lessons in government from William Richards led to a Declaration of Rights in 1839, and the institution of a constitutional monarchy in 1840.

Hawaiian independence survived threats from the French (in 1839) and the British (in 1843). The former were diffused after concessions were made permitting certain French goods and Catholic missionaries into Hawaii. The British incident involved one Lord George Paulet who, acting on his own initiative, occupied the fort at Honolulu and claimed Hawaii for the British crown. His superiors

Kamehama III and Queen Kalama

and Queen Victoria herself were vastly unamused and control was handed back to the king, along with profuse apologies.

Land division Kamehameha III's single most significant move was to initiate the land division known as the Great Mahele. The concept of private ownership was alien to the Hawaiian people, who had previously worked

Sugar mills arose from cane fields

Filipino cane workers

the land for the *alii* (chiefs), and later for the king. Encouraged by his foreign advisers, the king divided the Hawaiian lands into three portions: part to remain in the possession of the crown, part allotted to the government; and the remaining portion set aside for the Hawaiian people, though few of them followed the official claiming procedure. Just two years later, in 1850, *haoles* (foreigners) were allowed to buy land freehold. Needless to say, many missionaries and their families were at the front of the line when the Hawaiians happily sold off their unaccustomed property.

King Sugar The first sugar-cane plantations in Hawaii appeared on Kauai as early as 1835, but it was not until the California Gold Rush in the late 1840s that there was much demand for Hawaiian sugar. Though this initial interest was short-lived, the disruption to the sugar supply from the southern States during the Civil War was a further boost for the Hawaiian crop.

What had become painfully obvious by the mid-1800s was the dramatic and seemingly irreversible demise of the Hawaiian people. From an estimated population of around 300,000 at the time of Captain Cook,

the Hawaiians now numbered a mere 50,000. The plantations required a massive, cheap labor force, but the Hawaiians were both too few in number and disinclined to abandon their traditional lifestyle to slave for the *haole*. The plantation owners' solution was to import workers from abroad.

The first contract laborers from China arrived in 1852, to be followed in 1878–87 by some 12,000 Portuguese from the Azores and Madeira, many of whom were skilled workers and hence joined the *luna* (overseer) class. After a shaky start, large-scale immigrations from Japan began in the 1880s when the Emperor relaxed the restrictions on Japanese emigration after a visit from Kelakaua.

Typical plantation conditions were grim. A back-breaking 12-hour day, six days a week was the norm. Pay was low, facilities minimal and restrictive regulations abounded. There were severe penalties for desertion. Many of the early immigrants, particularly the Chinese, returned home at the end of their contracts. But, equally, many stayed and moved into business. In all, approximately 395,000 immigrants came to Hawaii to work in the cane fields between 1852 and 1946. Their common experience forged lasting cross-ethnic links.

■ The thorny question of some form of reciprocity agreement with the U.S. to protect the fledgling Hawaiian sugar industry was first discussed in the 1850s. Naturally, plantation owners supported the plan, which would allow Hawaiian sugar to be exported duty-free to the U.S. in return for similar trading concessions on U.S. goods coming into Hawaii. ■

Anti-U.S. feeling Reciprocity did not appeal to Kamehameha IV, who had succeeded to the throne in 1854. An anglophile who distrusted the Americans, the king was wary of closer ties with the U.S., preferring to keep his options open.

In 1864 Kamehameha V overturned the liberal constitution of 1852, and also reduced the powers of the American-influenced legislature while attempting to invest further authority in the crown. He died without naming an heir in 1872, the last of the Kamehameha dynasty, and the new king was elected from another branch of the family.

The reign of the "People's King,"

King David Kalakaua (1836–91)

King William Lunalilo (1873–4), was brief but popular. When Lunalilo came to the throne, the whaling industry was a fraction of its former size, and he recognized the necessity for reciprocity with the U.S. to secure Hawaii's economic future. There were serious discussions about what form the Hawaiian concessions should take, and at one point it was suggested that Hawaii might offer the Americans rights to develop Pearl Harbor as a naval base, but public concern over U.S. influence saw the plan dropped.

The Merrie Monarch King David Kalakaua, Lunalilo's successor, was no Kamehameha, but he was a powerful force and greatly beloved

The last Hawaiian royal, Queen Liliuokalani (1834–99)

by his countrymen. He visited Washington to promote negotiations in 1875, and the Reciprocity Treaty was implemented the following year. The king made quite a hit in the U.S., but he was a great deal less popular with the American community in Hawaii. His autocratic rule, coupled with heavy taxes imposed on planters and businessmen, led to considerable resentment amongst the *haoles* (foreigners), an influential group of whom banded together to form the pro-American Hawaiian League.

Kalakaua's lavish lifestyle, which included building the Iolani Palace and traveling on a world tour, was balanced by a genuine concern for Hawaiian history and culture. He revived the *hula* (native dance form), compiled a book of Hawaiian legends, and generally restored the Hawaiians' pride in their national heritage. But the country's coffers were empty, and the business-like Hawaiian League stepped in with a list of demands which led to the Bayonet Constitution of 1887. Kalakaua was forced to concede considerable power to the League-influenced legislature; the vote was restricted to a coterie of wealthy or land-owning figures, mainly the *haoles*; and the Reciprocity Treaty was renegotiated, giving the U.S. title over Pearl Harbor.

Royalty overthrown Kalakaua died on a visit to San Francisco in January 1891, to be succeeded by his sister, Lydia Liliuokalani. A passionate nationalist, Queen Liliuokalani and her supporters were determined to reassert royal authority and preserve "Hawaii for the Hawaiians." Court intrigues abounded, and two years later Liliuokalani announced her intention to do away with the 1887 constitution. In a hastily convened session of the Annexation Club, led by Lorrin Thurston (a founding member of the Hawaiian League), a group of some 30 U.S. business-men resolved to replace the queen with their own candidate.

They turned to the U.S. Minister to Hawaii, John Stevens, who summoned the U.S.S. *Boston* with-out consulting Washington. On January 16, 1893, 160 U.S. marines occupied strategic sites around Honolulu, and the following day the queen was forced to abdicate. The Hawaiian monarchy, after less than a century in power, was replaced by a Provisional Government headed by American plantation owner, Sanford B. Dole.

■ **When news of the American-led coup against the Hawaiian monarchy reached President Grover Cleveland, he was appalled and dispatched an emissary, James Blount, to assess the situation. Blount, who found an indignant ex-queen Liliuokalani and a resentful populace, reported to Cleveland that "a great wrong has been done to the Hawaiians."** ■

From Republic to U.S. territory

Both Cleveland and Blount favored reinstating the monarchy, but the Provisional Government in Honolulu ignored Washington and declared the Republic of Hawaii in July 1894, elevating Sanford Dole to President. In 1895 Liliuokalani plotted a counter-revolution, but it was nipped in the bud by the Provisional Government, the co-conspirators were rounded up and the ex-queen was put under house arrest in the Iolani Palace, now known as the Executive Building. In 1898, the new Republican president, William McKinley, signed an annexa-

tion agreement, and the Islands officially became a U.S. Territory in 1900.

The Hawaiian economy

By the early 20th century, economic power was concentrated in the "Big Five" sugar companies, which soon began to diversify into shipping, ranching, and land development. James Drummond Dole founded the Hawaiian Pineapple Company in 1901, and soon the pineapple industry was second only to sugar. Immigrants flowed into Hawaii to work the plantations, until 75 percent of the workforce was Asian. By the time immigration from Japan was ended in the 1920s, 42.7 percent of the Hawaiian population was Japanese. Further demand for labor was answered by 100,000 Filipino immigrants, who arrived between 1907 and 1941.

Besides the plantations, Hawaii's

Hawaiian pineapple power

biggest revenue earner was the U.S. military, which had started arriving in force from the beginning of the century. Pearl Harbor was dredged and equipped to service the Pacific Fleet, and the army occupied the huge Schofield Barracks complex in central Oahu. Tourism also began to play an important role, as luxury liners steamed into Honolulu Harbor, and the bright young things of the 1920s leisured classes danced and drank the tropical nights away in Waikiki's grand hotels. Air transportation arrived in the 1930s, and the first fare-paying air passengers flew in aboard the *Hawaii Clipper* from San Francisco on April 8, 1935.

World War II The Japanese attack on Pearl Harbor on December 7, 1941 both brought America into the war and marked the start of a period of profound change in Hawaiian society. Martial law was immediately declared, but although there was some initial unease about the Japanese population, given the numbers internment was not a serious consideration. When the AJA (Americans of Japanese Ancestry) 100th Battalion was formed in 1942, over 10,000 Hawaiian AJAs applied for 3,000 places. Renamed the 442nd Regimental Combat Team, the AJAs fought with distinction

U.S.S. West Virginia *at Pearl Harbor*

in Europe, North Africa, and the Pacific to become the most highly decorated World War II unit in the U.S. forces.

The war did more to Americanize Hawaii's various ethnic communities than half a century of annexation. New industry combined with a unionized workforce eroded the power of the "Big Five"—C. Brewer, Castle & Cooke, Alexander & Baldwin, Theo Davies and Amfac, Hawaii's biggest landowners and businesses, all originally sugar based—and Hawaii's servicemen and women received higher education under the Veterans Act. As racial and economic barriers came tumbling down, they began to demand a voice in Hawaii's future.

Hawaii achieves statehood The AJAs were particularly active in government, lobbying strongly for statehood, which was finally granted by President Eisenhower. Hawaii was admitted as the 50th state in the Union on August 21, 1959. That same year the first regular jet air-service to the mainland was started, and tourism and the construction industry associated with it boomed. As first sugar and then the pineapple industry have been forced into decline by cheaper southeast Asian competitors, tourism has grown to match military spending as Hawaii's chief source of revenue.

49

OAHU

A map of Oahu with the following labels:

Kahuku Point

Kawela Bay

Kawela

83

Kahuku Sugar Mill

Kahuku

Malaekahana State P

Sunset Beach

COMSAT

Kahikilani (Washington Stone)

Banzai Pipeline

Puu O Mahuka Heiau State Monument

Mormon Temple

Waimea

Waimea Bay

Polynesian Cultural Center

Laie

Kawailoa Beach

Waimea Falls Park

Kahuku Forest Reserve

Haleiwa Beach

Haleiwa

Koolau Range

Hauula

Kaiaka Bay

Anahulu

Kawailoa

Sacred Falls Par

Kaena Point

Keana Point State Park

Kuaokala Forest Reserve

Mokuleia Beach

Mokuleia

Waialua

Kamoolaa

99

Leilehua

Plateau

Forest

Reserve

Kaliuw (Sacred Fa

Channel

Kauai

Yokohama Bay

Makua

Kaneana Cave

Waianae

Makua Keaau Forest Reserve

4,038ft

Schofield

Waionae Kai

Forest Reserve

Kaala

Barracks

Forest

Reserve

Dole Plantation

Sacred Birth Stone

Schofield Barracks

Botanic Garden

Wahiawa

Ewa Forest Reserve

Ewa

Kepuhi Point

1,784ft Kokekole Pass

Waikele

Waipio Acres

Makaha

3,126ft Puu Kaua

Kunia

Milani Town

Ewa

Fore

Waianae Regional Park

Pokai Bay

Waianae

Mountains

Honouliuli Forest Reserve

H2

Waipi

Waiawa

Pacific Palisades

Maili

Hawaii's Plantation Village

Waipahu

Pearl City

Aiea

Maili Point

93

Nanakuli

H1

USS Bowfin Submarine Museum

H1

Nanakuli Beach Park

Makakilo

Ewa

Pearl Harbor

USS Arizona Museum

Hickam Air Force Bay

Honol Internati Airpo

Hawaii Raceway Park

Barbers Point

Barbers Point Naval Air Station

Barbers Point Beach Park

Ewa Beach

Mamala Bay

0   5   10 km
0   5 miles

A   B   C

4

3

2

1

Aloha attire

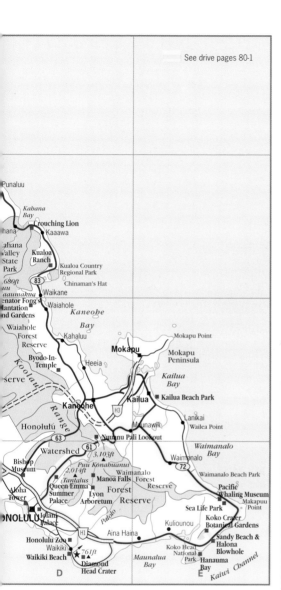

Punaluu

Kahana Bay

Crouching Lion

hana　Kaaawa

ahana
Valley
State
Park　Kualoa
Ranch

680ft　Kualoa Country
Regional Park

aau
aaumakua　Waikane　Chinaman's Hat

enator Fong's
lantation　Waiahole
nd Gardens

Waiahole　*Kaneohe*
Forest　*Bay*
Reserve　Kahaluu　Mokapu Point

Byodo-In-
Temple　Heeia　**Mokapu**

serve　Mokapu
Peninsula

*Kailua
Bay*

Kaneohe　**Kailua**　Kailua Beach Park

Honolulu

Nuuanu Pali Lookout　Lanikai
Wailea Point

Watershed　3,103ft　*Waimanalo
Bay*

Bishop
Museum　Waimanalo

Puu Konahuanui
2,014ft　Waimanalo

Queen Emma
Summer　*Tantalus*　Manoa Falls　Forest
Reserve　Waimanalo Beach Park

Aloha
Tower　Palace　Lyon
Arboretum　Reserve　Pacific
Whaling Museum

Palolo　Sea Life Park　Makapuu
Point

NOLULU　Iolani
Palace　Koko Crater
Botanical Gardens

Kuliounou

Honolulu Zoo　Aina Haina

Waikiki　Koko Head
National Park　Sandy Beach &
Halona
Blowhole

Waikiki Beach　761ft

Diamond
Head Crater　*Maunalua
Bay*　Hanauma
Bay

Kaiwi Channel

Pacific honeypot

The second oldest and third largest of the main Hawaiian islands, Oahu is also the most populous, most developed and most visited volcanic dot in the middle of the Pacific. A mere 604 square miles in area, the island is home to some 80 percent of Hawaii's total population of 1.1 million, and the capital, Honolulu, hosts around 4.5 million visitors a year.

However, although Oahu certainly lives up to its nickname of the "Gathering Place," these statistics do not tell the whole story. Often dismissed as an overcrowded tourist ghetto by its detractors, Oahu has room to spare. Of the mountainous interior terrain, 46 percent is just too steep to develop, and the heavily populated urban areas are confined to the southern portion of the island. Yet

OAHU

Makapuu Beach: body-surfers' favorite

Long weekend itinerary
Day one: Waikiki Trolley (suggested stops Hawaiian Maritime Museum, Foster Botanical Garden, and Chinatown for *dim sum* lunch). Relax on Waikiki Beach or visit Waikiki Aquarium.
Day two: U.S.S. *Arizona* Memorial. Aloha Marketplace for lunch. Historic Honolulu Walk.
Day three: rent a car for the Southern Drive.
Day four: Diamond Head or relax on Waikiki Beach. Shopping at the Ala Moana Center.

even here, less than half an hour from the concrete and glass heart of Honolulu, there are stunning azure-blue bays harboring more than 150 different types of tropical fish, terrific body-surfing beaches virtually deserted on weekdays, and a choice of upcountry hiking trails.

Attractions There is no avoiding Honolulu. It is, after all, the main gateway to the islands, and its high-rise skyline seems to reach up and draw the jumbo-loads of pale vacationers down into its sunny embrace. For many visitors the charms of Waikiki—luxury shopping, fine restaurants, well-appointed beachfront accommodations, and a lively nightlife—prove equally magnetic, and some never venture farther afield. But Oahu is well worth exploring and rewards tourists with a plethora of quiet beaches, beautiful gardens and more exotic attractions, from the popular Sea Life Park at Waimanalo to the South-Sea-Island delights of Laie's Polynesian Cultural Center.

Topography and climate Public transportation on Oahu is better than anywhere else on the Islands, and private bus companies serve several of the more far-flung attractions, but independent travelers should still consider renting a car. The simple island road plan is dictated by local geography, namely Oahu's two mountain ranges. The Koolau Mountains, which rise behind Honolulu, run almost the length of the windward (east) coast, tailing off opposite the famous surfing beaches of the north coast. Here, the frenetic activity in the water is in complete contrast to the laid-back, hippy-surfer attitude of Haleiwa, the only settlement of any size in this part of the island. South of Haleiwa, the Central Plain is given over to fields of sugar cane and pineapple plantations, while the Waianae Mountains reach over 4,000 feet before tipping down to the rugged west coast. As a rule of thumb, the windward coast is wetter, particularly in the November–March rainy season, and things get drier as you move west.

Honolulu and Waikiki

Sheltered bay The tenth largest city in the United States, Honolulu sprawls in the lee of the Koolau Mountains, extending its concrete arms from the Diamond Head end of Waikiki all the way around to the industrial jumble beyond Pearl Harbor. This is the financial center of the mid-Pacific, a top vacation destination and springboard to the Neighbor Islands, and the home of America's only royal palace.

The origins of Honolulu's success can be found on the downtown waterfront, where the original *hono-lulu*, or "sheltered bay," lies at the foot of the landmark Aloha Tower. The finest natural anchorage in the Islands was put on the map by English seafarer Captain William Brown in 1792–3, and became a useful mid-Pacific stop for sailing ships plying the ocean between the Americas and the Orient. The port settlement boomed with the arrival of whalers and New England missionaries in the 1820s, prompting King Kamehameha III to move the Hawaiian capital here from Maui in 1845. And the rest, as they say, is history.

Downtown Honolulu is contained within a few compact blocks. The historic financial district is sandwiched between the harbor and Iolani Palace, and provides a buffer zone between the old mission headquarters and present-day Chinatown, where the whalers once caroused and philandered along Hotel Row.

Pearl Harbor To the west, beyond the airport, are the lagoons of Pearl Harbor, dredged out in the early 1900s. As the home port of the U.S. Pacific Fleet, this key naval base witnessed the infamous Japanese aerial attack which brought America into World War II.

Window-cleaners hang out against a life-size whale leaping up a wall in Ala Moana

One week itinerary
Days one to three: as for long weekend itinerary (see panel opposite).
Day four: Haleiwa, the Northern Beaches, and Wailea Falls Park. Polynesian Cultural Center *luau*.
Day five: Punchbowl Crater and Tantalus Drive. Lunch at the Contemporary Museum. Lyon Arboretum and Manoa Falls Walk.
Day six: Kodak Hula Show (Tue–Thu), Honolulu Zoo and Diamond Head.
Day seven: relax on Waikiki Beach. Shopping at Ala Moana Center.

Life on the ocean wave

Keneohe
Kailua
Kaneohe

Manoa
Falls

Honolulu Watershed Forest Reserve

1,870ft
Napuumaia

Kekoalele Ridge

Rainforest
Drive

Lyon
Arboretum

(63)

Kalihi Valley
Park

PALI HIGHWAY

Kalihi

(61)

KALIHI
VALLEY

1,414ft
Waolani

DOWSETT
HIGHLANDS

2,014ft
Tantalus

Contemporary
Museum

UPPER
MANOA

Kapalama

Oahu
Country
Club

ALEWA
HEIGHTS

Queen
Emma
Summer Palace

NUUANU

Nuuanu Valley Park

PACIFIC
HEIGHTS

Rainforest

Roundtop
Forest
Reserve

Punchbowl
Lookout

1,046ft
Roundtop

LIKELIKE HIGHWAY

KAMEHAMEHA
HEIGHTS

Waolani

Nuuanu

MAKIKI
HEIGHTS

MANOA

Contemporary
Museum

Royal Mausoleum

Pagoda Lookout

TANTALUS DRIVE

KAPALAMA

NUUANU AVENUE

PALI HIGHWAY

PAUOA

MAKIKI

PUNAHOU

Bishop Museum

LANAKILA

Punchbowl Crater
National Memorial
Cemetery of
the Pacific

PUNAHOU

H1

N KING STREET

VINEYARD BLVD

Foster Botanical
Garden

Honolulu
Academy
of Arts

LUNALILO FREEWAY

BERETANIA STREET

S KING STREET

KAPIOLANI

H1

KALAKAUA AVE

Aiea

KALIHI

DILLINGHAM BLVD

Kuan Yin Temple
Cathedral of Our Lady of Peace
Chinatown Cultural
Plaza

Washington
Place

State
Capitol

Thomas Square

Neal S
Blaisdell
Center

NIMITZ HIGHWAY

Dole Cannery
Square

CHINA
TOWN

Island
Palace

City Hall

Ala Moana
Shopping Center

Ala Moana
Beach Park

IWILEI

Oahu
Market

Kawaiahao Church

Mission
Houses
Museum

Honolulu
International
Airport Reed Harbor

(92)

KAPALAMA

*Kapalama
Basin*

DOWNTOWN

Aloha
Tower
*Honolulu
Harbor*
(The Falls of Clyde)

Hawaii
Maritime
Center

KAKAAKO

ALA MOANA BLVD

(92)

Aina
Moana
State
Park

Sand Island

Honolulu Channel

Kakaako
Waterfront
Park

Sand
Island
State
Park

Mamala Bay

Mokouea
Island

N

4

3

2

1

A   B   C

*Waikiki Beach
surfboard park*

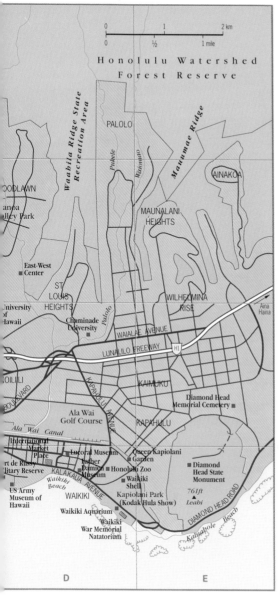

Catching the last rays of the day

"Spouting water" East of downtown Honolulu, there is an area which the Hawaiians called "Spouting Water." This former swamp, with its 1½-mile-long beach guarded by Diamond Head, is better known as Waikiki. Long before mass tourism, Queen Kaahumanu surfed here, and the 19th-century Scottish writer Robert Louis Stevenson "talked story" in a little grass hut. Drained and reclaimed, the square-mile resort boasts some 30,000 hotel rooms and 240 restaurants, plus diversions galore. It may not be everyone's cup of coconut milk, but, like Disneyland, it is a crowd-pleaser through and through.

Aloha and welcome

Princess Bernice Pauahi
Destined to marry into the Royal Family, Princess Bernice Pauahi defied her family and married American banker Charles Reed Bishop instead. The couple dedicated their considerable energies to the preservation of Hawaii's cultural heritage. Princess Bernice also founded the Kamehameha Schools to provide a first-rate education for students of Hawaiian or part-Hawaiian blood. These are still funded by the Princess Bernice Pauahi Estate, which controls vast tracts of Honolulu and the outer islands.

Eastern promise

▶ **Aloha Tower**   54B1

Pier 9, Downtown
Open: Sun–Thu 9–9, Fri–Sat 9AM–10PM. Admission free.
Bus 19, 20, 47; Waikiki Trolley Stop 7
The ten-story Aloha Tower was the tallest building in town when it was completed in 1926, a welcome beacon on the quayside overlooking Honolulu Harbor where the cruise ships of yesteryear were greeted by a bevy of *hula* girls with fragrant *leis* (garlands). Although long since dwarfed by modern skyscrapers, the tower still affords splendid views of downtown and the harbor from its outdoor observation decks. Orientation boards point out local landmarks and there is a bird's-eye view of the four-masted sailing ship *Falls of Clyde* directly below. The surrounding Aloha Tower Marketplace, decked out in a nautical turquoise and white trim, offers a range of attractive boutiques and waterfront restaurants.

▶▶▶ **Bishop Museum**   54A2

1525 Bernice Street, Honolulu (tel: 808/847-3511)
Open: daily 9–5; Planetarium, daily shows at 11 and 2, and Fri–Sat at 7 (reservations required). Admission charge: moderate. Bus 2; Waikiki Trolley Stop 10
This notable State Museum of Natural and Cultural History was founded in 1889 by Charles Reed Bishop, the husband of Princess Bernice Pauahi, great-granddaughter of King Kamehameha I. The princess was an enthusiastic collector, and her peerless hoard of Hawaiiana formed the basis for the museum's very impressive catalogue of Hawaiian and Pacific artifacts (some 187,000 pieces), widely regarded as the finest in the world.

In the Victorian main building, exhibits in the Polynesian Hall cover the island cultures of Melanesia and Micronesia in the Pacific southwest. Artifacts range from flutes and fish hooks to jewelry, finely carved from human bone, and elaborate costumes constructed with great skill and flair from animal, vegetable, and even mineral components.

The three floors of the Hawaiian Hall delve into every aspect of Hawaiian history, society and culture. Beneath the skeleton of a 55-foot sperm whale hoisted to its present position as a tribute to the whaling industry in 1902, displays unravel the complexities of the ancient social hierarchy alongside magnificent ceremonial capes made from the feathers of up to 80,000 birds apiece. There are Stone Age tools and utensils, and sections on war, migrant heritage and traditional crafts. In addition to frequent guided tours, daily demonstrations feature the likes of *lei*-making (garland-making) and quilting.

Beyond the main halls, look for the exhibitions in the Castle Building, *hula* performances in the Atherton Hall, and daily shows in the Planetarium.

▶ **Chinatown**   54B2

West of Nuuanu Avenue, between Ala Moana and
Vineyard Boulevards
Bus 2, 19, 20, 47; Waikiki Trolley Stop 11
A stone's throw from the bustling dockside where the first Chinese indentured laborers would have landed in the 1850s, Honolulu's Chinatown is a compact and

evocative grid of colorful Asian markets, stores selling Chinese medicines and joss sticks, noodle shops, and *dim sum* restaurants. Open-air activities and cultural performances take place in the Chinese Cultural Plaza on North Beretania Street. Nearby, a statue commemorates the "Father of Modern China," Sun Yat-sen, who founded the revolutionary Hsing Chung Hui secret society in Honolulu in 1895, before overthrowing China's Manchu dynasty in 1911.

One of the best ways to explore the area and come to grips with its colorful history is to take a guided walk with the Chinatown Historical Society (Asia Mall, 1250 Maunkakea Street, tel: 808/521-3045).

▶ **Contemporary Museum**   54C3

2411 Makiki Heights Drive, Honolulu (tel: 808/526-0232) Open: Tue–Sat 10–4, Sun 12–4. Admission charge: moderate

Try to visit this elegant museum around lunchtime to take advantage of the excellent Contemporary Café. The permanent collection of modern art (predominantly Hawaiian) is augmented by temporary exhibitions. Take a turn around the pretty gardens, and do not miss David Hockney's 1983 stage model for the Ravel opera *L'Enfant et les Sortilèges,* a theatrically lit, naive-style woodland environment housed in the Milton Cades Pavilion.

History and culture at the Bishop Museum

Charlie Chan
Honolulu's Chinatown was home to Charlie Chan, the world-famous Asian sleuth of Earl Derr Biggers' best-selling crime stories. Biggers drew the inspiration for his hero from a real-life Hawaiian-Chinese detective, Chang Apana, who died in 1933.

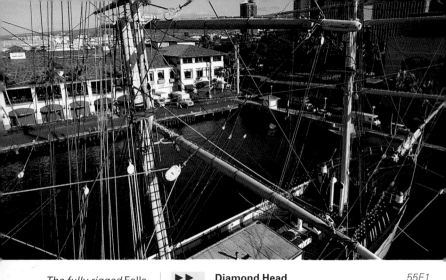

The fully rigged Falls of Clyde

Local directions
If, when asking directions of local people, you are told to walk "Diamond Head, two blocks" for your destination, it means head toward that mountainous landmark. There are three other local direction terms which are less easy to understand: *makai* (toward the sea), *mauka* (toward the mountains), and *ewa* (west toward the Ewa Plain beyond Pearl Harbor).

Heading makai *in the lee of Diamond Head*

▶▶ **Diamond Head**   55E1

Diamond Head State Monument, Diamond Head Road
Open: daily 6–6. Admission free
The crest of Diamond Head, Honolulu's most arresting natural landmark, towers over the southern end of Waikiki Beach. The headland, site of an ancient Hawaiian *heiau* (temple), gained its *haole* (foreign) name from a band of British soldiers who found calcite crystals here in 1825, and mistook them for diamonds.

For a great view of Honolulu, follow Diamond Head Road into the crater. A strenuous trail leads up from the parking lot, through a tunnel and up to the summit.

▶ **Dole Cannery Square**   54A2

650 Iwilei Road, Downtown
Open: daily 9–5. Admission free. Free bus from Waikiki
(schedule, tel: 808/548-6601); Bus 19, 20;
Waikiki Trolley Stop 8
Now that the Dole canning factory has closed, the Square has to employ somewhat drastic measures to entertain customers such as a multi-media presentation devoted to Jim Dole and his pineapples (see page 151) and a display of pineapples from all over the world.

▶ **East-West Center** 55D3

1777 East-West Road, Honolulu (tel: 808/944-7111)
Open: Mon–Fri 8–4:30. Admission free
Inaugurated to promote relations between the U.S. and Asian-Pacific nations, the East-West Center's chief attraction is its setting on the University of Hawaii campus at Manoa. The Center boasts a Thai Pavilion donated by the King of Thailand, a Center for Korean Studies inspired by the Kyongbok Palace in Seoul, the Imin Conference Center designed by I.M. Pei (architect of the John Hancock Tower, Boston), Japanese gardens and numerous oriental artworks. Maps of the center are available at John A. Burns Hall.

▶ **Father Damien Museum** 55D1

130 Ohua Avenue, Waikiki (tel: 808/923-2690)
Open: Mon–Fri 9–3. Admission charge: donations
Behind St. Augustine's Catholic Church on Kalakaua Avenue, this simple museum houses a smattering of memorabilia and a video presentation on the story of Father Damien de Veuster. De Veuster came to Hawaii as a theology student in 1864. From 1873 until his death from leprosy in 1889, he devoted his life to tending the lepers of Kalaupapa (see pages 116–17).

Denizens of the deep in the Hawaii Maritime Center

59

▶▶ **Foster Botanical Garden** 54B2

50 North Vineyard Boulevard, Downtown
Open: daily 9–4. Tours Mon–Fri at 1. Admission charge: inexpensive. Waikiki Trolley Stop 11
In 1853, William Hillebrand, a young German doctor, leased this leafy 14-acre plot from the Crown, built a home, and planted several of the exotic trees that tower over visitors today. Look out for the explosive flowers of the cannonball tree, the panama-hat tree, specialty orchids, heliconias, palms, ferns, and the boulder-strewn Prehistoric Glen.

▶▶▶ **Hawaii Maritime Center** 54B1

Pier 7, Honolulu Harbor (tel: 808/536-6373)
Open: daily 9–5. Admission charge: moderate. Bus 19, 20, 47; Waikiki Trolley Stop 7; free parking
Start a visit to this world-class maritime museum with an audio-guided tour of the main hall (personal stereos provided). Here, exhibits trace the seagoing history of the Islands, from the rafts of the early Polynesians to the heyday of the steamship by way of models and all manner of nautical knick-knacks. Beside the museum, the world's last fully rigged, four-masted sailing ship, *Falls of Clyde*, has been restored. Built in Glasgow in 1878, the ship once plied the San Francisco–Honolulu route.

▶▶ **Honolulu Academy of Arts** 54B2

900 South Beretania Street, Downtown (tel: 808/532-8701)
Open Tue–Sat 10–4:30, Sun 1–5. Admission charge: donations. Bus 2; Waikiki Trolley Stop 5
Housed in a charming 1927 Mediterranean-style building, the Academy is a pleasure to explore. The Asian section, which includes author James Michener's collection of Japanese *ukiyo-e* prints, is one of the finest in the U.S. Notable Western artworks include paintings by Picasso, Gauguin, and Van Gogh, plus sculptures by Rodin.

Legend of Diamond Head
The Hawaiian name for Diamond Head is Leahi ("Brow of the Ahi"). Ancient Hawaiian legends say it was named by the fire goddess Hiiaka, who thought it resembled the profile of a yellowfin tuna (*ahi*). The Hawaiians venerated the site and constructed a *heiau* (temple) here, probably on the western slopes. Kamehameha I is reputed to have both worshipped at the temple site and, after his victory over Oahu's chieftain, Kalanikupule, at the Battle of Nuuanu Valley in 1795, presided over some of the last human sacrifices in Hawaii.

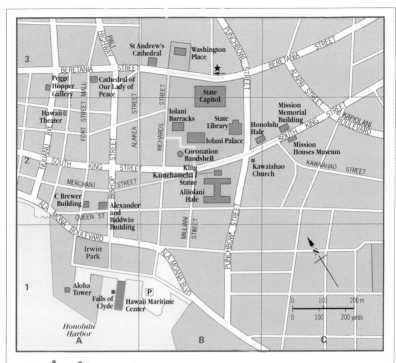

60

Walk Historic Honolulu

This walk offers a full half-day of sightseeing through the historic heart of downtown Honolulu. If you want to include a visit to the Iolani Palace, do remember to make reservations in advance (see page 62).

Start at the **State Capitol** (from Waikiki take Bus 2 or Waikiki Trolley Stop 6 to South Beretania Street). Surrounded by a moat and flanked by pillars which represent palm trees, the 1969 Capitol building gathers its architectural inspiration from Hawaii's volcanic origins. A striking 600,000-tile mosaic in shades of ocean blues dominates the central courtyard. From the Capitol, head across Beretania Street to **Washington Place**, an elegant Greek Revival mansion of the 1840s which was built by Queen Liliuokalani's in-laws. It now houses the Governor's official residence.

Next to Washington Place, the neo-Gothic **St. Andrew's Cathedral** was

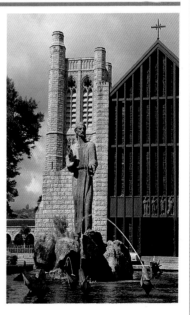

St. Andrew's Cathedral

A resplendent Kamehameha the Great

built in the 19th century partially from stone cut in England and then shipped around the Horn. Above the porch a stained-glass window depicts the church's founders, King Kamehameha IV and Queen Emma. From here, take Richards Street, opposite Washington Place, to the side entrance into the grounds of the **Iolani Palace**. A royal palace for a mere ten years, it takes its name from the Hawaiian for "Hawk of Heaven," the highest symbol of royal authority. The American Florentine-style building has been carefully restored and furnished with many original pieces (see page 62).

Leave from the Iolani's main gate and turn left along South King Street, crossing the junction with Punchbowl Street. On the far left of the junction, the Mediterranean-Revival-style city hall, **Honolulu Hale,** was opened in 1929. Farther along the street, and used as an annex, is the gracious red-brick **Mission Memorial Building**, its façade lined with elegant white columns beneath a triangular tympanum. Built in honor of the New England missionaries, the Mission Memorial faces the original Sandwich Islands Mission buildings, now a museum.

Cross King Street to the **Mission Houses Museum**, the oldest surviving Western-style buildings in the Islands. The buildings were erected by New England missionaries here at the headquarters of the Sandwich Islands Mission, and offer a fascinating insight into life in the Islands from the 1820s to the end of the missionary era (see page 64).

Leave the museum and cross Kawaiahao Street to the churchyard gate of **Kawaiahao Church** (see page 63). Though the missionaries arrived in Honolulu in 1820, the construction of this Protestant church was not completed until 1842.

If you have had enough exploring for one day, Waikiki Trolley Stop 13 is across the street. If not, retrace your steps along King Street to the **Kamehameha Statue** opposite the Iolani Palace. Set on the lawn in front of the Aliiolani Hale, this replica gold-caped statue of Kamehameha I is a famous downtown landmark (the original remains on Kamehameha's home island of Hawaii).

Now take Merchant Street on the far side of the Aliiolani Hale, off Milliani Street, walk the two blocks to Bishop Street, then turn left and continue to the **Alexander and Baldwin Building** at 822 Bishop Street. This venerable building belongs to one of Hawaii's "Big Five" trading companies. Admire its splendid carvings, glazed tiles depicting Hawaiian marine life, and the plethora of oriental motifs.

Continue down Bishop Street to the waterfront. To the right, the **Aloha Tower Marketplace** offers shopping, eateries, and great views from the tower itself (see page 56). To the left is the excellent **Hawaii Maritime Center** (see page 59), opposite Waikiki Trolley Stop 7.

Iolani Barracks

Within the Iolani Palace grounds lies the Iolani Barracks building, a toytown castle with mini crenellated battlements and arrow slits, which now houses the ticket kiosk, visitor center and a gift shop piled high with Hawaiiana. To the left of the palace façade, the Royal Coronation Bandstand, erected for the coronation of King David Kalakaua and Queen Kapiolani in 1883, now hosts free concerts by the Royal Hawaiian Band every Friday at 12:15. Behind the palace, a statue of Queen Liliuokalani honors Hawaii's last monarch.

The Iolani Palace, completed at a cost of $360,000 in 1882

 Honolulu Zoo　55D1

151 Kapahulu Avenue, Waikiki (tel: 808/971-7171)
Open: daily 9–4:30. Admission charge: inexpensive; children under 12 free. Waikiki Trolley Stop 2

Honolulu Zoo occupies a 42-acre site in Kapiolani Park. The old-fashioned enclosures, currently being refurbished, are being phased out and replaced with natural habitat displays, such as the African Savannah area, with hippos and Nile crocodiles, antelopes, lions, giraffes, and chimps. The zoo is home to more than 1,250 animals, including giant Galapagos tortoises (the first bred in zoo conditions), kangaroos, and gibbons; there is a reptile house, plus the rare nene goose, Hawaii's state bird.

 Iolani Palace　54B2

South King Street, Downtown (tel: 808/522-0832)
Open: Wed–Sat 9–2:15 (no children under 5). Admission charge: moderate. Bus 2; Waikiki Trolley Stop 6

Hailed as "America's only royal palace," the Iolani was founded in 1879 and completed three years later under the direction of King David Kalakaua, Hawaii's "Merrie Monarch." The palace has been restored and the *koa*-wood interior is full of grand furnishings, Bohemian crystal, French porcelain and portraits of the Hawaiian kings and queens which recall King David's love affair with foreign royalty and its trappings. Guided tours (it is advisable to make reservations) reveal fascinating nuggets of royal history and palace gossip.

 Kapiolani Park　55D1

Kalakaua Avenue, Waikiki
Open site. Admission free

When King David Kalakaua dedicated the park in his wife's name in 1877, he declared "this breezy plain a place of innocent refreshment for all who wish to leave the dust of the town streets." The 300-acre park south of the Waikiki hotel district is still a favorite recreation area. The park is home to Honolulu Zoo and the Kodak Hula Show (see panel), and also hosts numerous events.

Kamaaina grannies join in the fun at the Kodak Hula Show...

▶ Kawaiahao Church 54B2

957 Punchbowl Street, Downtown
Open: daily 9–4. Admission free. Bus 2; Waikiki Trolley Stop 13

Kawaiahao is built from blocks of coral rock—around 14,000 of them weighing some 1,000 pounds apiece. It was completed in 1842, on the site of the first Christian church, and services are still held there. Two prominent Hawaiians are interred in the graveyard: King William Lunalilo, the "People's King"; and the Reverend James Kekela, Hawaii's first native Christian minister.

▶ Kuan Yin Temple 54B2

170 North Vineyard Boulevard, Downtown
Open: daily 8:30–2. Admission free. Waikiki Trolley Stop 11

The smell of incense wafting down the street near the Foster Botanical Garden greets you long before you catch sight of this ornate little temple, with its traditional curving roof, and red and gold trimmings. A statue of Kuan Yin, the Buddhist goddess of mercy, presides over the altar and carved and gilded pagodas contain the figures of other deities.

▶▶▶ Lyon Arboretum 54C4

3860 Manoa Road, Honolulu
Open: Mon–Sat 9–3. Admission charge: donations

These glorious gardens lie tucked in a cleft of the Manoa Valley cliffs. Winding paths traverse steep hillsides and there is a Fern Valley *en route* to Inspiration Point, which affords splendid views over the flowering trees. The Aeroid Valley path leads to plantations of colorful gingers and heliconias. Touring the gardens is quite a hike in itself, but if you still feel energetic, the start of the Manoa Falls walk (see page 69) is near the arboretum's entrance.

... and their daughters show how it should be done

Kodak Hula Show
A Waikiki institution, this popular hula show has been running since 1937. It is still great fun, with the added bonus that it is free. Be sure to arrive early in summer since the line snakes around the park. (Kapiolani Park, Tue, Wed and Thu at 10AM.)

Waioli Tea Room

Feeling thirsty after a morning's trek around the Lyon Arboretum? Hungry after the hike to the Manoa Falls? On the road back to town, look for the intersection of Manoa Road and Oahu Avenue, where the Salvation Army's Waioli Tea Room (3016 Oahu Avenue) serves good home-cooked pastries and offers an inexpensive lunch menu (Tue–Sun 11–1:30), with tables on the veranda. You can also see the old grass shack in which author and traveler Robert Louis Stevenson is supposed to have lived during his stay in Waikiki in the 1880s.

Up in the hills

Anyone renting a car in Honolulu should explore the hills behind the city. From Puowaina Drive (the road up to Punchbowl Crater), Tantalus Drive winds its way up into the Koolau Mountains, changes its name to Round Top Drive, then makes a grand circuitous tour through the lush rainforest and classy residential heights of the city. There are several viewpoints, public paths and hiking trails *en route*, and the Contemporary Museum (see page 57) makes a good lunch stop on the way back.

▶▶▶ Mission Houses Museum   54B2

553 South King Street, Downtown (tel: 808/531-0481)
Open: Tue–Sat 9–4 (tours every hour 9:30–11:30 and
1–3), Sun 12–4 (tours every hour 1–3). Admission
charge: moderate. Bus 2; Waikiki Trolley Stop 13

When the first New England missionaries arrived in Hawaii in 1820, they established their headquarters here in Honolulu. This small group of historic buildings, its exhibits and guided tours trace the lifestyle of the missionaries and their relationship with their native hosts. Amongst the period furnishings of the 1821 frame house, built of pre-cut timbers shipped from New England, is a rocking chair which belonged to Queen Kaahumanu, whose conversion to Christianity was a major coup for the mission brothers. The Hale Pai (printing office), completed in 1841, displays a working press which was used to print Hawaiian and English tracts and books.

▶▶ Punchbowl Crater National Memorial
Cemetery of the Pacific   54B2

2177 Puowaina Drive, Honolulu
Open: daily 8–5:30 (until 6:30 Mar 2–Sep 29). Admission
free. Bus 2 to Beretania and Alapai streets, then Bus 15

The national cemetery, located in the crater of an extinct volcano whose name means "Hill of Sacrifice," contains the graves of 25,000 servicemen and -women who fought in World War II, Korea and Vietnam. The site is dominated by the Columbia Memorial, where the Courts of the Missing flanking the monumental staircase list a further 26,000 military personnel whose bodies were never recovered. Behind the 30-foot-high statue of Columbia is a chapel, and galleries on either side illustrate major World War II battles in the Pacific.

A road leads up from the cemetery to a lookout point which affords spectacular views across Waikiki to Diamond Head.

The Columbia Statue at Punchbowl Crater National Memorial Cemetery of the Pacific

Weddings in Paradise

■ "Suitably masked and flippered, the bride wore a white one-piece, while the groom was attired in tuxedo and board shorts. After the ceremony, the happy pair swam away to a reception held aboard a 65-foot pirate schooner, accompanied by the priest, his parrots and 15 close friends." It could only happen in Hawaii. ■

The big day Hawaii's wedding industry is booming. Around 43 percent of the marriages performed in the state are for visitors from the mainland or overseas, and providing both partners are over 18 and hold a valid Hawaiian marriage license (see panel), getting married in Hawaii is easy. Most large hotels have their own wedding co-ordinator, and offer special packages with extras such as a champagne breakfast in bed or a sunset sail for the newlyweds.

Pirates and *paniolos* On Oahu, the Reverend Howie Welfeld of **Above Heaven's Gate** (tel: 808/259-5429) is a big fan of alfresco weddings in what he calls "the Lord's Outdoor Cathedral"; couples employing his services can tie the knot on his schooner *Lotus Flower* or even under water! At **Kualoa Ranch** (tel: 808/237-8515), the happy pair can head off *paniolo*-style (cowboy-style) into the Koolau Mountains with a blue-jeaned minister for a short ceremony followed by a barbecue reception.

Surfboards to temples On Kauai, Wedding in Paradise (tel: 808/246-2779) are the local experts. On Maui, wedding options include a surfboard ceremony orchestrated by Angela Thomas of **Royal Hawaiian Weddings** (tel: 800/659-1866), or weddings at a Tibetan temple arranged by Alicia Bay Laurel of **A Wedding Made in Paradise** (tel: 808/879-3444).

On the Big Island, Debbie Cravatta of **Paradise Weddings Hawaii** (tel: 808/883-9067) fulfills her motto "Intimate to Outrageous" by organizing weddings in helicopters and submarines, on the golf course, on horseback, or even on Harley Davidson motorcycles.

For most couples, however, a traditional wedding in a Hawaiian setting is the order of the day. And for Hawaii's professional wedding organizers, no wedding is too big or too small, too grand or too simple, or even too weird!

Marriage rules
Hawaiian marriage licenses can be purchased from the Department of Health, Marriage License Office (1250 Punchbowl Street, Honolulu, HI 96813), or from a marriage licensing agent on any of the Neighbor Islands (details available from hotels and from wedding organizers). A birth certificate, driver's license or some other form of identification will be required. The names and birthplaces of both partners' parents must be filled in on the form. If either partner has been married before, he or she must state the date, county and state (or country) in which the divorce was finalized.

65

Tee-ing up for married life

Queen Emma Summer Palace in the hills above Honolulu

Kamehameha IV
The high regard in which Kamehameha IV held British royalty dated from a trip he made to Europe as a young prince in 1849–50. A stop in England resulted in a meeting with Queen Victoria, who later agreed to be a godmother to his son, Albert Edward (named after Victoria's husband Prince Albert). On returning to Hawaii via the U.S., the 15-year-old prince was mistaken for a black servant and ejected from his train carriage by the conductor. The incident left a lasting impression, and Kamehameha IV consistently favored British interests over those of the U.S.

▶▶   **Queen Emma Summer Palace**   54B3
2913 Pali Highway (tel: 808/595-3167)
Open: daily 9–4. Admission charge: moderate
Queen Emma's modest summer retreat, perched on the Nuuanu hillside with its green-shuttered windows carefully aligned to catch the slightest breeze, is about a ten-minute drive from downtown Honolulu. The building materials for the two-bedroom wooden home were shipped to Oahu from Boston in the mid-1800s, and the palace's Victorian furnishings include many souvenirs of the British royal family, with whom the queen and her husband, Kamehameha IV, maintained a cordial if long-distance acquaintanceship.

▶   **Royal Mausoleum**   54B3
Nuuanu Avenue, Honolulu
Open site. Admission free
During King Kamehameha V's reign, the original royal graveyard in the grounds of what is now the Iolani Palace was deemed overcrowded, so the burial site was moved here to the lower reaches of the Nuuanu Valley in 1865. All the Kamehameha kings except Kamehameha I are buried in this attractive plot, as are King David Kalakaua and Queen Liliuokalani.

▶▶   **U.S. Army Museum of Hawaii**   55D1
Fort de Russy, Kalia Road, Waikiki (tel: 808/438-2821)
Open: Tue–Sun 10–4:30. Admission free (charge for audio tours)
This well-laid-out and informative museum is housed in a former coastal artillery battery on the seafront. Tours begin with an introduction to Hawaiian history and warfare. Alongside other assorted Hawaiiana, a selection of vicious-looking barbed spears and *pua*-wood clubs inset with sharks' teeth give new meaning to the phrase "armed to the teeth."
   Displays of photographs, memorabilia and models, together with video presentations detail World War II in the Pacific, with extensive coverage of the Pearl Harbor

attack and the exploits of the famous AJA (Americans of Japanese Ancestry) battalion, which saw action in Europe, North Africa, and the Pacific. Further exhibits turn to more recent conflicts in Korea and Vietnam.

▶▶ U.S.S. *Arizona* Memorial 50C1

Pearl Harbor (Exit 15A from H-1 West) (tel: 808/422-0561) Open: Visitor Center, daily 7:30–5; daily programs, Sep–May 8–3, Jun–Aug 7:45–3. Admission free. Bus 20 and 47 from Waikiki direct; or 8, 19, or 58 to Ala Moana Center and transfer to 48, 49, 50 or 52

At 07:55 on December 7, 1941, two waves of Japanese fighter-bombers dropped out of the sky above Oahu and pulverized the American war machine massed on the "Gibraltar of the Pacific." The catalogue of military gaffes—from planes parked wingtip to wingtip and disarmed at night to prevent sabotage, to the officer of the watch deciding that the blips on the radar screen were probably reinforcements due in from California later that day—defies belief, and the losses were catastrophic. President Roosevelt described it as a "day of infamy" and the attack brought the U.S. into World War II.

The U.S.S. *Arizona* sank at her moorings on Battleship Row, and 1,102 members of her crew rest with her on the bottom of Pearl Harbor. The memorial was dedicated on May 30, 1962, to all service personnel killed in action during the attack. Visits to the striking white concrete structure which spans the 106-foot-wide and 608-foot-long hull begin at the *Arizona* Memorial Center on the dock. After a film presentation, which includes clippings from pre-War newsreels as well as actual footage shot during and after the attack, there is a boat trip out to the Memorial. The full visit takes approximately 75 minutes, and tickets are issued on a first-come-first-served basis. In the peak summer season you can wait up to three hours between collecting tickets and getting access to the theater, though the lines are more manageable early in the day. The Visitor Center has basic refreshment facilities and information.

The memorial building above the sunken U.S.S. Arizona

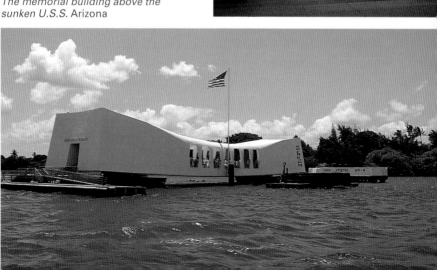

The roll-call of servicemen lost in the Pearl Harbor attack

The U.S.S. Bowfin *at Pearl Harbor*

A window on the underwater world

▶▶ **U.S.S. *Bowfin* Submarine Museum and Park**   50C2

11 Arizona Memorial Drive, Pearl Harbor
Open: daily 8–5. Admission charge: moderate. Bus 20 and 47 from Waikiki direct; or 8, 19, or 58 to Ala Moana Center and transfer to 48, 49, 50 or 52

This museum makes a welcome harbor-side diversion for visitors to the *Arizona* Memorial who may have a wait between ticket collection and access to the Center. It gives a history of submarines and tours of an actual World War II submarine, plus a free wander around its missile garden park.

The waterfront park positively bristles with hardware, from torpedo shells and gun batteries to an amputated conning tower and a captured Japanese suicide submarine. From the dock, you can go below deck into the cramped confines of the U.S.S. *Bowfin*, nicknamed the "Pearl Harbor Avenger" for her role in sinking 44 enemy vessels during nine tours of duty.

▶▶▶ **Waikiki Aquarium**   55D1

2777 Kalakaua Avenue, Waikiki (tel: 808/923-9741)
Open: daily 9–5. Admission charge: moderate (children under 12 free)

The third oldest public aquarium in the U.S. (founded 1904) lies right on the ocean shore and is just the place to come to grips with the exotic marine life of the Hawaiian Islands and South Pacific. Indoor and outdoor exhibits bring visitors face to face with denizens of the deep and not-so-deep, and interactive displays track the journeys of marine creatures across the Pacific to Hawaii.

Here you can meet the endangered Hawaiian monk seal, investigate the myriad life-forms of the coral reef at the Reef Machine exhibit, and ogle the predatory sharks at Hunters on the Reef. Then take in a couple of shows at the SeaVisions Theater; and learn about the life cycle of the *mahimahi* (dolphin fish) at the Mahimahi Hatchery, before trawling The Natural Selection gift shop for fishy gifts and other marine-related souvenirs.

Walks Two short walks around Honolulu

These two walks in the hills above Waikiki are easily accessible from Honolulu. They take in beautiful views, colorful trees and flowers, and glimpses of native birdlife.

Manoa Falls

This short but worthwhile hike through the lush hillsides of Mount Tantalus will take only an hour or so for the round trip, and begins at the top of Manoa Road, just beyond the Lyon Arboretum. Sensible shoes and mosquito repellent are advisable.

From the road, the marked path leads into the cool, green woodlands. At the first fork in the path, keep left and then navigate the main stream with the help of stepping stones. The trail clambers through the woods across a chaos of mossy boulders and twisted tree roots edged by ferns. A massive exposed root network serves as a slippery stairway before the path narrows, traverses a bamboo copse on duckboards, and winds up to the base of the falls, which cascade down the bare cliff face in a plume of white water.

Waahila Ridge

This trail makes another short walk above Honolulu, beginning from the Waahila Ridge State Recreation Area up in St. Louis Heights. Take St. Louis Drive and Peter Street up to Ruth Place, and park in the State Recreation Area. It can get very hot and breezy up here, so bring water and sunscreen.

From the parking lot, the first leg of the hike is a strenuous ten-minute uphill climb through the ironwood forest. Then the trail alternately scales the peaks and plunges down the troughs of the narrow, 2-mile ridge top. There are bird's-eye views across the Manoa and Palolo valleys on either side, but some of the prettiest things to be seen are the wildflowers which grow in abundance up here. In addition to the blankets of miniature passion-flower vines, hibiscus-like yellow-orange *ilima*

flowers and tuffets of spiky purple valerian, there are tunnels of gnarled trees tortured into bizarre shapes by the wind.

Manoa Falls

Shopping

Souvenir City: Waikiki's International Marketplace

Kamakas all
What have Tiny Tim, Laurel and Hardy, astronaut Scott Carpenter, and just about every celebrated Hawaiian slack key guitarist got in common? They have all owned a Kamaka ukelele. These *koa*-wood Stradivariuses of the ukelele world are handcrafted by the family firm of Kamaka Hawaii, Inc., under the direction of the sons and grandsons of its founder, Sam Kanaka Sr., who turned out the first Kamaka ukes from the basement of his home in 1916. Kamaka ukeleles are on sale in good music shops, and *aficionados* are always dropping in for a chat at the family factory at 550 South Street, Honolulu.

Shopping (the fun stuff, not the routine weekly trek to the supermarket) has always been one of life's little pleasures. Let the shop-'til-you-drop contingent rest assured that there is plenty of fun in store in the malls, markets, galleries and gift shops of Waikiki and Honolulu.

Waikiki Waikiki's Kalakaua Avenue is the home of two major shopping experiences: the **Royal Hawaiian Shopping Center**, whose three buildings are filled with 150 assorted designer boutiques and discount stores, perfumeries, T-shirt outlets and dining options; and the six-story **Waikiki Shopping Plaza**. Just down the block, the **International Marketplace** spreads its wares over a collection of open-air stalls beneath a banyan tree. This is strictly kitsch merchandise, but is still good for a browse. On palm-shaded **Kuhio Avenue**, you can upgrade your luggage at Louis Vuitton, drop in on Chanel, and then check out the latest designer-wear from Italy.

Honolulu Outside Waikiki, just across the Ala Wai Canal, Honolulu's biggest and best mall, the **Ala Moana Center**, offers 200-plus stores and Hawaii's largest food hall. The well-known department stores—Sears, J.C. Penney and the Hawaiian chain store, Liberty House—are here, as well as designer outlets and souvenir sellers. Closer to downtown, the **Ward Center** (1200 Ala Moana Boulevard), and neighboring **Ward Warehouse** (1050 Ala Moana Boulevard), with a more arts and crafts bias, both offer shopping, dining, and easy access via the Waikiki Trolley route (Stop 17).

Downtown's latest shopping mecca is the attractive, harbor-front **Aloha Tower Marketplace** complex, where the inevitable boutiques are augmented by elegant household shops selling Hawaiian quilts and furnishings crafted from native woods. Further west, the **Chinatown** district offers a cornucopia of Asian shops and markets, plus recently rediscovered and cleaned-up **Nuuanu Avenue**, nicknamed "Gallery Row," which is a showcase for Hawaii's vibrant contemporary arts scene.

Shopping

Arts and crafts For high quality, genuine Hawaiian-made souvenirs of the arts and crafts variety, the best choice and some of the fairest prices are often found in museum gift shops throughout the Islands. The **Iolani Palace, Mission Houses Museum,** and Bishop Museum all offer a selection of *kukui*-nut jewelry, Hawaiian quilting kits, *koa*-wood carvings, Hawaiian books, and specialty guides. The Iolani Palace is particularly good on things royal; the Mission Houses Museum sells Hawaiian food-stuffs such as coffee and tropical fruit jellies, as well as inexpensive prints produced from period plates on the original mission press; and the **Honolulu Academy of Arts** shop sells all sorts of handicrafts by local artists, including pottery and glassware.

Clothes Probably the most classic Hawaiian souvenir of all is the *aloha* shirt. This boxy, short-sleeved evergreen introduced in the 1930s is on sale everywhere, from the hotel foyer to hippy beach stalls. The female equivalent, the sack-like *muumuu*, is also a popular buy. **Hilo Hattie** has become a byword in the Islands for the greatest choice of *aloha*-wear, general resort-style clothing and value-for-money local souvenirs. The Honolulu branch provides free transportation from Waikiki, and is on the Waikiki Trolley route (Stop 9). Another favorite tourist shopping spot is the **Maui Divers' Jewelry Design Center,** which specializes in jewelry made from Hawaiian coral and shells (Waikiki Trolley Stop 4).

Foodstuffs If you would like to take home a taste of Hawaii, macadamia nuts are a real local specialty and are widely available. So are jams, jellies and preserves made from exotic fruits such as guavas, pineapples, and mangoes, and coffee blends from the Big Island's Kona Coast (notably light and easy to pack). Many tourist attractions stock these items in their gift stores, though better deals can be found in supermarkets.

Shell shopping

Looking for *leis*?
Then make tracks for Chinatown's Maunakea Street. Here, dozens of shops and street stalls offer the best choice of *leis* in town from the intricate and rare to the simply fragrant. Maunakea Street is also the place to buy tropical blooms such as gingers, anthuriums, proteas, and orchids. Several flower shops can arrange delivery to the mainland U.S.

Trawling the Mall

Nightlife

As yet another spectacular tropical sunset turns the Pacific horizon to fire, the *mai-tais* begin to flow, the bands tune up, and the great Waikiki entertainment scene shifts up a gear in preparation for another night on the town. Among the entertainments are cabaret and dinner shows, Hawaiian *luaus*, discothèques, comedy clubs and karaoke lounges full of Japanese Elvises. Weekly listings of diversions on offer are published in the Friday edition of the *Honolulu Advertiser*, and in free publications such as *This Week* and *Spotlight on Oahu* (available in hotel lobbies and on the street). The latter are also a good source of discount-entry and free drinks coupons.

A little cocktail music For a sundowner accompanied by ocean views and a little local music, the classiest spot on "The Strip" must be the Halekulani Hotel's **House Without a Key** (2199 Kalia Road, tel: 808/923-2311), which has some of the best old-style Hawaiian music in town. The **Sheraton-Waikiki** (2255 Kalakaua Avenue, tel: 808/922-4422) features local singer-musicians in three bars and *hula* at the poolside; and there is always an entertaining show at the **Hilton Hawaiian Village's** open-air **Tapa Bar** (2005 Kalia Road, tel: 808/949-4321).

For something a little more lively, whoop it up with margaritas and tortilla chips at **Compadres Bar & Grill** (Building 3, Ward Center, 1200 Ala Moana Boulevard, Honolulu, tel: 808/591-8307).

Dinner shows and *luaus* Polynesian-style dinner shows are perennial favorites with visitors, and probably the biggest on the beach is the **Sheraton Princess Kaiulani's Polynesian Revue** (120 Kaiulani Avenue, tel: 808/971-5300), with earlybird and 8PM seatings. **Hilton Hawaiian Village's Magic of Polynesia** (2005 Kalia Road, tel: 808/941-0924) is a good family show with the

Top entertainments
Keep an eye out for acts such as the excellent singing duo The Brothers Cazimero, who play in the Monarch Room at the Royal Hawaiian Hotel (tel: 808/923-7311); crooner Don Ho at the Waikiki Beachcomber (tel: 808/922-4646); and others such as Teresa Bright, Sons of Hawaii, and the Makaha Sons. Comedian Frank De Lima plays at the Polynesian Palace (tel: 808/923-9861); and the pick of local and mainland comedy acts can be seen at the Honolulu Comedy Club (tel: 808/922-5998).

72

Partytime Polynesian-style in Waikiki

added attraction of magician John Hirokawa, while the **Outrigger Main Showroom** (2335 Kalakaua Avenue, tel: 808/923-0711) features the Society of Seven show band, which spices up its act with impressions and comedy routines.

Out of town, on the Windward Coast, the **Polynesian Cultural Center** (Kamehameha Highway, Laie, tel: 808/293-3333) offers the most spectacular revue of them all with a cast of hundreds. On the north coast, **Waimea Falls Park** (59-864 Kamehameha Highway, tel: 808/638-8511 or 808/942-5700) has a weekend program including story-telling, song, dance, a buffet, and a dramatic night dive down the park's 45-foot waterfall.

Terrible liberties have been taken with the traditional Hawaiian *luau* (see pages 16–17), and vacationers expecting a genuine Hawaiian experience may well be disappointed. Yet commercial *luaus,* accompanied by music and *hula,* are very popular with people who enjoy a crowd. Oahu's leading *luau* operations are **Paradise Cove Luau** (tel: 808/973-5828) and **Germaine's Luau** (tel: 808/949-6626).

Discothèques and dancing Want to dance the night away? At the top end of the market is the chic **Maharaja** (Waikiki Trade Center, 2255 Kuhio Avenue, tel: 808/922-3030), where the visiting celebrities go. Night-owls should try **Rumours** (Ala Moana Hotel, 410 Atkinson Drive, Honolulu, tel: 808/955-4811), open until 4AM Friday and Saturday. **Studebaker's** (500 Ala Moana Boulevard, Honolulu, tel: 808/526-9888) is in Restaurant Row. If you prefer dancing in the old-fashioned way to 1940s', 50s' and 60s' music, try the **Maile Lounge** (Kahala Hilton, 5000 Kahala Avenue, Honolulu, tel: 808/734-2211) or the **Esprit Lounge** (Sheraton Waikiki Hotel, 2255 Kalakaua Avenue, tel: 808/922-4422), where the band covers an impressive range of rock, disco, and big-band favorites.

Honolulu lights up for another action-packed night on the town

Hawaii Symphony Orchestra
The Hawaii Symphony Orchestra strikes a more classical note from its base at the Neal Blaisdell Concert Hall, 777 Ward Avenue, Honolulu (box office, tel: 808/591-2211; administration office, tel: 808/527-5400). The Symphony's August–May season covers a wide range of classical music and pop, and also hosts Hawaiian artists and special holiday concerts. Outdoor concerts at the Waikiki Shell in Kapiolani Park are a favorite summer feature.

Eating and drinking

Kau-kau *wagon*

Honolulu's eclectic restaurant scene leaves very few gastronomic stones unturned. You can eat your way around the globe, from China to California, a pizza to Pacific Rim (see panel), Creole to continental and Thai to Tex-Mex, all within a short walk of most hotel lobbies. The choice often starts in the hotel itself with, for example, a California-style courtyard café, a seafood broiler, and a chic dining-room serving French, Italian, or New American/Pacific Rim cuisine.

Home cooking The most difficult ethnic cuisine to find amidst this wealth of international influences is authentic Hawaiian food. Several commercial *luaus* (feasts) and dinner shows (see page 72) offer tame Hawaiian dishes with distinctly American trimmings, but visitors who want the real thing in Waikiki should try chef Gary Strehl's excellent Hawaiian buffet at the **Hawaii Prince Hotel**. Alternatively, for home cooking, Honolulu's best local restaurant is **Ono Hawaiian Foods** (see page 200), where you can enjoy a mountainous plate lunch (see panel).

Asian influences The greatest influence on the local cuisine after all-American is Japanese, or to be more specific, *teriyaki*. *Teriyaki* beef, *teriyaki* chicken, *teriyaki* fish, even *teriyaki* hamburgers, are tried and tested Island favorites, though some palates (mainly non-American) may find meat treated this way cloyingly sweet. *Sushi* is also popular, as is *saimin*, a Japanese clear soup with noodles, scallions, and fish.

Chinese cuisine is also a strong influence. Chinatown is obviously the place to go if you want authentic *dim sum*, but there are several good Chinese restaurants in Waikiki. Korean, Vietnamese, and Thai restaurants are also gaining a toehold.

The plate lunch
A typical Hawaiian hybrid, the plate lunch is said to have its origins in World War II, when lunch wagons trundled around feeding workers on site. These cramped portable kitchens, known as *kau-kau* wagons, still exist, parked in city lots or down at the beach. They dish up plates of *teriyaki* beef and/or chicken, barbecue ribs, a fish dish such as *mahimahi* (dolphin fish), macaroni salad and the requisite "two scoops rice." The plate lunch is generally no culinary masterpiece, but it is fast, filling, and inexpensive.

Waterfront dining

Where to go Most major hotels offer a choice of dining options, from buffets and family-style eateries to elegant candle-lit "signature" restaurants. Shopping centers are a good source of affordable restaurants and snack stops. The **Ala Moana Center's Makai Market** food court has 18 eateries serving up a diverse range of cuisines. The **Royal Hawaiian Shopping Center** in Waikiki, and the **Ward Center** and **Ward Warehouse** on Ala Moana Boulevard also provide a successful mixture of shops and restaurants. The **Aloha Tower Marketplace** enjoys a waterfront setting; and Honolulu's **Restaurant Row** is at the downtown end of Ala Moana.

Several of Waikiki's top hotels combine superior cuisine with enviably romantic settings. A table on the terrace overlooking the ocean at the Halekulani Hotel's **Orchids** restaurant should ensure an unforgettable evening; or, if you are really pushing the boat out, try the sumptuous **La Mer**, in the same hotel, or **Michel's** at the Colony Surf.

What to expect On the whole, restaurant dress in Hawaii is casual, although one or two restaurants request that gentlemen wear a jacket. Reservations are advisable at all good restaurants. All restaurants have smoking and non-smoking sections, so make your preference clear when booking. Service is rarely included on the bill; a 15 percent tip is the norm.

Thirsty work There is nothing quite like a day on the beach for building up a thirst, and Waikiki boasts some 279 drinking venues, from pool bars to pubs. Most serve cocktails, American and imported beers, and Californian wines at resort prices. Local bars are often more reasonably priced than hotels, although daily specials and Happy Hours offer a few bargains, and every decent Hawaiian bar should offer a selection of *pupus* (bar snacks).

Pacific Rim Cuisine
Yet another new culinary title for the mystification of the uninitiated. Pacific Rim or Hawaiian Regional cuisine, as it is often known in the Islands, is an offshoot of the *nouvelle cuisine* revolution which also spawned the New American style. Pacific Rim/Hawaiian Regional cuisine style draws its inspiration from California and the Orient, marrying local ingredients with cooking styles from the Phillipines, Japan, Thailand, Korea, and Vietnam. Renowned local HRC chefs include Peter Merriman, Gary Strehl, and Amy Ferguson Ote.

75

Genuine luaus *are hard to find*

Accommodations

With well over 90 hotels providing around 30,000 hotel rooms, Waikiki offers its visitors a tremendous choice of accommodations ranging from relaxed family-style facilities, quiet "boutique" hotels and self-catering condominiums to luxurious beach-front properties.

On the one hand there is the Hilton Hawaiian Village's resort within a resort, boasting some 2,542 rooms in four separate highrise buildings in a complex of pools, bars, restaurants and entertainment areas. At the opposite end of the scale are intimate "boutique" hotels with elegant surroundings but few facilities.

Although nowhere in Waikiki is more than a ten-minute walk from the beach, location is important and, not surprisingly, accommodations on the beach command higher rates. An unimpeded panorama of the sparkling Pacific from an ocean-front room adds between 10 and 15 percent to the price of an identical room with a garden or mountain (inland) view.

Peak-season rates run from mid-December to March, with slight variations on either side. Some hotels also raise their prices during the June–August summer season. And remember Hawaii's 9 percent room tax.

Colonial elegance at the Sheraton Moana Surfrider

Value for money Waikiki hotels are seldom a bargain, and there are no chain motels to soften the blow for budget travelers. However, most of the hotels offer competitive package rates for stays of a week or more including extras such as car rental. Check what is on offer with a knowledgeable travel agent. Many larger hotel groups, such as the Hilton, Sheraton, and the Islands' own Outrigger and Aston groups (with 20 and eight hotels in Waikiki respectively), have charge-free reservations numbers in the mainland U.S.

Make sure the hotel's facilities will suit your needs. Most hotel rooms are equipped with air-conditioning, T.V.

Beachfront Waikiki

and phone, and non-smoking rooms are usually available on request. A swimming pool, different dining options and an activities desk providing advice on local sights and tours are frequently available, as well as children's programs and free evening entertainment.

Condominiums and self-catering Waikiki's wide range of condominium accommodations are an attractive option if you are staying for a while, and for families and groups of friends. These privately owned apartments are usually part of a highrise development which may or may not offer facilities such as a pool, concierge and maid service. Minimum stay is usually three to seven days, particularly during the peak season. The Hawaii Visitors Bureau can supply a comprehensive list of its member properties throughout the Islands (see page 192).

A number of moderately priced hotels offer efficiencies (hotel rooms equipped with basic cooking facilities), another popular money-saving option.

Beyond Waikiki Although Waikiki undoubtedly offers the greatest choice of accommodations, there are alternatives to The Strip. Just 5 miles east of Waikiki is the **Kahala Hilton** (see page 195), a luxurious beach-front retreat with dolphins swimming in a lagoon; and there is golf, tennis, and riding at the sister **Turtle Bay Hilton & Country Club**, on the windward coast at Kahuku (see page 195). Peace and quiet is guaranteed at the superbly appointed **Ihilani Resort & Spa** on the leeward coast, which has deluxe facilities, a championship golf course, tennis courts, watersports, three restaurants and shopping (see page 195). Look for more affordable bed-and-breakfast accommodations on the windward coast.

Kick back and relax by the hotel pool

Colonial and luxurious
For style that stands out by a mile, there are two *grandes dames* of the Waikiki hotel scene. The senior is the elegant, colonial-style Sheraton Moana Surfrider, built in 1901 around a banyan-shaded courtyard, where the good and the great take afternoon tea or a cocktail on the veranda. The rival Royal Hawaiian, a splendidly over-elaborate Spanish Moorish Revival edifice built in 1927, has been nicknamed the "Pink Palace" because of its rosy paintwork. This former playground of Douglas Fairbanks and Mary Pickford still offers some of the best dinner shows and most fabulously decorated public rooms in town.

Practicalities

Airport transfers Honolulu International Airport lies a 15-minute drive northwest of downtown and 30 minutes from Waikiki. The international and inter-island terminals are linked by the free **WikiWiki bus service**. Reasonably priced **shuttle buses** to Waikiki hotels depart every 20 minutes or so from the medial strip outside the arrivals areas. Round-trip tickets are available; the Waikiki–airport trip should be reserved 24 hours in advance. There is always a plentiful supply of **taxis**, including capacious family-size limousines.

Car rental All the major car-rental companies have offices at the airport and in Waikiki. For further details, see pages 184–5.

Crime Sadly, crime does exist in Paradise, but the main danger for tourists is petty theft, so do not carry large amounts of cash; do not leave valuables unattended on the beach or in easily identifiable rental cars; and keep to brightly lit streets after dark.

The bus and the Waikiki Trolley Honolulu and, in fact, the whole of Oahu, has the best public transportation service in the Islands. It is called **The Bus**, and it serves 65 routes covering most of the island and it is a bargain. Buses stop only at marked bus stops, and the number and destination are written on the front. One-price tickets (there is a reduction for students, and children under six go free) are issued on board and cover single continuous trips in one general direction, including transfers (tell the bus driver your destination). Payment must be made with exact money; no change is given. For specific route information tel: 808/848-5555 between 5:30AM and 10PM, for recorded information on how to get to more than 50 top attractions and places of interest, tel: 808/296 1818, followed by code 8287.

The distinctly touristy **Waikiki Trolley**, though hardly a bargain, is convenient and easy to use. These open-sided, rubber-wheeled trolleys depart from outside the Royal Hawaiian Shopping Center every 15 minutes from 8AM to 4:30PM on a two-hour circuit of Waikiki and downtown Honolulu, stopping off at all the major sights. Passengers are free to get off where they choose and to stay there for as little or as long as they like. In addition to its one-day passes, the Trolley also offers a five-day Multi-Day Pass. For further details tel: 808/596-2199.

Tourist information Information for Oahu and the other islands can be obtained in advance from the **Hawaii Visitors Bureau**'s U.S. mainland or overseas offices (see page 192), or direct from the main information office at the Waikiki Business

Honolulu's finest

The WikiWiki Shuttle links the terminals at Honolulu International Airport

Plaza (2270 Kalakaua Avenue, 7th Floor, Honolulu, HI 96815, tel: 808/923-1811), Monday to Friday 8–4:30. Most Waikiki hotels have a selection of maps and brochures in their reception areas covering the island's main sightseeing attractions, dinner shows, and tours. Larger establishments may have an information desk offering assistance with inquiries and a reservations service.

Tours Dozens of operators, both large and small, offer tours of Oahu. Two of the best known are **E Noa Tours** (tel: 808/591-2561) and **Polynesian Adventure Tours** (tel: 808/833-3000), both of which offer a range of downtown Honolulu and around-the-island tours as well as visits to specific attractions, in air-conditioned buses or mini-buses. (See also panel opposite.)

Explore Honolulu aboard the Waikiki Trolley

Drive Southern Oahu

See map on pages 50–51.

This leisurely day-long driving tour from Waikiki explores the southern corner of Oahu. Leave plenty of time for sightseeing along the 60-mile circular route which takes in a royal retreat, the Sea Life Park, surfing beaches, and a crater garden.

From Waikiki, take Kapahulu Avenue off Kalakaua Avenue, and follow the signs to the H-1 freeway. Take H-1 west to Exit 21B, exit on to the Pali Highway (HI-61), and drive uphill for about 3½ miles before beginning to look for the red and yellow HVB sign-post (on the right, but difficult to see) outside the **Queen Emma Summer Palace.** This upcountry retreat of one of Hawaii's most beloved queens has just five rooms leading off its broad central hall. Royal furnishings and ornaments include splendid *koa*-wood beds, feathered *kahili* (royal standards) and jewelry, plus poignant reminders of Emma's only child,

Prince Albert Edward, who died aged four. (See also page 66.)

Back on the Pali Highway, continue for about 3 miles to the exit for the **Nuuanu Pali Lookout.** This was the scene of Kamehameha I's victory over the king of Oahu's army in 1795. It is said that the defenders jumped or were pushed over the sheer cliff, which affords a magnificent view over the Kailua and Kaneohe bays.

Beyond the Lookout, HI-61 cuts through the Pali Tunnels and descends towards the leeward coast. Take the Kalanianaole Highway exit (HI-72) and head southeast via Waimanalo to **Sea Life Park** (8 miles). One of the island's top attractions, Sea Life Park combines a little gentle education about the marine world with a host of great shows, and there are fascinating exhibits next door in the free **Pacific Whaling Museum.** The on-site family-dining restaurant is a convenient place to

Sea Life Park ocean view

stop for lunch. (See also pages 87 and 88.)

Continue on HI-72 for approximately 2 miles to the right turn onto Kealahou Street, and follow signs to the Koko Crater. Inside the crater are the **Crater Botanical Gardens**, a relatively new outpost of the Honolulu Botanical Gardens. The 200-acre site is being planted with desert-loving plants such as cacti, aloes and other hardy types (*Open: daily 9–4. Admission free*).

Return to HI-72; **Sandy Beach** is almost directly across the main road. This beautiful white-sand beach is famous for its splendid though treacherous surf, so if the waves are up do not swim unless you are an expert. However, it is a great place to unfurl a beach towel and escape the car. Just down the coast is the **Halona Blowhole**, where waves forced up a narrow lava tube spout like a giant geyser.

Still hugging the coast, continue on HI-72 until it reaches **Hanauma Bay**, a gorgeous aquamarine inlet

Stunning Hanauma Bay

encircled by the walls of a sunken crater. This is one of the most popular places on the island, so in order to preserve its fragile marine ecostructure visitor numbers are restricted. There is fabulous snorkeling around the reef, home to more than 150 types of tropical fish so tame they approach the flippered and masked visitors.

Return to Waikiki via HI-72/H-1 (15 miles) or follow the signs to Diamond Head for a scenic detour.

Hitching a ride

Central Oahu and the North

Waimea Adventure Tours
After a couple of slow days on the beach, let off steam with Waimea Adventure Tours – a real favorite with children. There are three-hour ATV (all-terrain vehicle) rides along wilderness trails to the top of the valley, with a stop for a bit of exercise in a rope jungle, as well as archery and paintballing. There is also a 45-minute ATV Mini-Challenge obstacle course, downhill mountain-bike tours, kayak trips down the Waimea River, and a 2½-hour Nature Quest Tour which includes a stop at Puu O Mahuka Heiau (see panel opposite). For further details, tel:808/638-8511.

82

▶▶ Banzai Pipeline   50B4
Ehukai Beach Park, Kamehameha Hwy (HI-83), northeast of Waimea
Flanked to the west by Waimea Bay, and to the east by Sunset Beach, Banzai Pipeline must rate as the most evocatively named surfing beach in the world. It is also, along with its immediate neighbors, one of the best. Winter waves can reach heights of around 30–40 feet, and international competitions are held here regularly. In summer the tamed ocean can resemble glass, but these are tricky waters, so snorkel and swim with care. (See also pages 84–5.)

▶ Dole Plantation   50B3
64-1550 Kamehameha Hwy (HI-99), 2 miles north of Wahiawa (tel: 808/621-8408)
Open: daily 9–5:30. Admission free
Surrounded by the pineapple fields of James Drummond Dole's original plantation, this is the home of pineapple power. The Dole Plantation Visitor Center is a gift shop laden with pineapple-themed souvenirs, from beach bags and oven gloves to T-shirts and confectionery. There are fresh pineapples for sale whole, sliced or juiced (but none of them a bargain). Other diversions include horse-riding and an international pineapple garden.

▶▶▶ Haleiwa   50B3
Kamehameha Highway (HI-83)
Little more than an hour's drive from Waikiki, but light years away in style, this delightfully laid-back north coast settlement displays the casual signs of surfer culture everywhere—faded Billabong T-shirts and thongs, sun-bleached locks, and trucks loaded with beatboxes and boards. Spread haphazardly along HI-83, clapboard buildings with creaky *lanais* (verandas) house all sorts of boutiques and galleries with fluttering tie-dye creations and shell jewelry on display. You can rent a bike or a surfboard, charter a deep-sea fishing boat, cool down

Watching for waves at the Banzai Pipeline

Sea shell souvenirs

Puu O Mahuka Heiau
For a wonderful view of the north coast, its jagged volcanic fingers inset with white-sand beaches stretching off either side of Waimea Bay, turn off the highway onto Pupukea Road, just east of Waimea. The road winds up to Puu O Mahuka Heiau, an ancient Hawaiian temple site, where locals still leave offerings of fruit, flowers, and shells on the piles of ancient stones. It is said that the *heiau*, one of the largest on Oahu, was used for human sacrifices, and that three English sailors from HMS *Daedalus* were slaughtered here in 1794.

with one of the famous shave ices (Hawaii's answer to the snow cone) from the Matsumoto Store, pick up sandwiches from a delicatessen, eat a plate lunch from a *kau-kau* wagon on the beach, or dine at a linen-clad table overlooking the marina. The one thing you shouldn't do is hurry. It's just not cool, man.

► **Wahiawa Botanic Garden**   50C3
1396 California Avenue, Wahiawa
Open: daily 9–4. Admission free
A good reason to stop off in Wahiawa, these leafy botanic gardens—27 acres of rainforest—lie a short distance east of the highway, and are planted with spice trees from the Indies (smell the bark of the cinnamon tree), tropical conifers, palm trees, lobster-claw helico-nias, bird-of-paradise plants, brownleas with their orange pom-pom flowers, and many other native varieties. From the upper level, paths lead down into a shaded ravine. This lower area is still being developed, so watch your step on the mini-trek past palms, ferns and brightly colored banks of impatiens. There is an information desk and an explanatory booklet with maps to guide visitors around the gardens.

►►► **Waimea Falls Park**   50B4
59-864 Kamehameha Highway (HI-83 east of Haleiwa)
Open: daily 10–5:30. Admission charge: expensive.
Guided tours are available; narrated tram rides leave every 20 minutes from the entrance; for information
tel: 808/638-8511
A lush 1,800 acres, reaching back into the Waimea Valley, this park offers something for just about every-one. Landscaped botanic gardens lead gently up to the falls themselves, with plenty of stops along the way. The colorful blooms provide photo opportunities galore, and garden lovers can take guided tours. An arboretum contains more than 5,000 varieties of plants, many of them endangered. More than 30 species of birds live in the park, special exhibits add a historical angle, and there are interactive areas such as the Kauhale Kahiko, where visitors can learn about traditional crafts, Hawaiian food, and medicinal plants. Do not miss the entertaining *hula* show; but do join in the Hawaiian games; and try to time your arrival at the falls for a cliff-diving demonstration.

Cliff diving at Waimea Falls

■ **The Hawaiians have been surfing for a thousand years. Stick-men surfers can be found amongst ancient petroglyphs carved into the volcanic rocks of the Big Island, and age-old *mele* (chants) celebrating surfing exploits, and *pohuehue* (prayers to the sea for perfect waves) have been passed down from generation to generation.** ■

Surf or boogie?
Waikiki remains one of the best places in the world to learn how to surf. There are around a dozen long-ride breaks between Diamond Head and the Hilton Hawaiian Village. In addition to reliable year-round surfing conditions, locals and board rental operators are usually around to offer advice. If you want to ride a wave, but don't rate your chances on a surfboard, boogie boards are a fun alternative. These 3-foot-long foam boards, which support the upper body while leaving the legs free to kick, are inexpensive to buy or can be rented for a nominal fee.

Duke Kahanamoku

"Sliding on a wave" The Hawaiian word for surfing was *heenalu*, or "sliding on a wave," an apt description of this demanding sport with its vital combination of grace and power. The *mele* tell of hotly contested competitions, animated betting and sizable wagers won and lost, as well as days when the surf was up and the fields lay unattended as the Hawaiians rode the great winter waves which have their origins in the stormy Arctic.

When Captain Cook and his men arrived by sea, the Hawaiians paddled out on their surfboards to greet them, and the first Europeans to clap eyes on these upstanding, wave-riding Hawaiians were fascinated and impressed in equal measure. Farmers and fishermen were not the only *heenalu* addicts. Women and children of all ages took to the water whenever possible, and the *alii*, or Hawaiian royalty, reserved some of the best surfing beaches for themselves. Royal surfing beaches, such as Queen Kaahumanu's favorite Waikiki, were *kapu* (forbidden) to commoners, and trespassers were punished with death.

The "Father of Modern Surfing" By the end of the 19th century, however, surfing was a dying art. The combined influences of the all-work-no-play missionary era and increasing Westernization had taken their toll. The writer Jack London is often credited as the man responsible for reviving interest in the sport through articles written after his stay in Waikiki in 1907. The *haole* (foreigners') Outrigger Canoe Club, founded in 1908, and the Hawaiians' own Hui Nalu club, both helped to preserve the Hawaiian surfing and outrigger traditions. But the man who really put surfing on the map, and took it all over the world, was Duke Kahanamoku (1890–1968), the acknowledged "Father of Modern Surfing."

A full-blooded Hawaiian raised in Waikiki, "The Duke" first hit the headlines in 1912, when he took an Olympic gold for the 100-meter freestyle at the Stockholm Games. Between 1912 and 1932, Kahanamoku's Hawaiian crawl style added a further two gold, two silver, and four bronze medals to his personal haul. Meanwhile, The Duke starred in films and acted as Hawaii's unofficial "Ambassador of Aloha," introducing surfing to Australia, Europe and the U.S. eastern seaboard, before being elected Sheriff of Honolulu for 13 consecutive terms from 1934 to 1960.

Surf's up! From humble beginnings, surfing is now a world-class sport with a generous purse. The professional circuit has spread from the Americas to Australia, Europe and South Africa, but the world's tallest rideable surf is still found in Hawaii—more precisely at Waimea Bay on Oahu's north shore. Waimea Bay is one of the hosts for winter surfing classics such as the Hawaiian Pro and Triple Crown (see panel). Even if no official competition is in progress, when the surf is up spectators take positions on shore to watch the daring few paddle out on their big "elephant gun" boards. At the relative calm of the "lineup," the surfers judge the swell and pick their moment to ride the most thrilling waves the ocean can produce.

In recent decades, modern technology has brought about a revolution in surfboard design. The *koa*-wood boards of the ancient Hawaiians, which measured between 18 and 20 feet and could weigh in at around 150 pounds, have been replaced by lightweight hollow shells filled with polyurethane foam, laminated with fiberglass and measuring only 8 to 12 feet in length. Skegs (rudder-like fins) can be selected for increased maneuverability in different wave conditions. And the search for the perfect hydrodynamic board goes on as the prize money rises.

Throughout the Islands, the local press, radio stations, and even television news broadcasts offer up-to-the-minute surf reports.

Riding the big blue

Surfing championships
Hawaii's top winter surfing classics, the Hawaiian Pro and Triple Crown of Surfing, take place from mid-November to mid-December at several locations along Oahu's north shore. They make a great day out even for non-surfers. The actual competition days depend on how the waves are shaping up over a set time period, so check the local papers for details. Another hot date in the surfing calendar is mid-February's Makaha World Surfing Championships on the leeward coast.

85

Competitive spirit

The Windward Coast

Kualoa Ranch
This family-owned cattle ranch on HI-83 south of Kaaawa, opposite Kualoa Country Regional Park, has now diversified into the adventure-tour market and offers activities ranging from horse-riding and mountain-biking to diving, catamaran cruises, jet-skiing, snorkeling, and even helicopter trips. Reservations should be made in advance, and prices vary according to the activity, tel: 808/237-7321.

▶ **Byodo-In Temple** 51D2
47-200 Kahekili Highway (HI-83), Kaneohe
Open: daily 9–4. Admission charge: inexpensive
Tucked behind the rolling lawns of the Christian cemetery in the Valley of the Temples is a traditional-style Japanese Buddhist temple, set in a peaceful dell backed by the volcanic folds of the Koolau Mountains. The temple was completed in 1968 to mark the centenary of the arrival of the first Japanese immigrants in Hawaii, and its design is based on the famous 900-year-old Phoenix Hall of Byodoin at Uji, Japan. The ocher-painted buildings with their yellow trimmings and graceful curving roofs are surrounded by gardens and carp ponds, and guarded by rather predatory pecking peacocks.

▶▶ **Kualoa Country Regional Park** 51D3
HI-83 south of Kaaawa
Open: daily 7–7. Admission free
A popular windward-coast beach park with a long, grassy strip backing the beach, good swimming and snorkeling, and facilities that include picnic tables, toilets and campsites. It can get windy, but that is good news for kite-flyers. The distinctive little **Chinaman's Hat** island, just offshore, is accessible at low tide.

▶▶▶ **Malaekahana State Park** 50C4
HI-83, just north of Laie
Open: daily 7–dusk. Admission free
Hidden behind a swath of coastal woodlands, this secluded beach park is a well-kept secret, invisible to the average passerby. There is a beautiful, though narrow, stretch of white sand facing Goat Island (a pint-sized offshore seabird sanctuary), picnic tables and barbecue grills in the woods, and a spacious grassy area as well as campsite facilities.

Japanese heritage is celebrated at the Byodo-In Temple

▶ Mormon Temple 50C4

55-600 Naniloa Loop (off HI-83), Laie
Open: Visitor Center, daily 9–8. Admission free
The first Mormon mission arrived in Hawaii in 1850, and moved to Laie in 1864. The town's population is 95 percent Mormon, and its temple, the first to be built outside the mainland U.S., is the second most visited after that in Salt Lake City, Utah. Dedicated in 1919, the square white wedding-cake structure stands in impressively landscaped grounds. Fresh-faced young Mormon guides patrol the grounds. Non-Mormons are not allowed to enter the temple.

▶▶ Pacific Whaling Museum 51E1

HI-72, Waimanalo
Open: daily 9:30–5, Fri until 10. Admission free
This free museum, alongside the Sea Life Park complex, gives a fascinating account of whaling history. Its displays are laid out beneath the 38-foot-long skeleton of a sperm whale that was washed up off Barbers Point in 1980. Informative (and occasionally pithy) signboards, photographs, models and memorabilia detail the dangers that the whalers—and the whales—faced. There are also many fine examples of scrimshaw carvings, the traditional folk art made by sailors in the long empty hours on board (see panel).

▶▶ Polynesian Cultural Center 50C4

55-370 Kamehameha Highway (HI-83), Laie
(tel: 808/293-3333)
Open: Mon–Sat 12:30–9. Admission charge: expensive.
Ticket options offer admission only; admission and show; and admission, show and a choice of buffets
One of Oahu's top attractions, the Polynesian Cultural Center opened in 1963 and has been playing to packed houses ever since. It features traditional-style buildings and entertainment from the seven main Polynesian nations of Tahiti, Fiji, Tonga, the Marquesas, Samoa, New Zealand's Maoris and, of course, Hawaii. The Center is set in attractively landscaped grounds, and the interactive village settlement areas highlight traditional building styles and crafts. Canoe tours paddle around the 42-acre site, and a giant IMAX film show explores Polynesian history.

The all-singing, all-dancing 90-minute evening show, a Polynesian revue with fire-walking and other high-octane pursuits, features 100-plus performers, many of whom are Pacific Island students at the neighboring Brigham Young University.

Music and dance at the Polynesian Cultural Center

Scrimshaw knick-knacks
Faced with long months at sea and intermittent work, many whalers whiled away the hours whittling scrimshaw masterpieces from whales' teeth and jawbones. The scrimshaw collection at the Pacific Whaling Museum contains dozens of expertly carved pieces, including children's toys and games such as cribbage boards, intricately decorated canes and knife handles, sewing-kits and pastry cutters, intended as presents for girlfriends and wives. The famous whalebone stays which enforced the hour-glass figures of Victorian and Edwardian women were made not from bone but from baleen, a tough, flexible material found in the whale's mouth.

*Turtle-watch at Sea
Life Park*

"Wholphin"
What's in a "wholphin"?
Astonished marine
biologists at Sea Life Park
were treated to a scientific
wonder on May 15, 1985.
One of the park's female
bottlenose dolphins gave
birth to a calf that was a
half-bottlenose dolphin
(*Tursips truncatus*) and a
half-false killer whale
(*Pseudorca crassidens*).
Christened Kekaimalu, the
600-pound, almost 10-foot-
long "wholphin" is about a
third larger than an
average dolphin and has 66
teeth compared to a
dolphin's 88 and a whale's
44. Being a native
Hawaiian, she also dances
the *hula* in daily shows.

Sea lion parked

▶▶▶ Sea Life Park 51E1

*41-202 Kalanianaole Highway (HI-72), Makapuu Point
(tel: 808/259-7933)
Open: daily 9:30–5, Fri until 10. Admission charge:
expensive. Free round-trip transportation six times daily
from several Waikiki hotels, telephone for schedules*

A noted marine research facility and a top attraction, the
park takes visitors straight to the heart of the matter
just inside its gates as they descend the curving ramp
which circles the 300,000-gallon Hawaiian Reef Tank.
Giant windows reveal more than 2,000 marine
specimens, from moray eels and rays to the bizarre scal-
loped hammerhead shark with its eyes literally out on
stalks. There are striped convict tangs, horned unicorn
fish, sex-changing wrasses and, of course, the tongue-
twisting *humuhumunukunukuapuaa*, Hawaii's multi-
colored state fish.

Bottlenose dolphins, sea lions, and penguins perform
regularly in the Hawaii Ocean Theater. At Whaler's Cove,
the replica whaling ship *Essex* offers a view of the park's
dolphins and whales through sunken porthole windows.
This is also the place to spot a "wholphin," the park's rare
(if not unique) bottlenose-dolphin/killer-whale hybrid (see
panel). Other attractions include a touch pool, a seabird
sanctuary, a penguin habitat, a sea lion feeding-pool, a
turtle lagoon, and a care center for Hawaiian monk seals.

Guided tours (40 minutes) are offered five times daily,
and include a close-up look at animal-training techniques,
and a visit to the maternity tanks, not open to the general
public (telephone for schedules). Friday night is
"Kamaaina Night," when visitors can enjoy dinner and an
evening of Hawaiian music at the park's Sea Lion Café.

▶▶ Senator Fong's Plantation
and Gardens 51D2

*47-285 Pulama Road (off HI-83), Kaneohe
Open: daily 10–4 (last tram at 3). Admission charge:
moderate*

Since his retirement, former U.S. Senator Hiram Fong (the
first Asian-American senator in Congress) has devoted his
energies to tending this lush 725-acre estate. Open-
sided trams make 45-minute guided tours of the
extensive rain-forest gardens and orchards,
where more than 100 varieties of tropical
fruits and nuts are cultivated.

The West

Heading *ewa* (west) of Honolulu, H-1 streaks past the industrial jumble of Aiea, the old sugar town of Waipahu, and sprawling Ewa almost as far as the Ko Olina resort, a surprising oasis for golf and spa lovers at the southern end of the Waianae Coast, Oahu's arid leeward side. The old Farrington Highway, a slow local traffic and truck route, parallels H-1 all the way, and then continues as HI-93 north up the coast for 17 miles through a smattering of virtually tourist-free local towns. The road disintegrates into a track at Yokohama Bay, renamed for the Japanese cane-workers who came to fish here.

This is largely undiscovered Oahu. Traditionally poor and with a bad reputation, the Waianae Coast has vigorously resisted development, but there are some fine sandy beaches at Maili and Makaha, and a long, clean sand strip at Kaena Point State Park, where the road runs out. The challenging surf attracts some of the island's real hot shots, and February's Buffalo Big Board Surfing Contest at Makaha is a major event on the surfing calendar.

▶▶ Hawaii's Plantation Village   50C2
94-695 Waipahu Street, Waipahu (Waikele/Paiwa Street exit off H-1)
Open: Mon–Fri 8–4:30, Sat 9–4, Sun 10–4:30, tours on the hour. Admission charge: moderate
Somewhat off the beaten track for most visitors, but well worth searching out, this little historical park in the shadow of the old sugar mill has preserved a real chunk of Hawaiian history. There is a small but interesting museum displaying artifacts and memorabilia from the heyday of Hawaii's sugar industry. Clothing, tools, domestic utensils, photographs, and even the dog-tags the immigrants were forced to wear by their employers, paint a vivid picture of hardship and fortitude. Then it's off on a guided tour of a plantation settlement, with a genuine period store, camp office, infirmary and workers' houses in as many styles as there were nationalities: Chinese, Portuguese, Japanese, Puerto Rican, and Filipino.

On the beach
There is good rock pooling to be had at the far end of the Kaena Point State Park Beach, where wave action has also eroded several natural arches in the rocky cliffs on this northwestern tip of Oahu.

Makaha Beach on Oahu's Waianae Coast

KAUAI

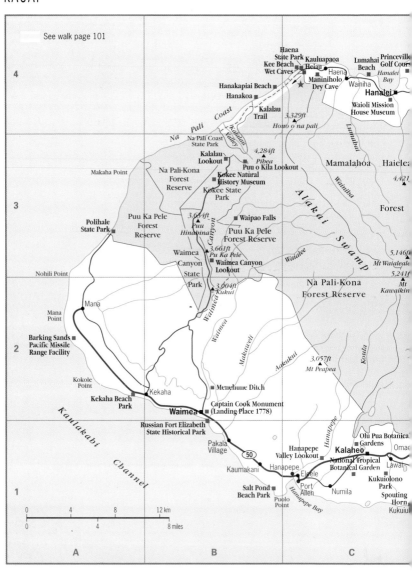

See walk page 101

4

Haena
State Park ■ Kauluapaoa
Kee Beach ■ Heiau ■ Lumahai Princeville
Wet Caves Beach Golf Course
Haena *Hanalei*
Hanakapiai Beach ■ Maninholo *Bay* ■
Hanakoa Dry Cave Wainiha **Hanalei**
Kalalau Waioli Mission
Trail *3,329ft* House Museum
Hono o na pali ▲ *Lumahai*

Na Pali *Coast*

Na Pali Coast
State Park *4,284ft* **Mamalahoa** **Haielea**
Kalalau *Pihea* ▲
Lookout ■ Puu o Kila Lookout
Na Pali-Kona ■ Kokee Natural *4,421*
Forest History Museum *Wainiha*
Reserve Kokee State **Forest**
Park

Makaha Point

3

3,654ft
Puu Ka Pele *Puu* ■ Waipao Falls
Forest *Hinabina* Puu Ka Pele
Polihale Reserve Forest Reserve *5,146ft*
State Park *3,661ft* *Mt Waialeale*
Waimea *Pu Ka Pele* *Walalee* *5,241ft*
Canyon ■ Waimea Canyon *Mt*
State Lookout *Kawaikini*
Park *3,004ft* Na Pali-Kona
▲ *Kukui* Forest Reserve

Nohili Point

Mana
Mana *Waimea* *3,057ft*
Point *Mt Peapea* ▲

2

Barking Sands ■
Pacific Missile *Makaweli* *Kohla*
Range Facility

Kokole *Aakukui*
Point *Hanapepe*
Kekaha

Kekaha Beach ■ Menehune Ditch Olu Pua Botanica
Park ■ Gardens
Waimea ■ Captain Cook Monument **Kalaheo** Omao
(Landing Place 1778) National Tropical ■
Russian Fort Elizabeth ■ Botanical Garden Lawai
State Historical Park Hanapepe *Kukuiolono*
Pakala Valley Lookout Park
Kautakabi Village *50* **Kalaheo** Spouting
Hanapepe Horn
Kaumakani Eleele *Kukuiul*

1

Channel Salt Pond ■ Port Numila
Beach Park Allen
Puolo *Hanapepe Bay*
Point

```
0    4    8    12 km
0    4    8 miles
```

A   B   C

weonui
int
Princeville

Kalihiwai
Kilauea Mokuaeae Island
Lighthouse
■ Kilauea Point National Wildlife Refuge

Hanalei
Lookout
Kalihiwai
Kilauea
Christ Memorial Church
St Sylvester's Church
Kepuhi Point

aalei
seum
Hanalei National Wildlife Reserve
■ **Guava Kai Plantation**
Moloaa Bay

■ **Kapinao Heiau**

Moloaa Forest Reserve
Makaleha Mountains
Anahola
Hole-in-the-Mountain
■ **Anahola Beach**
Anahola
Kahala Point

Kalihiwai

3,254ft
▲ Mt Wekiu
Kealia Forest Reserve

Kapaa

56

Kumukumu

eserve

Keahua Arboretum
Nonou Forest Reserve
Kapaa Kapaa Beach Park
Sleeping Giant
Waipouli

Kaholalele Falls
Wailua
Opaekaa Falls
Wailua
■ **Royal Coconut Grove**
■ **Holo-Holo-Ku Heiau**
■ **Smith's Tropical Paradise**

Wailua River State Park
Fern Grotto
Lydgate State Park

Wailua Falls ■

ihue-Koloa Forest Reserve

Kalepa Forest Reserve

1,132ft
▲ Kilohana Crater
Kapaia
Hanamaulu
Ahukini State Park

Lihue
■ **Kauai Museum**

Kilohana Plantation
Puhi
51
Lihue Airport

50
Grove Farm Homestead
Lighthouse
Ninini Point

Huleia
Niumalu
58
Nawiliwili
Harbor

Kipu
Menehune Fish Pond
Kawai Point

Tunnel of Trees
Haupu Forest Reserve
Queen Victoria's Profile

First
gar Mill
Waita Reservoir
Koloa

■ **Old Koloa Church**
■ **St Raphael's Catholic Church**
■ **Prince Kuhio's Birthplace**

Poipu
Beach
Park
■ **Poipu**
Makahuena Point

Kauai Channel

D   E

The "Garden Isle" Lush and beautiful Kauai was named the "Garden Isle" by admiring 19th-century visitors, and it can still do justice to the name. The island is swathed in a rich mantle of luxuriant greenery, from the flanks of its ancient mountains to its rippling lowland cane fields and vivid emerald checkerboards of taro patches. Kauai, the oldest of the main Hawaiian islands and the result of a single massive volcano, has an unmistakable maturity to its grandeur. Several million years of rain, wind and waves have sculpted dramatic sea cliffs and broad valleys, and the latter have been cultivated for almost 1,000 years. From the 5,148-foot central crown of Mount Waialeale, "the wettest spot on earth"—with an average annual rainfall of 486 inches—seven rivers and dozens of

Take a helicopter
Helicopter tours offer unparalleled access to the remotest corners of Kauai's mountainous heartland and the Na Pali Coast. They swoop above twisting chasms, dangle within a few yards of 1,000-foot-high waterfalls in the misty heights of Mount Waialeale, hover over hanging valleys and flit around the whole island pointing out landmarks. Reservations should be made in advance (use every ploy in the book to secure a window seat). For further information, contact: Ohana Helicopter Tours, Lihue (tel: 808/245-3996); Papillon Hawaiian Helicopters, Hanalei (tel: 808/826-6591).

Brilliant emerald green taro fields in the Hanalei Valley

streams and waterfalls have furrowed the mountainsides and carved the monumental Waimea Canyon. Meanwhile, offshore reefs have been ground away to create the island's fine white-sand beaches which are backed by the ever-encroaching jungle.

Resorts and attractions Despite stealing an evolutionary march on the younger islands to the south, Kauai has been rather more reticent in the tourism stakes. Visitors in search of hotel balconies with dizzying views, late-night discothèques, and vast shopping malls stacked with designer boutiques should avoid Kauai. Its charms are low-key and scenic, though there is no lack of luxury and style if required. The three main resort areas—Poipu in the south, Kapaa-Wailua on the east coast, and Princeville-Hanalei in the north—boast accommodations ranging from comfortable seaside condos to luxurious hotel suites. Backpackers are equally welcome.

Activities on Kauai include horseback-riding, biking, some of the most spectacular hiking in the Islands, canoeing and boat trips as well as sport fishing and a choice of glorious golf courses (see pages 24–5). On the sightseeing front, natural beauties are augmented by the historic homes of early missionaries and plantation owners, and one of the state's best museums, in Lihue, the capital. And Kauai is *the* place to take a helicopter tour (see panel).

A bit of history Kauai may have been inhabited up to 500 years before the other Hawaiian islands by early Polynesians, who were possibly Kauai's legendary "little people," the *menehune* (see panel on page 100). Several ancient sites, including irrigation ditches and stone-walled fishponds, have been attributed to the *menehune.* Though most of them are supposed to have sailed away to preserve their bloodline from contamination by the first Tahitian immigrants, a few are said to have missed the boat and continue to live on in Kauai, hiding out in the hills.

The Tahitians settled Kauai's fertile valleys, building stone terraces into the hillsides, cultivating taro, sweet potatoes, and bananas. Captain Cook noted several coastal settlements around Waimea Bay when he landed on Kauai on January 20, 1778 (see pages 36–7). Waimea later developed into a busy port, the center for the sandalwood trade in the early 19th century and a whaling station in the 1840s.

Taken by stealth During the great Kamehameha I's campaign to unite the Islands at the end of the 18th century, Kauai was twice saved from invasion fleets by the weather. In 1810 the Kauaian king, Kaumualii, managed to negotiate a face-saving agreement with Kamehameha to relinquish his role as monarch and become instead the governor of the island.

In 1815 Georg Anton Schaeffer, sent to salvage a wrecked ship belonging to the Russian-American Company, secured Kaumaualii's permission to build a fort at Waimea and raised the Russian flag on it. Fort Elizabeth's construction in 1817 alarmed Kamehameha who, fearing the threat of Russian annexation, expelled Schaeffer from Kauai. The unfortunate Kaumualii was eventually kidnapped by Kamehameha II, and forced to marry Kamehameha I's widow, Kaahumanu, thus firmly securing Kauai for the Hawaiian kingdom.

Missionaries and plantations The first missionaries arrived in Kauai in 1821, and the first sugar plantation in the Hawaiian Islands was established at Koloa by New Englanders in 1835. They were joined by German Lutheran planters in the 1850s, and by Asian and Portuguese immigrant laborers, and thousands of acres of sugar cane were planted in the south of the island.

Modern Kauai Kauai's strong agricultural tradition has enabled the island to retain much of its quiet rural aspect and lifestyle. Most of the population lives on the "Coconut Coast," between Lihue and Kapaa on the east of the island. Beyond here, villages are small and friendly, served by "mom and pop" stores and farmers' markets. A coastal road loops around three-quarters of the island before running into the impassable Na Pali Cliffs, and there are no shortcuts across the interior. Here, remote areas such as the Alakai Swamp have been preserved by their very inaccessibility as rich and rare sanctuaries for plant and bird life, some of it unique to this lovely island.

On location
Hollywood has had a long love affair with Kauai ever since some canny location scout decided the Garden Isle would make a splendid backdrop for "Bali-Hai" in the smash-hit film *South Pacific*. After Mitzi Gaynor washed that man right out of her hair on the North Shore's Lumahai Beach, Elvis Presley came along for some *Blue Hawaii* at the Coco Palms Resort, Jessica Lange squealed her way through a remake of *King Kong*, and dinosaurs rampaged around the primordial Na Pali Coast in Spielberg's *Jurassic Park*—to name but a few...

Wailua Falls

The Fern Grotto

Approximate driving times from Lihue
- Kapaa: 20 minutes
- Kilauea: 45 minutes
- Kokee: 1 hour 30 minutes
- Poipu: 30 minutes
- Princeville and Hanalei: 1 hour
- Wailua: 15 minutes
- Waimea Canyon: 1 hour 15 minutes

History in Lihue

The East Coast

▶▶ Coconut Coast and Lihue 91E2

The Coconut Coast, a stretch of the island's east coast, takes its name from a 19th-century coconut grove near Wailua. Kapaa, Wailua and neighboring Waipouli together form "Garden Island Central," a seaside strip of tourist-oriented hotels and restaurants, plus two popular shopping malls in the attractive Coconut Marketplace complex and the Kauai Village respectively. Wailua also has a fine 18-hole municipal golf course.

To the south is Lihue, Kauai's chief town, located midway along the coastal highway (see panel for driving times). Lihue's airport is the main gateway to Kauai, but the town has little for the visitor save the excellent Kauai Museum (see opposite) and the Kukui Grove Shopping Mall (2 miles southwest), which has department stores, supermarkets, and an information booth.

▶▶ Fern Grotto 91E2

Wailua Marina
Open: daily, regular departures with Waialeale Boat Tours (tel: 808/822-4111) and Smith's Motorboats (tel: 808/822-4654). Admission charge: moderate
This extravagantly fern-draped grotto is one of the most popular attractions on the island and the most touristy. To reach it, visitors are ferried on flat-bottomed river boats along the only stretch of navigable river in the Hawaiian Islands. The 1½-hour, 6-mile round trip is accompanied by local entertainers. Bring a raincoat.

▶▶▶ Grove Farm Homestead 91D2

Nawiliwili Road, near Lihue (tel: 808/245-3202)
Open: tours by reservation: Mon, Wed–Thu 10–1.
Admission charge: moderate
A visit to the old Wilcox homestead gives a fascinating insight into Hawaiian plantation life. Tours (by reservation

only) are limited to preserve the 80-acre property, which was founded in 1864 by George Wilcox, one of eight sons born to Hanalei missionaries Abner and Lucy Wilcox. The comfortable family home is still furnished with original antiques. Although sugar has been abandoned, the present farm is self-sufficient, relying on its orchards, cattle pasture, timber, and a vegetable garden.

*Grove Farm
Homestead in the
foothills above Lihue*

95

►►► Kauai Museum 91D2
4428 Rice Street, Lihue (tel: 808/245-6931)
Open: Mon–Fri 9–4:30, Sat 9–1. Admission charge:
moderate
Rated second only to the prestigious Bishop Museum in Honolulu, this small museum is a must for those with an interest in local history and Hawaiiana. The collections and informative storyboards trace the development of the Islands from the Stone Age to the plantation era and also cover immigrant workers, Kauai's leading families, geology and natural history. There is a very good museum shop for gifts and souvenirs.

► Keahua Arboretum 91D3
7 miles along HI-580 from Wailua
Open site. Admission free
A great place for a picnic, this country park sits up in the hills above Wailua. There are mountain views, open meadows and picnic benches in the shade, plus a swimming hole with a rope swing on the Keahua Stream.

► Nawiliwili Harbor 91E2
Waapa Road, off Nawiliwili Road (HI-58) south of Lihue
Nawiliwili is a small working harbor and marina on a sheltered bay at the mouth of the Nawiliwili Stream. There are kayaks for rent here, and Kauai River Adventures (tel: 808/245-9662) offers guided kayak tours up to the **Menehune Fishpond** (see panel) and to the lush backwater country where parts of *Raiders of the Lost Ark* were filmed. Sport-fishing operators Gent-Lee Charters Inc (tel: 808/245-7504) are also based here.

Shrimp pay
There are two notable *menehune* sites on the south coast of Kauai. The first is the neat semicircular Menehune Fishpond in the Huleia River valley behind Nawiliwili Harbor; there is a good view of it from a point on Hulemalu Road. The other is Kiki a Ola, or the Waimea Ditch, an earthwork near the Waimea River, reached from Menehune Road (off HI-50 at Waimea). The Ditch is said to have been built for Ola, an ancient chief of Waimea, who paid the *menehune* workers in shrimp.

Wailua Valley
The Wailua Valley was cultivated by Kauai's *alii* chiefs in ancient times, and there are a number of historic sites in its vicinity. Along the upriver trail, once known as the King's Highway, the remains of several *heiau* (temples) can still be seen, while *kapu*-breakers (taboo-breakers) could find refuge at the *honaunau* (sanctuary) which occupied part of what is now Lydgate State Park. Royal women would make their way down to the shore at Wailua to give birth at the *pohaku-hoo-hanau*, or royal birthing-stones, near what is now the Coco Palms Resort.

▶▶ Opaekaa Falls 91E2

HI-580, 1½ miles west of Wailua
Open site. Admission free
The picturesque Opaekaa Falls plunge down the cliff face in a veil of mist to a deep pool hedged in by forest, and are a favorite destination for visitors. Across the street from the parking lot there is a good view of the Wailua River and the river boats making their way upstream to the Fern Grotto (see page 94).

▶ Smith's Tropical Paradise 91E2

174 Wailua Road, off HI-56 (gardens, tel: 808/822-4654)
Open: gardens, daily 8:30–4; luau, Mon, Wed, Fri 7–9
(pageant only, 7:30). Admission charge: gardens,
moderate; luau, expensive
Situated on 30 prime acres at the mouth of the Wailua River, Smith's Tropical Paradise has three strings to its bow. The first is river boats, which make their way at a leisurely pace up to the Fern Grotto from the dock (see page 94). The second and third are a botanical garden and a *luau* (feast), which share the same landscaped site. Tram tours circle the gardens and central lagoon, taking in Polynesian-style villages and a mature show of local and exotic plants and trees. The evening *luau* features *kalua* pig—cooked in the traditional way in an *imu* (underground oven)—and a pageant.

▶▶ Wailua River and Falls 91D2

The 12-mile-long Wailua River starts life on the slopes of Mount Waialeale. The slow-flowing lower portion of the river is a good spot for a half-day's boating, and kayaks can be rented from a number of operators on the main highway. KBTC (4-746 Kuhio Highway/HI-56, tel: 808/822-7759) throws in useful extras such as a drinks cooler, tarpaulin, dry bag, and so on.

About five miles north of Lihue, off HI-583, the river's south fork plummets down the 80-foot **Wailua Falls**. It is said that ancient Hawaiian chiefs used to dive into the pool from the top of the falls to test their courage. Today, it is not even recommended to attempt the trail down.

A floating carpet of water-lilies at Smith's Tropical Paradise

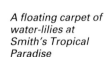

Language of the lei

■ The Hawaiian *lei* (garland) is pure *aloha*, a traditional symbol of friendship and affection exchanged in greeting or farewell, and is often given as a gift to celebrate a special occasion. ■

Traditional decoration

A *lei* for every season
A *lei* is not only a thing of beauty, but can be a scented sensation as well. In addition to plumeria and carnations, two of the most sweet-smelling types of flower used in *lei*-making are heady tuberoses and *pikake* (the Hawaiian name for jasmine). White ginger flowers exude a delightfully subtle fragrance, while some types of orchid have a delicate vanilla scent. The aromatic leaves of the *maile* vine are popular, and the locals favor the unusual *puakenikeni leis*, which not only smell divine, but gradually change color as well.

Origins The origins of the *lei* are a mystery, though some believe the custom began during the days of the earliest European explorers, when plants were presented as gifts. Today, *lei*-making is one of the Islands' most visible craft forms, adorning the necks of tourists and *hula* dancers, *kamaaina* grannies and grinning politicians, not to mention the Kamehameha I statue in downtown Honolulu, which is festooned in dozens of multi-colored *leis* on May 1, Hawaii's official Lei Day.

The basic *kui*-style *lei*, which is made of either fragrant plumeria flowers or carnations strung end to end, is child's play, but wondrous *haku*-style *leis*, intricate braids of greenery and flowers, are skilled works of art. Many hotels offer demonstrations and simple *lei*-making lessons. For *leis* galore, head for Maunakea Street in Honolulu's Chinatown; better still, attend a prestigious local *hula* competition, such as the springtime Merrie Monarch Festival on Hawaii.

Flowers and shells Each Hawaiian island has its own special *lei*. On Oahu, look for the orange ruffle of an *ilima*-flower *lei*; on Maui it is the rosy-pink *lokelani*. Kauai's *leis* are scented by little square *mokihana* berries, which smell of anise and were used by the ancient Hawaiians to perfume their clothes. Hawaii has adopted Madame Pele's feathery red *lehua* blossoms, while Lanai has a twist of orange *kaunaoa*. Molokai combines the silver-green leaves of the *kukui* (candlenut) tree with its small white flowers, though many visitors prefer a polished *kukui* nut necklace as a permanent souvenir of the Islands. Barren Niihau harvests the beach for *lei*-making purposes. The "Forbidden Island's" delicate shell *leis*, made from tiny white and speckled *pupu* shells, make expensive but lasting souvenirs of a trip to the *aloha* islands.

Lei-*making is an art form*

Newell's shearwaters
During October and November hundreds of Newell's shearwaters flock to Kauai's north shore. These endangered, pigeon-sized black-and-white seabirds fly only at night, so they easily become confused and disoriented by bright lights (to which they are attracted), and frequently crash into buildings and telephone wires. Locals rescue dozens of dazed birds from the roadside every year.

The North Shore

▶ Guava Kai Plantation 91D4
South of Kuhio Highway (HI-56), Kilauea
Open: daily 9–5. Admission free
With 480 acres of guava trees yielding around 14 million pounds of fruit a year, it is no wonder that this plantation is called the "Guava Capital of the World." Introduced from South America in 1791, the delicious pink-fleshed guava makes excellent jams, jellies and sweet syrups. The fresh juice is even better and can be sampled for free in the plantation shop, which also sells guava preserves and other foodstuffs. There is a short "nature trail" through a garden where bird-of-paradise flowers, gingers, taro, bananas, pineapples, and other food plants grow behind an intoxicatingly scented gardenia hedge.

▶▶▶ Hanalei 90C4
Approaching Hanalei from the east on HI-56, stop off at the **Hanalei Scenic Lookout** just beyond Princeville for a preview of the green and fertile Hanalei Valley. The valley, backed by 3,500-foot-high mountains streaked with waterfalls, has been cultivated for centuries. Its colorful patchwork of taro fields and wetlands, irrigated by the Hanalei River, is one of the last refuges of the Hawaiian coot, and is busy with ducks, gallinules, golden plovers, and dozens of visiting waterfowl.

The road continues down to the Hanalei Bridge, a narrow span with a sharp right-angled bend at the far side which discourages tour buses. Here, Ohike Road strikes off into the valley and the 917-acre **Hanalei National Wildlife Refuge**. Birdwatchers can walk or drive along the track, but the farm land is private property.

Sleepy downtown Hanalei straggles along the main street in a collection of old wooden houses. There are galleries, cafés and restaurants in the attractive open-air **Hanalei Center**, where the Old School House has filled its former classrooms with surf and sailboard stores, boutiques and craft shops. The **Ching Young Village**, opposite, offers much of the same and also has a supermarket. The town has several adventure-tour operators, offering bicycle rental, kayak outings, and boat trips along the magnificent Na Pali Coast.

Aku Road, adjacent to Ching Young village, leads down towards **Hanalei Bay,** where whaling boats and traders once anchored. Turn right for the beach park and pier.

Kauai's mountainous interior rises above Hanalei Bay

This is a good surfing spot, and kayak tours leave from the mouth of the Hanalei River.

On the road out of town to Haena and Kee Beach is the little green and white shingle **Waioli Huiia Church** (1912), and a timber-framed **Mission Hall,** completed in 1841. Inside the American Gothic-style church, pretty stained-glass windows cast a cool, green light. The bell tower contains the original mission bell brought from Boston in 1843. The mission house lies across the park and is now a museum (see page 100).

▶▶ Kee Beach   90C4

At the end of the road on the Na Pali Coast is pretty Kee Beach, part of Haena State Park. Along the route from Hanalei are several small bridges and a couple of popular beaches in Lumahi (the "*South Pacific* Beach") and the surfers' favorite, Makua, also known as "Tunnels Beach". Just across the Limahuli Stream, look for the entrance to the Maniniholo Dry Cave, which was hollowed out of the cliff face by ancient surf.

Kee and the neighboring beaches are protected by reefs, and are great for swimming and snorkeling; they also have basic facilities. The challenging Kalalau Trail along the Na Pali Coast (see page 101) starts at Kee Beach, and returning hikers are all too grateful to flop down on the sand and dip their weary toes in the lagoon. On a rather less intrepid note, paths lead up through the undergrowth to the ruins of the Kauluapaoa Heiau where, it is said, the *hula* dance form was first enacted in honor of the goddess Laka.

Kee Beach at the northern end of the Na Pali Coast

Limahuli Gardens
Next to the entrance to Haena State Park a sign points to the Limahuli Gardens, an outpost of the National Tropical Botanical Gardens. Flanked by 2,000-foot forested cliffs, this 17-acre site in the isolated Limahuli Valley is stunningly beautiful. Limahuli Gardens support important areas of native forest, as well as a more conventional garden of colorful interlopers such as heliconias and gingers. The stone-terraced hillsides, constructed by ancient Hawaiians as much as 700 years ago, have been repaired and recultivated. (Tours by reservation only, Tue–Thu, Sat at 10 and 1; tel: 808/826-1053.)

Kilauea lighthouse

► Kilauea

This old sugar village lies just off the main road and has a brace of churches: the little coral-rock Christ Memorial Church, and St. Sylvester's. A clutch of shops on the road to Kilauea Point includes the delectable Kong Lung Store (purveyor of designer furnishings, knick-knacks and fashions) and a delicatessen. A 1913 lighthouse boasting the world's largest clamshell lens overlooks the cliffs and coves of **Kilauea Point National Wildlife Refuge**. Here, nesting colonies of boobies, shearwaters, albatrosses, tropic birds and turnstones cling to the precipitous cliffs, and whales can be spotted offshore in spring.

►►► Na Pali Coast State Park　　90B3

Rearing up from the ocean in a series of magnificent fluted and ridge-backed cliffs inset with deep, green valleys, the Na Pali Coast is breathtakingly beautiful. The remote and difficult to access Na Pali valleys were inhabited and cultivated right up until the early 20th century. The valleys can be reached only by boat, or via the 11-mile Kalalau Trail (see opposite). For views alone, nothing can beat a helicopter tour (see panel on page 92). There is also a spectacular lookout over the Kalalau Valley from Kokee State Park (see page 102).

►► Waioli Mission House Museum　　90C4

HI-56, Hanalei (tel: 808/245-3202)
Open: Tue, Thu, Sat 9–3. Admission charge: donations
The Reverend William Alexander and his family arrived at Hanalei in a double canoe from Waimea in 1834. Their first home was a thatched hut, but the pastor built a sturdier house in 1837. The descendants of their successors at the Mission, the Wilcox family, restored this house in 1921, furnishing it with some original family possessions, from mission furniture and china to leather-bound volumes of uplifting reading material.

The last of the *menehune*
Local legend relates that the *menehunes'* last trek to self-imposed exile led to the Na Pali Coast through the Kalalau Valley. Two *menehune* princesses died on the trail, giving their names to the Hanakoa and Hanakapiai valleys . Some *menehune* stayed behind, however: a 19th-century census recorded 65 living in the Wainiha Valley!

Na Pali Coast

Walk **Na Pali Coast Kalalau Trail**

The Kalalau Trail is surely one of the best short treks in the world. The challenging 11-mile, one-way trail cuts a strenuous path via five valleys from Kee Beach (see page 99) to the Kalalau Valley, about halfway along the Na Pali Coast.

Most people tackling the full trail will be advised to make an overnight camping stop in the Kalalau Valley. Drinking water, sun lotion, mosquito repellent, and wet-weather gear are essential equipment.

The first (and easiest) 2-mile section of the trail to Hanakapiai is a popular short hike. Beyond Hanakapiai it is necessary to have a permit, free from the State Parks Office, 3060 Eiwa Street, Lihue (tel: 808/241-3444. *Open:* Mon–Fri 8–2:15).

A reasonably fit walker can tackle the trail between Kee and **Hanakapiai** in about an hour. There are terrific views along the coast as the narrow path hugs the cliff sides, which are edged by banks of ferns, papaya trees and groves of *hala* (screw pine). A worthwhile, although

Hala *trees on the trail*

tough, 2-mile detour is possible from the beach by the mouth of the Hanakapiai Stream up to the 300-foot **Hanakapiai Falls**. You pass old taro terraces and mango trees to reach a great swimming-hole below the falls.

Back on the trail, between Hanakapiai and Hanakoa (4 miles/2–3 hours), the main path climbs 800 feet before tumbling down into **Hoolulu Valley**. This is the hardest section. The scale of Hoolulu is awe-inspiring and there is plenty of shade as you trek on to **Waiahuakua**. The trail then drops down to **Hanakoa Valley**, another lush, shaded spot with an abundance of mountain apple, mango, guava and *ti* trees.

On the final 5-mile stretch to **Kalalau** (3 hours), the landscape and vegetation become more arid as the trail leaves the island's windward side. The Kalalau Valley, 2 miles wide and 3 miles deep, studded with freshwater pools, was a Hawaiian settlement. There is camping on the beach and near the trail.

The South

Moa on the run
On the drive up to Kokee you may be forgiven for thinking that there has been a mass break-out from the local chicken farm. The glossy brown fowl feeding at the roadside are not domestic hens, but wild jungle fowl, or *moa*, introduced by the Polynesians. *Moa* now survive only on Kauai, which has no mongooses. The mongoose, which has a penchant for birds' eggs, was introduced into Hawaii to control the rat problem in the 1880s, but the consignment for Kauai was tipped off the dock by the irate recipient of a mongoose bite, to the everlasting gratitude of the *moa*.

▶   Hanapepe   90C1
West of the Hanapepe Valley, which was featured in scenes from *Jurassic Park*, is the small plantation town of Hanapepe. It has also had its moment of screen fame, masquerading as outback Australia in the television version of *The Thorn Birds*. Here tin-roofed homes and false-fronted wooden shops bake quietly in the hot sun. There are a couple of small galleries, restaurants and delicatessens where you can find picnic items for lunch at **Salt Pond Beach Park**, a sandy beach west of town with safe swimming, basic facilities, and picnic pavilions that provide shade and protection from falling coconuts.

▶▶   Kilohana Plantation   91D2
HI-50 (1½ miles south-west of Lihue) (tel: 808/245-5608) Open: Mon–Sat 9:30–9:30, Sun 9:30–5; carriage rides Mon–Sat 11–6:30, Sun 11–5; reservations for wagon tours and Gaylord's, tel: 808/245-9593. Admission free; charge for carriage rides and wagon tours
Built in 1935 by a member of the Wilcox family as a private home, this brick and shingle manor house has been transformed into a collection of craft shops and galleries, with Gaylord's restaurant in the courtyard. Souvenir hunters can stock up on "Kauai made" products, Niihau shell *leis*, Hawaiian quilts and more. The 35-acre grounds, which include tropical gardens and a working farm, can be explored on foot or by horse-drawn carriage. Wagon tours venture into the surrounding cane fields.

▶▶▶   Kokee State Park   90B3
HI-550 (15½ miles north of Waimea) Open: Museum, daily 10–4. Admission free
An outing to Kokee encompasses two of Kauai's most spectacular sights in a single expedition. On the road up to

A rainbow strikes the ridge above Hanapepe

The Wilcox sitting room at Kilohana Plantation

Two short walks
For an easy-to-access short walk in Kokee, look no further than Camp 10 Road near the park headquarters, which winds its way through moss-covered *ohia* and fern forests. Another relatively easy hike is the first section of the Pihea Trail from the Puu O Kila Lookout, 5 miles beyond the park's headquarters. A mile out and a mile back, the walk takes about an hour and affords views of the 3-mile-long, 2-mile-wide Kalalau Valley and the Alakai Swamp. However, be warned: both trails get very slippery after heavy rains.

the 4,345-acre state park there are lookouts over the dramatic 10-mile-long Waimea Canyon (see page 108), and in the park itself the Kalalau Lookout gazes out from the 4,000-foot-high cliffs at the head of the Na Pali Coast's deepest valley.

At an altitude of 3,800 feet, Kokee's cool, forested heights seems a million miles from the hot sands of Polihale, which in reality are just 30 miles away down on the coast. Temperatures are around 12˚F cooler than those at sea level. The weather is changeable, and for the best views of the Kalalau Valley it is advisable to make an early start, arriving at the Lookout before 10AM when the clouds can close in.

At the park headquarters, the **Kokee Natural History Museum** contains collections of plants and geological specimens as well as samples of petroglyphs found on Kauai. It has an information center selling hiking maps, books and souvenirs. There is also a restaurant, Kokee Lodge, which is the contact point for cabin rental in the park (see page 196).

The park's rugged terrain is criss-crossed by 45 miles of hiking trails. These range in lenth and degree of difficulty from a 15-minute nature walk near the museum to forest walks along unpaved jeep tracks (see panel) and arduous treks down into the precipitous gorges of the Na Pali Coast.

The boggy and remote Alakai Swamp is a naturalist's dream but demanding hiking terrain, as it is frequently swathed in mist and rain. Rainwater from Mount Waialeale gathers in the giant caldera of Kauai's only volcano to form the 30-square-mile Alakai. Here, native plant species flourish in conditions unsuited to introduced species. Rare birds—perhaps even the *oo aa* which has not been seen for decades—flit amongst the stunted *ohia* trees, which barely reach knee-height. Hikers in the Alakai must be well prepared, with wet-weather gear, drinking water, and decent maps. Anyone thinking of hiking down to the Na Pali Coast should be aware that there are no facilities or quick routes out. Information can be obtained from the State Parks Service (tel: 808/241-3444).

Muddy trails at Kokee State Park

Old-time Koloa

Hurricane Iniki
Originating off the coast of Central America, hurricanes usually dissipate before they reach Hawaii, but on September 11, 1992, Hurricane Iniki caught Kauai head on. Winds gusting up to 227m.p.h. damaged 14,000 buildings, and the costs of rebuilding—all the major hotels have been refurbished—and property compensation have been enormous.

Baking white sands at Polihale State Park

▶ **Koloa**   91D1

On the main road to Koloa (HI-520), a mile-long leafy tunnel of eucalyptus trees momentarily blocks out the view of cane fields. The former plantation town of Koloa was the center of the Kauai sugar industry, and the first successful plantation in Hawaii, with its sugar mill (now gone), was founded here in 1835.

The town's restored wooden stores and houses are clustered around the site of the old Ladd & Company mill. Nearby, Old Koloa Church reveals New England origins in its white-painted clapboard and Classical Revival columns. Out near the existing sugar mill, off Weliweli Road, the 19th-century Catholic Church of St. Raphael is a more typically European stone-built affair. The mortar used in the original construction was made from pounded coral collected from the offshore reefs by hand and then hauled overland for 3 miles back to the church site.

▶▶▶ **National Tropical Botanical Garden**   90C1

Off HI-50, Lawai Valley
Tour information, tel: 808/332-7361; reservations, tel: 808/742-2623. Admission charge: expensive

There are in fact two glorious gardens here. The NTBG's 186-acre Lawai Garden contains collections of tropical plants from around the world, including bromeliads, palms and heliconias, with a special emphasis on rare and endangered Hawaiian species. The neighboring Allerton Garden, which was founded in the 1870s, is a masterpiece of garden design. Laid out around Queen Emma's ocean-side summer cottage, the garden has meandering paths which link a number of plant-filled and individually landscaped outdoor "rooms," many of them ornamented with pools and fountains.

▶▶ **Olu Pua Botanical Gardens**   90C1

HI-50, 1 mile west of Kalaheo (tel: 808/332-8182)
Open: daily, tours every hour from 9:30 to 2:30.
Admission charge: moderate

This is another lovely garden, with the added bonus of a 1930s plantation home designed by architect C.W. Dickey for the Alexander family. The 12½-acre landscaped site is full of unusual trees and plants, colorful hibiscus bushes (the state flower), and water-lilies in a hibiscus-shaped pond. There is also a rainforest section

where orchids flourish amidst giant gingers, lobster-claw and parrot's beak heliconias. The plantation house is decorated with exquisite oriental furnishings and porcelain, and overlooks a little Japanese garden.

A plume of spray from Spouting Horn, Poipu

▶▶ Poipu 91D1

A popular resort area on the sunny southern tip of the island, Poipu's string of crescent-shaped sandy beaches spreads 1½ miles along the coast. Accommodations range from deluxe beachfront resorts and well-appointed condominiums (none of them taller than a coconut palm) to bed-and-breakfast operations. There is great snorkeling, fishing, sailing, windsurfing and scuba off the coast, plus golf, tennis and horseback-riding for landlubbers. Of the beaches, Poipu Beach Park is a favorite. In the grassy park, there are picnic tables and barbecue grills under the trees. Brennecke's store and restaurant opposite offers everything from a fish dinner and sandwiches to boogie-board rental and boat tours.

At the western end of Poipu, the tour buses roll up to watch the antics of **Spouting Horn**. It is best seen on a blustery day when the waves are driven powerfully through an old lava tube in the volcanic rock promontory, creating a massive geyser-like plume of spray with an eerie accompanying moan, rather like whale song.

▶ Polihale State Park 90A3

A 5-mile-long red dirt track leads through the cane fields to this magnificent beach in the driest corner of the island. Its sprawling dunes end abruptly in the towering buttresses of the Na Pali Coast, and the only shade is provided by spiky thorned *kiawe* trees. There are showers and barbecue grills; camping permits are available from the Division of State Parks (tel: 808/241-3444).

Lappert's ices
One of the most popular pit-stops in Koloa is the Lappert's ice-cream emporium. A home-grown family business founded in Hanapepe in 1983, Lappert now sells its exotic sorbets and diet-shattering rich ice-creams throughout Hawaii. One generous serving is almost guaranteed to soothe frayed tempers and fractious children after a long drive or a day at the beach. Try the caramel-coconut-macadamia ice-cream, or "Hana Road," with marshmallows, walnuts, and white-chocolate chunks.

■ **Dip beneath the glassy surface of the Pacific Ocean, and you find a spectacular and colorful marine world set to rival—and perhaps even surpass—the diversity and beauty of Hawaii's scenery on land.** ■

Night dives

Night dives are an amazing experience. All sorts of nocturnal creatures desert their daytime hideaways to feed, stony corals appear to blossom against the backdrop of a darkened ocean, and the reef's colors are, if anything, magnified by flashlight beams, which also attract fish. For an unforgettable experience, Kona Coast Divers on the Big Island of Hawaii (tel: 808/329-8802) present Manta Ray Madness, a spectacular night dive where rays between 8 and 10 feet long glide past on their spreading "wings" in the beams of halogen lamps.

Scanning the seabed

Coral reefs The Hawaiian Islands form the most isolated archipelago in the world, and local marine life is every bit as unusual as the flora and fauna found on dry land. About a third of the marine species living in Hawaiian waters are endemic to the islands, fish and molluscs that have evolved on and around the offshore reefs and are found nowhere else in the world.

Hawaii's coral reefs have taken millions of years to develop in the mid-Pacific, where the water is relatively cool for coral. The hard corals, which form the basis of the reef, are the limestone exterior skeletons of polyps (soft-bodied relatives of sea anemones and jellyfish), and grow slowly but surely as each generation of corals builds on the skeletal remains of its ancestors. Hard coral reefs are generally found on the sheltered leeward sides of the islands, and are practical as well as beautiful. They act as a breakwater for the coast and make a safe anchorage for soft corals and shellfish, as well as creating the dazzling white-sand beaches which are the result of reef erosion.

Living color The bizarre though beautiful submarine landscape, fashioned from corals and lava outcrops carved into

pinnacles, archways and dark caverns, is only the beginning of the wonders in store. Down beneath the waves, golden butterfly fish, neon wrasses, and striped convict tangs streak past masked divers like shivers of liquid color. Puffed-up and speckled balloon fish and parrot fish, which can bite off chunks of coral with their sharp, beak-like mouths, move at a more sedate pace. Stripy orange-brown lionfish shimmy by in a fluttering of lacy fins, while Moorish idols trail a delicate white streamer in their wake and surgeon fish swim about their business sporting tail spines that resemble scalpels.

One of the most colorful reef dwellers is Hawaii's state fish, the *humuhumunukunukuapuaa*, or painted triggerfish. Triggerfish are named for the sharp spine in their dorsal fin which can be used to see off predators. Keeping a low profile, crabs, lobsters, and sinister moray eels lurk in convenient crevices.

In deeper water, yellowfin tuna, amberjack, dorado, marlin, and mackerel swim with the sharks—black- and white-tipped sharks, hammerheads, and even great whites—as they patrol their ocean territories. One peculiar resident here is the huge toothless whale shark, the largest fish in the world. Another huge creature is the blanket-sized manta ray, its giant body soaring through the ocean in a stunning display of grace and power.

Sighting a sea turtle is always a thrill. These primitive leviathans glide slowly above the coral beds, and can grow shells more than 3 feet long. Another treat is the sudden arrival of a pod of spinner dolphins, performing effortless underwater acrobatics and chattering furiously in a welter of whistles and clicking sounds. In winter, divers can occasionally pick up the electrifying echo reverberations of whale songs.

Snorkel and dive The best time for diving in Hawaii is in the summer, when the seas are calm and visibility is exceptional. Each island offers a choice of snorkel and dive sites (see panel), some suited to beginners and others requiring experience. Snorkeling equipment (flippers and masks) is available to rent on several busy public beaches and from many hotels. Local diving operators will offer scuba-diving courses with certified instructors, rent equipment out to bona fide divers, and run day- and night-diving expeditions for divers of all levels. Some can also rent underwater cameras and supply waterproof housings to fit most standard cameras and camcorders.

Snorkel and dive trips drop in on the underwater world

Top snorkel and dive sites
- Hanauma and Maunalua Bays, Oahu
- Haena State Park and Poipu, Kauai
- Mokuhooniki Island, Molokai
- Honolua Bay, Ahihi Bay and Molokini, Maui
- Cathedrals off Hulopoe, Lanai
- Kealakekua Bay and Pine Trees, Hawaii

Waimea Canyon, the "Grand Canyon of the Pacific"

► **Russian Fort Elizabeth State Historical Park** 90B1

HI-50, ½ mile east of Waimea
Open site. Admission free

Strategically placed at the mouth of the Waimea River, Georg Anton Schaeffer's Fort Elizabeth dominated the once-bustling port of Waimea. After Schaeffer was sent packing by King Kamehameha (see page 92), the Hawaiians occupied the European-design star-shaped fort until 1864, then demolished most of its 30-foot-thick walls and dismantled its guns. It is difficult to conjure up the full picture from the dark and dusty basalt rock ruins, but try to imagine the bay full of trading schooners and whaling ships. The views are suitably commanding.

► **Waimea** 90B2

This old port and whaling station, a mere shadow of its former self, is the last supply stop on the way up to the Waimea Canyon (see below) and Kokee State Park (see pages 102–3). The main road, flanked by some classic 1920s plantation-era buildings, runs straight through town. In the town center a monument commemorates Captain Cook, who first set foot on Hawaiian soil here on January 20, 1778, and the town throws off its dusty torpor once a year at the end of February to celebrate the Captain Cook Carnival.

►►► **Waimea Canyon** 90B3

Waimea Canyon Road (HI-550)
Open site. Admission free

Mark Twain called this the "Grand Canyon of the Pacific," and as the road climbs (over 1,000 feet in the first mile) and glimpses of the massive red, purple, and green cliffs appear, it is clear he was right. Measuring 10 miles long, over a mile across and over 3,000 feet deep, the canyon has been carved with deeply scoured valleys by centuries of wind and rain. Wooded gullies etched by waterfalls and streams burrow back into the multicolored volcanic rock, and rainbows sprout like fairy bridges. There are spectacular views from the Waimea Canyon Lookout, just beyond Mile Marker 10; serious hikers can tackle the Kukui Trail (see panel).

Kukui Trail

The name "Waimea" means "red water," referring to the color of the Waimea River after heavy rain as flood waters carry away the rich red-brown topsoil. There is a strenuous but rewarding hike down the precipitous canyon sides to the river via the 2½-mile Kukui Trail. From the trailhead at the Iliau Nature Loop (Mile Marker 8.5), a steeply graded, knee-trembling path zigzags down to the canyon floor where it hooks up with the Waimea Canyon Trail leading back to Waimea (8 miles). Hikers should wear sturdy boots, and carry drinking water and sunscreen.

The "Forbidden Island" Separated from the west coast of Kauai by the Kaulakahi Channel, the "Forbidden Island" of Niihau is a tantalizing shadow on the horizon. The island was bought for $10,000 by Mrs Elizabeth Sinclair in 1864, and it remains in the hands of her descendants, the Robinsons of Kauai.

Climate and way of life Bleak and arid Niihau (18 miles by 6 miles) is caught in the lee of neighboring Kauai, which siphons off most of the rain. The island is inhabited mainly by pure-bred Hawaiians, who make a living from cattle and sheep ranching, producing charcoal from *kiawe* trees, collecting honey, and gathering the shells to make precious Niihau shell *leis,* or "necklaces" (see page 97). There are no telephones, electricity, alcohol, or jails on Niihau. Most people live in simple wooden houses in the main village of Puuwai on the central west coast, and get around on horseback or by truck.

Hawaiian is Niihau's first language, though English is taught in the elementary school; children leave the island to attend high school on Kauai or Oahu. The people of Niihau are free to come and go, but the only way for an outsider to visit the island is as a guest of the Robinson family or via helicopter tours from Kauai operated by Niihau Helicopters (tel: 808/335-3500), which land at a remote spot far away from habitation.

109

Forbidding cliffs greet visitors to Niihau

Battle of Niihau
One unwelcome guest on Niihau was a Japanese Zero pilot who was forced to ditch his plane after bombing Pearl Harbor. Having escaped his Hawaiian captors, the pilot retrieved a machine gun from his plane and held out for five days before local resident Benehakaha Kanahele went out to try to persuade him to give himself up. Kanahele was shot several times, but nevertheless managed to overpower the Japanese interloper. Kanahele was later awarded the Congressional Medal of Honor for his part in what became known as the "Battle of Niihau."

MOLOKAI

Map

2

Kaiwi Channel

Ilio Point
Anapuka Cave
Mokio Point
Kawakiu Beach
Kepuhi Beach
Kaluakoi
Papohaku Beach Park
Lauhue
Molokai Ranch Wildlife Conservation Park
Kaluakoi
Moomomi
Paualaia Point
Purdy's Macadamia Nut Farm
Hoolehua
Hoolehua Airport
Mahana
Malulani Estate
Phallic Rock
Palaau State Park
Kalae
Kalaupapa Peninsula
Oceanview Pavilion
Kauhako Crate
Kahiu Point
Kalaupapa
Kalaupapa National Park
Kalaupapa Lookout
RW Meyer Sugar Mill and Molokai Museum
Awahua Bay

Kaunakakai
1,381ft
Puu Nana
Maunaloa
Waikane
Kolo Wharf
Laau Point
Oahu Outrigger Canoe Race
Hale o Lono Harbor
Halena
Kualapuu Reservoir
Umipaa
Kiowea Park & Coconut Grove
Church Row
Kaunakakai
Kamiloloa
Kawela Place of Refug
Kawela
Molokai Tunne

460

1

Kalohi Channel

0   4   8   12 km
0   4   8 miles

A   B   C

Lahaina, Maui

Ancient stone-walled fishponds line the south coast bays of Molokai

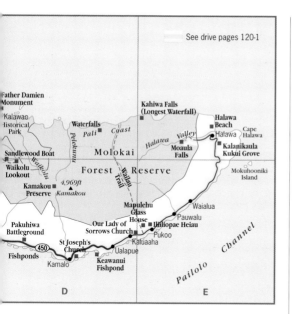

See drive pages 120-1

Father Damien Monument
Kalawao
Kalaupapa Historical Park
Waterfalls
Pali Coast
Pelekunu
Sandlewood Boat
Waikolu Lookout
Kamakou Preserve
4,969ft Kamakou
Molokai
Kahiwa Falls (Longest Waterfall)
Halawa
Halawa Beach
Cape Halawa
Kalanikaula Kukui Grove
Mokuhooniki Island
Forest Reserve
Wailau Trail
Halawa Valley
Moaula Falls
Pakuhiwa Battleground
Mapulehu Glass House
Our Lady of Sorrows Church
St Joseph's Church
Kaluaaha
Ualapue
Iliiliopae Heiau
Pukoo
Waialua
Pauwalu
Fishponds
450
Kamalo
Keawanui Fishpond

Pailolo Channel

D   E

The "Friendly Isle" The second smallest of the main Hawaiian islands, the "Friendly Isle" of Molokai measures a modest 38 miles by 10 miles. With no natural harbor to attract ships, the development of the island has always been slow, but this has worked in Molokai's favor. Although the island lies just 9 miles across the Pailolo Channel from Maui, or a 20-minute air hop from Honolulu, it remains a 260-square-mile haven of rare, unspoiled natural beauty and quiet rural charm.

On the central south coast, the chief settlement of Kaunakakai lies about midway along the single east–west main road. A laid-back country town, Kaunakakai (and indeed Molokai) does not boast a single traffic signal, shopping center or movie theater, and no building taller than a coconut palm. The 7,000 residents, of whom around half are native Hawaiians (the highest proportion of the population in the main islands), are quite content to leave the big-time tourism industry to Waikiki and Lahaina over the water. Instead, they proudly point out the fact that over half their visitor figures are made up of Neighbor Islanders who come to relax, play a little golf, go fishing or hunting, or simply enjoy the peace and quiet.

Scenery and climate The island was formed by two volcanoes—Kamakou in the east and Maunaloa in the west—linked together by a central plateau, and its scenery varies dramatically from one end to the other. Battered by wind, rain and the relentless ocean, the windward, northern slopes of Kamakou have been sculpted into dramatic 3,300-foot-high *pali* (cliffs). These are amongst the tallest seacliffs in the world, and rise like an impenetrable moss-coated bulwark slashed by narrow valleys that glint with waterfalls.

The waterfalls are fed by rain clouds snared by the summit of Mount Kamakou (4,970 feet), at the heart of the mountainous East End. Here, in the cool depths of the

forest reserve, there are areas of eerie, mist-clad swamp, where primitive, stunted plants creep among lava boulders. At lower, and markedly warmer, altitudes, the steep hillsides falling down to the coast are swathed in luxuriant rainforest, and there is a looping necklace of ancient stone-walled fishponds along the shore.

The central plateau is given over largely to agriculture. The old pineapple plantation town of Kualapuu now experiments with coffee groves, fresh vegetables are a burgeoning business, and there is a macadamia nut orchard. To the west is open ranch country.

Molokai's West End receives a fraction of the East End's rainfall. Here, the island's only resort, Kaluakoi, perches on the shore amidst an emerald-green golf course that is flanked by beaches. Inland, the Molokai Ranch (the island's largest, with some 60,000 acres) offers photographic safaris through its African and Asian animal reserve where giraffe, eland, and zebra roam in a surprisingly African-looking landscape.

History Molokai was one of the first islands to be settled by the Polynesians (the fertile Halawa Valley in the East End was cultivated from around AD 650), but it was not always so friendly. During the 16th and 17th centuries neighboring islanders, wary of Molokai's powerful *kahuna* (priests), used to call Molokai the "Lonely Island" and avoided contact with it.

Captain Cook sighted Molokai in 1778 but did not stop. Kamehameha I did not allow the threat of the *kahuna* to interfere with his all-conquering sweep through the islands, and took Molokai in 1795. The missionaries,

Halawa Bay was a favorite surfing spot of Molokai's ancient alii chiefs

probably the first Westerners to set foot ashore, arrived in the 1830s. Sheep and cattle ranches were established in the 1840s, and Kamehameha V later secured the prime Molokai Ranch for himself, built a house near Kaunakakai, planted a coconut grove and introduced axis deer, a present from the Emperor of Japan.

In the mid-1800s leprosy appeared in Hawaii, possibly introduced by Chinese migrant workers. A decision was made to isolate the victims on Molokai, casting them adrift off a remote and inaccessible cove on the Kalaupapa peninsula. In 1873, a Belgian priest, Father Damien de Veuster, arrived at the god-forsaken colony and devoted his life to caring for the lepers in one of the most famous true-life stories of Hawaii (see pages 116–17).

Sugar was introduced to Molokai in the 1870s but the crop, and several later attempts to harvest cane, failed because of irrigation problems. In the 1920s, Del Monte and Dole set up pineapple plantations and associated fruit operations, which kept the island's economy afloat until the 1970s. Diversified agriculture is now the name of the game, though low-key tourism is essential to the island's shaky economy.

Getting around Molokai airport lies 8 miles northwest of Kaunakakai. Cars can be rented at the airport (reservations essential, especially at weekends). Kukui Tours & Limousines (tel: 808/553-5133) offer a 24-hour taxi service. There is no public transportation on the Island. The *Maui Princess* provides a boat service to Maui (tel: 808/667-6165; or 808/661-8397, Lahaina).

Zebras graze at the Molokai Ranch Wildlife Park

Madame Pele's Ohia lehua *blossom*

Sandalwood
In 1810 Western traders discovered sandalwood in the Hawaiian Islands. The Chinese could not get enough of the fragrant timber, and the Hawaiians logged their forests until the last groups of mature sandalwood were destroyed in the late 1820s. Up in the Kamakou preserve, a deep depression alongside the trail is known as Ka Lua Na Moku Iliahi, "The Pit of the Sandalwood Ships." The pits were dug to resemble a ship's hold. Local people felled the sandalwood trees and filled the pit, then sold it as a job lot to trading vessels.

Isolated Kalaupapa

►►► Kalaupapa   110C2

Several daily five-minute shuttle flights with Air Molokai (tel: 808/553-3636)
Open: daily tours by reservation only, contact Damien Tours (tel: 808/567-6171); minimum age limit 15 years.
Admission charge: expensive

The Kalaupapa peninsula, a volcanic after-thought tacked onto the central north coast of Molokai, at the foot of the *pali*, was reckoned to be the most isolated outpost of the Hawaiian kingdom when Kamehameha V decided to round up leprosy sufferers in 1865 and incarcerate them in a quarantine colony in a remote area far from the rest of the population.

The first arrivals were literally tossed overboard in Kalawao Cove and left to struggle for survival. Later, Father Damien (see pages 116–17) moved the colony to the more hospitable western shore, where its inhabitants remained cut off from the world until the introduction of sulphone drugs, which arrest the effects of the disease, in the 1940s. Around 50 permanent residents remain in the Kalaupapa village, now open for official tours.

The only land access to Kalaupapa is by foot via the steep 3-mile trail from Palaau State Park, near the Kalaupapa Lookout (see page 119). Hikers must make reservations in advance and will be met at the foot of the trail by Damien Tours for a guided visit.

▶▶▶ Kaluakoi and the West Coast Beaches 110A2

At the end of the road on the west coast, the Kaluakoi resort offers hotel and condominium units, an 18-hole oceanfront golf course, tennis courts, a swimming pool and an activities center (see panel).

There is a trio of terrific beaches close to Kaluakoi: the golf course actually borders lovely **Kepuhi Beach**; **Kawakiu Beach**, with excellent swimming, lies a short walk to the north; and **Papohaku Beach Park** (Mile Marker 15), to the south, boasts the largest white-sand beach in the state. Beyond a small shady park, where barbecue grills and picnic tables stand beneath *kiawe* trees, a strand of coastal woodland borders the dunes.

▶▶ Kamakou Preserve 111D1

Off HI-470 at Mile Marker 4
Open: Permission from the Nature Conservancy (tel: 808/553-5236). Admission free

The Kamakou Preserve, a 2,774-acre tract of land on the slopes of Kamakou, was established by the Nature Conservancy in 1982 to protect one of the best remaining areas of native Hawaiian forest. A muddy jeep-track winds its way up through the forest past groves of eucalyptus where sandalwood once grew, to a viewpoint on the edge of the Waikolu Valley. *Ohia* trees cling to the cliffsides and the rainforest harbors five endangered bird species, including the *olomao* and *kakawahie*, a thrush and a creeper respectively, both found only on Molokai. Near the top of the mountain, a slippery path-cum-boardwalk through moss-wrapped trees and bracts of *amau*, *hapuu,* and *uluhe* ferns leads up to the mysterious Pepeopae Bog.

▶ Kaunakakai 110C1

Reminiscent of an Old West trading post, Kaunakakai probably looks much as it did when *The Cockeyed Mayor of Kaunakakai* was a hit song in the 1930s. Among the false-fronted shops, Molokai Fish & Dive does an eclectic line in souvenirs and equipment for snorkeling, fishing, diving, and hunting. Down on the dock, you can catch the *Maui Princess* ferry to Lahaina, sample *poke* (raw fish) salad, and arrange sightseeing, diving, or sport-fishing trips at the marina.

A short drive (3 miles) west of town takes you to the half-dozen small chapels of picturesque **Church Row**. Across the street is the coconut grove, which was planted by Kamehameha V in the mid-1800s.

Downtown
Kaunakakai

115

Outdoor activities
Molokai can offer a host of outdoor adventures. Fun Hogs at Kaluakoi (tel: 808/552-2555) specializes in kayak, mountain-bike, fishing and camping rental. Molokai Charters (tel: 808/553-5852) offers day sails to isolated beaches with snorkeling and whale-watching (in season). Alternatively, try Bill Kapuni's Snorkel & Dive (tel: 808/553-9867). As well as snorkelling, diving and spear fishing, Maa Hawaii (tel: 808/558-8184) arranges a guide service for hikers, and can organize rifle and bow-hunting excursions.

■ **A remote leper colony created in 1865 on an isolated peninsula of northern Molokai became one of the most godforsaken spots on earth. Its wretched inhabitants were reduced by starvation and sickness to little more than animals until a Belgian priest arrived in 1873 and dedicated his life to relieving their suffering.** ■

Restricted area
Though no longer a place of exile since its remaining inhabitants are now free to come and go as they please, the Kalaupapa peninsula remains a restricted area. Today, some 50 people (all aged 60 plus) still prefer to stay on voluntarily, and the settlement will continue to be their home for as long as they wish. Sulphone drugs and pharmaceutical developments have contained Hansen's disease, and "former patients" now welcome visitors on a guided tour program that was inaugurated in the late 1950s (see pages 114–15).

St. Joseph's Church

Chinese legacy Leprosy was first seen in Hawaii in the 1830s. The locals called it *mai pake*, "comes from China," and by the 1860s the incurable, chronically contagious and horribly disfiguring disease was causing such concern that Kamehameha V agreed to the establishment of a quarantine colony. An isolated site was chosen on the north coast of Molokai, a barren, windswept peninsula bordered on three sides by treacherous seas and more or less cut off from the main body of the island by a natural barrier of towering cliffs. The peninsula was originally known as Makanalua, the "Given Grave."

The schooner *Warwick* transported the first boatload of leprosy sufferers to Molokai in January 1866, where they were tossed into the sea at Kalawao on the harsh east coast of the peninsula. Those who survived the waves and rocks were forced to live like wild animals, some constructing rude shacks on the shore or living in caves. There they preyed on new arrivals and fought for the few basic supplies that were occasionally dumped ashore. Fear of the disease was such that unrelated skin diseases were often diagnosed as leprosy; bounty hunters roamed the Hawaiian kingdom wrenching sufferers and non-sufferers alike from their villages and families. The victims were then incarcerated in cages on the ships' decks, taken to Molokai and dumped in the surf.

Father Damien

Our Lady of Sorrows

The "Martyr of Molokai" Four years before Norwegian scientist Armauer Hansen isolated the bacterium that causes leprosy (thereafter known as "Hansen's disease"), Joseph Damien de Veuster arrived in Hawaii. Born in Tremeloo, Belgium, in 1840, he attended the Catholic Seminary of the Sacred Heart in Louvain, before being posted to Hawaii. De Veuster was ordained at Honolulu's Cathedral of Our Lady of Peace in 1864, and then sent to Puna on the Big Island of Hawaii.

By 1873, a few concerned missionaries had begun to organize a small-scale relief operation for the victims of Hansen's disease on Molokai. Father Damien heard about the mission on a visit to Maui, and volunteered to go there for a few months to help out. His stay lasted 16 years.

The scene which greeted the priest had already sent several sickened volunteers scurrying back to civilization at the first available opportunity. Although the mission distributed a few meager scraps of food and clothing, medical assistance was non-existent, and physical contact with the contagious, unkempt and disfigured exiles was forbidden.

Father Damien flouted these rules. He bathed and dressed the suppurating wounds of the living and buried the dead himself. An accomplished carpenter, he built shelters, churches, orphanages and hospitals, investing dignity and hope in the lawless and dispirited vacuum of the colony. It was moved to the more sheltered west coast of the peninsula, Kalaupapa or the "Flat Plain," and the priest lobbied government and mission agencies for supplies. A 3-mile trail carved down the *pali* in 1886 allowed mule trains to bring provisions, and Father Damien sold the produce of his vegetable plot for nails and bandages. Although many admired his extraordinary dedication and achievements, the good father nevertheless also stirred up resentment amongst both mission and government circles.

The first tell-tale lesions of Hansen's disease appeared on Father Damien's body in 1885. Despite his illness, he continued his work to improve the lot of the people of Kalaupapa right up until his death, aged 49, in 1889. He was buried beside St. Philomena's, the church he built at Kalawao, although his remains were returned to Belgium in 1936.

Honors and decorations
What Father Damien would make of the present attention focused on him is hard to say. He rarely wore the Cross of the Royal Order of Kalakaua awarded to him in recognition of his selfless contribution to the plight of Hansen's disease sufferers on Kalaupapa, and later remarked "The Lord has decorated me with his own particular cross — leprosy." Honored more recently by a modern statue erected near the State Capitol in Honolulu, the "Martyr of Molokai" was also beatified by the Roman Catholic Church in 1995, the penultimate step before elevation to sainthood.

A courageous priest

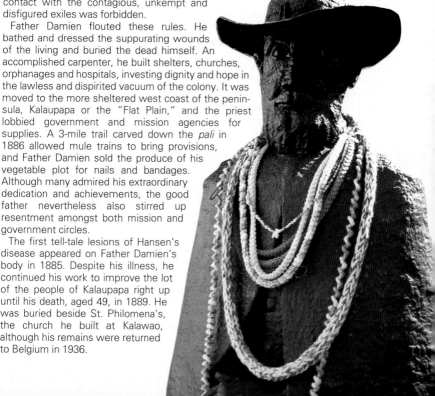

Molokai Ranch Trail Rides
A terrific way to explore outback Molokai is on horseback with Molokai Ranch Trail Rides (tel: 808/552-2681). Local guides are full of information as the 1½-hour (or longer) rides follow trails across the private ranchlands above Kualapuu. There are views down the *pali* to the Kaluapapa peninsula and across to the sand dunes of Moomomi Beach. During whale-watching season (November–April), humpback whales may be seen off shore. The ranch also offers mountain-bike rental and trophy game hunting, and hosts rodeos several times a year.

As good as new, this engine once powered Hawaii's smallest sugar mill

▶▶ **Malulani Estate Coffees of Hawaii** *110C2*
Off HI-470 at Kualapuu
Open: Plantation Store daily 10–3; tours by reservation, Mon–Fri . Admission charge: plantation store, free; tours, expensive
Coffee is now grown instead of fruit on 450 acres of former Del Monte pineapple land around the plantation village of Kualapuu. There are free coffee-tastings in the Plantation Store, which also houses a good souvenir shop. On weekdays, mule-drawn wagons tour the coffee groves, and there are visits to the aromatic processing plant—Malulani means "Heavenly Aroma."

▶▶ **Maunaloa** *110B1*
The town that pineapple built: Libby, McNeill and Libby literally shipped Maunaloa to Molokai in 1923. From a consignment of prefabricated houses, they constructed a plantation town amongst the pineapple fields, but now that the pineapples have gone, Maunaloa is a dozy sort of place, with an old-fashioned country store and neat rows of houses tucked behind bougainvillea hedges.

A colorful collection of fluttering windsocks and pennants opposite the shop heralds Maunaloa's main diversion. Jonathan Socher's Big Wind Kite Store is the place to learn how to fly a *hula* dancer, a hibiscus flower, or a shark. Socher makes many of the kites on sale in his on-site workshop, and there are serious (and expensive) competition models and stunt kites, too (*Open:* Mon–Sat 8:30–5, Sun 10–2).

▶ **R.W. Meyer Sugar Mill and Molokai Museum** *110C2*
Off HI-470 at Kalae
Open: Mon–Fri 10–2. Admission charge: inexpensive
Rudolph Meyer arrived in Molokai from Hamburg, Germany, in 1850. He married a local chieftess, had 11 children, farmed, managed Kamehameha V's Molokai Ranch, and still found time to take on more than a dozen public offices. Meyer experimented briefly with growing sugar, but without success. However, his old mill, which operated from 1878 to 1889, and which was the smallest in Hawaii, has been restored to show the crushers and vats, the steam engine and the clarifier.

▶▶▶ Molokai Ranch Wildlife Conservation Park 110A2

Molokai Ranch Outfitters Center, Maunaloa
Open: Tue–Sat, tours at 10 and 1; reservations
tel: 808/552-2681. Admission charge: expensive
Molokai Ranch boasts a little corner of its vast acreage that is forever Africa. Guided safari tours set off from the Maunaloa Outfitters Center and trundle through rolling, sunbaked grasslands to an enclosure of some 300 acres which is home to African and Asian grazing animals. Eland and zebra roam while giraffes snack on *kiawe* trees. There are photo opportunities galore and animal-feeding activities, too.

▶▶ Palaau State Park 110C2

Central north coast via HI-470
The chief reason to visit this 234-acre forested park on the crest of the *pali* (cliff) is for the eagle's-eye view it affords of Kalaupapa and the Makanalua peninsula, 1,500 feet below. The Kalaupapa Lookout is a five-minute walk through the woods from the parking lot.

Another path fetches up at the **Phallic Rock**. It is no surprise that the ancient Hawaiians recognized this 6-foot protuberance as a fertility symbol. Infertile women, they say, need only stroke it...

▶▶ Purdy's Macadamia Nut Farm 110B2

Off HI-480, Hoolehua
Open: Mon–Sat 9:30–3. Admission free
Macadamia nut trees were first introduced to Hawaii in 1882 from Queensland, Australia, and the Islands now produce around 90 percent of the world's crop. After a short introduction to the nut and its cultivation, visitors to Tuddie Purdy's 1-acre, 70-year-old macadamia grove then get down to the serious business of tasting. There is a slab of granite and a hammer to crack open the rock-hard shells. Tuddie also sells pre-cracked roasted and salted kernels, and macadamia-flower honey. The latter can be sampled on slivers of coconut.

Guzzling giraffes

Celebrating the *hula*
It is said that Maunaloa ("Long Mountain") was the birthplace of the *hula*, where the goddess Laka learned the dance from her sister Kapo. Laka traveled all around the other islands teaching the *hula*, and set up a sacred *hula* school at Haena on the island of Kauai. These days *hula* dancers from the Neighbor Islands come to Molokai on the third Saturday in May for Molokai Ka Hula Piko, a celebration of the birth of *hula*, and a day of free *hula* performances, Hawaiian music and crafts.

Tough nuts

Drive **From Kaunakakai to the East End**

See map on pages 110–111.

A single road (HI-450) runs out from Kaunakakai along the coast to the Halawa Valley at the eastern tip of Molokai. Apart from great scenery, there are several low-key sites to visit along the way. History buffs wanting to visit the Iliiliopae Heiau, which is on private land, should obtain advance permission from Pearl Petro (tel: 808/558-8113). At the time of writing, the hiking route to the Halawa Valley's Moaula Falls is closed to the public because of a dispute about

The 250-foot Moaula Falls, Halawa

access, but check for developments with the Molokai Visitors Association (tel: 808/553-3876). Pack a picnic, fill up with gas (there are no gas stations *en route*) and allow a couple of hours to follow the scenic 30-mile road to Halawa at a leisurely pace.

The road heads out east towards Kamalo along the sea. Once, more than 60 ancient fishponds fringed Molokai's southeastern coast, lassoing the shallow waters in neat arcs of lava and coral boulders. Some of the fishponds date from the 13th century and are in use again for breeding mullet. **Keawanui** is the biggest, enclosing 54½ acres within its 2,000-foot seawall. Several other fishponds along the route are visible from the road.

At Kamalo (Mile Marker 10.5), **St. Joseph's Church** is a simple white-painted wooden church that was built by Father Damien in 1876. In addition to his work with the lepers at the Kalaupapa colony, the priest also ministered to other settlers on the island. He built four churches outside Kalaupapa, of which only St. Joseph's and one other still stand. A statue of him stands by the entrance to the Gothic-style building.

A couple of miles farther on, the other Father Damien church, **Our Lady of Sorrows**, dates from 1874 but was rebuilt in 1966. There is a fine view from the open lawn past a giant wooden cross to the shallow waters of an ancient fishpond.

Just beyond Mile Marker 15.5 is **Mapulehu Glass House**, a 9-acre flower farm open to visitors on weekday mornings (Mon–Fri 7–noon). In addition to the tropical gardens, the hothouse is filled with orchids, 43 varieties of gingers and heliconias, and much more.

A 15-minute walk from the road over private land takes you to **Iliiliopae Heiau** (for directions see above), one of the largest (if not oldest) temple sites in Hawaii. The vast rock-strewn platform of the *heiau* stands 22 feet high and is surrounded by rainforest jungle.

Archaeologists date the vast platform, which measures an astonishing 320 feet by 120 feet, to between the 11th and 13th centuries. Powerful priests who carried out the most sacred and complex religious rites at Iliiliopae, possibly including human sacrifice, earned the island the name of *Molokai pule oo*, the "place of mature prayer."

Beyond Pukoo, the views along the rocky coast are tremendous. As the road climbs around hairpin bends into the Puu O Hoku ranchlands, look for **Mokuhooniki Island**, an offshore seabird sanctuary.

Panoramic views of the **Halawa Valley**, cut deep into the *pali* (cliffs), open up after Mile Marker 25. The valley was a major settlement site up until 1946, when a massive *tsunami* (tidal wave caused by an undersea earthquake or volcanic eruption) wiped out many of its farms. Now the jungle is reclaiming dozens of home and temple sites and choking terraces once irrigated by the Halawa Stream. At the mouth of the stream there is a small crescent-shaped beach. It is not safe to swim here, but the bay was a favorite surfing spot for the *alii* (chiefs).

A 2-mile trail starts from near Jerusalem Hou Church and leads up the valley to the **Moaula Falls** (see above). The pool beneath the falls is said to be guarded by a giant *moo*. Bathers should throw a *ti* leaf onto the pool to check the mythical lizard's mood: if the leaf floats it is safe to go in the water, if it sinks, steer clear.

Iliiliopae Heiau

MAUI

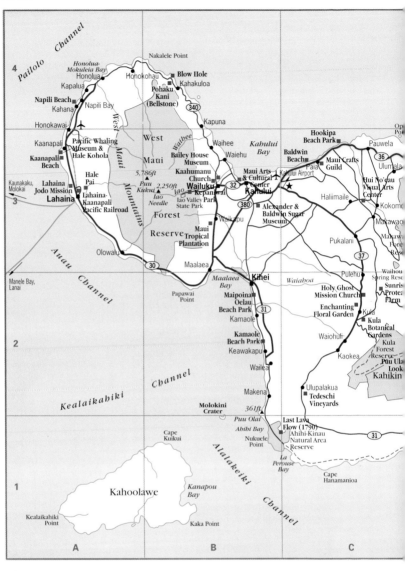

MAUI

See drive pages 138-9

123

Mokupapa Point
Kaulanapueo Church
Huelo · Kailua
Puohokamoa Falls
Kaumahina State Wayside Park
Keanae
Keanae Arboretum
Wailua
Nahiku
Wailua Valley State Wayside Lookout
Koolau Forest Reserve
Kalahu Point
360
Kaeleku
Waianapanapa State Park
Park Headquarters
Leleiwi Lookout
Hana Gardenland Nursery
Hawaiiana Museum & Hana Cultural Center
Kauiki Head
Hana
Wananalua Church
Kalahaku Lookout 8,905ft Hanakauhi
Haleakala National Park
Hana Forest Reserve
Koki Beach
Hamoa
Visitor Center
10,020ft Puu Ulaula
8,200ft Haleakala Crater
Pahihi
Forest Reserve
31
Muolea
Kipahulu Forest Reserve
Waimoku Falls
Catholic Monument
Oheo Gulch
Loaloa Heiau
Kipahulu
Palapala Hoomau Congregational Church
Kaupo
Mokulau
Natural Arch
Kailio Point
Alenuihaha Channel

0 4 8 12 km
0 4 8 miles

D   E

The "Valley Isle." Named for the legendary demi-god Maui, whose feats of cunning and superhuman strength included lifting the sky so that Man could walk upright, slowing down the sun, and giving Hawaiians the secret of fire, the "Valley Isle" is almost as full of surprises as its namesake. Maui is the second largest island in the Hawaiian archipelago, some 124 square miles bigger than Oahu but with just 10 percent of the population. Although Maui's tourist industry is well developed (it is number two in the tourism stakes, welcoming around 2 million visitors each year), the main resort areas of the island are confined to pockets along the sunnier, drier west coast and it is easy to escape into unspoiled, open countryside.

MAUI

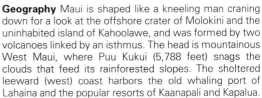

Transportation
Public transportation is limited on Maui, so most visitors rent a car for a couple of days. Trans Hawaiian (tel: 808/877-7308) operates a daily shuttle between Kahului airport and locations in the Kaanapali resort area. Akina Airport Shuttle (tel: 808/879-2828) serves the East Maui resort areas of Kihei, Wailea, and Makena. Free shuttle buses operate within the Wailea resort area. The main center for information about car rental is the airport at Kahului.

Silver-green pine-apple fields on the north shore

Geography Maui is shaped like a kneeling man craning down for a look at the offshore crater of Molokini and the uninhabited island of Kahoolawe, and was formed by two volcanoes linked by an isthmus. The head is mountainous West Maui, where Puu Kukui (5,788 feet) snags the clouds that feed its rainforested slopes. The sheltered leeward (west) coast harbors the old whaling port of Lahaina and the popular resorts of Kaanapali and Kapalua.

Maui's commercial centers, modern Kahului and the older county seat of Wailuku, lie at the northern end of the neck, a low-lying valley which gives the island its soubriquet. Most visitors arrive at Kahului airport and then head across for Lahaina-Kaanapali, or to East Maui's Wailea-Makena resort areas.

East Maui is the kneeling man's torso, and at its heart is magnificent Haleakala (the "House of the Sun"), the largest dormant volcano in the world. At 10,023 feet, with a crater that could comfortably accommodate Manhattan, Haleakala is quite literally the high spot of the island and a "must see" on any tourist itinerary.

On Haleakala's gentle western slopes, the cane fields of the valley give way to upcountry ranchlands and flower farms. Cattle country extends around to the south via the Tedeschi vineyards, where Hawaiian pineapple wine is made, and eventually runs into the rainforest belt that circles the windward portion of the mountain. The road to Hana along the lush windward coast is another visitors' "must"—54 miles and 600 curves of twisting tarmac edged by forest and waterfalls on one side, and startling views of the deep-blue sea and the rocky and windswept shore on the other.

Warriors and whalers When Captain Cook discovered Hawaii, Maui was ruled by powerful Chief Kahekili. In the 1780s, Kahekili brought Oahu and Molokai under his control and proved a formidable opponent to the great Kamehameha I (whom some say was his son). Kamehameha eventually took control of Maui after Kahekili's death in 1794, and later established a royal seat at Lahaina, where his sons held court until the 1840s.

The whalers beat the missionaries to Maui by about four years, and during the mid-1800s turned the sheltered harbor of Lahaina into the whaling capital of the world.

The first Western visitors to Maui landed at rocky La Pérouse Bay

Meanwhile, the missionaries did battle for the Hawaiians' souls, and tried every means to counter the licentious and alcohol-fueled antics of the whalers.

After the royal court was moved to Honolulu and the whaling ships left town for good, Lahaina slipped back into obscurity and waited for a new foreign invasion in the form of tourism. In recent years its picturesque wooden buildings have been restored and refitted, and it has emerged as Maui's leading tourist town. Along Front Street, where tour operators hustle good-naturedly for the tourist dollar, there are plenty of boutiques and galleries, bars and restaurants, and self-conscious new owners of garish *aloha* shirts pack the pavements three or four deep in a lively and entertaining street parade.

Vacation activities The sheltered waters of Lahaina Roads, where hundreds of whaling ships once rode at anchor, now buzz with sailing yachts and charter boats heading for Lanai or the snorkel and dive sites around Molokini. Other popular options are whale-watching excursions and deep sea fishing charters. On Lahaina's main street it is possible to book boat trips, or sign up for bus tours, surfing lessons, parasailing, helicopter flights, submarine adventures, horseback-riding and even bicycle rides down Haleakala.

Perfect vacations on Maui come in all shapes and sizes. For some, the ideal is a long weekend relaxing by the pool of a Kaanapali hotel within a stone's throw of a wonderful restaurant; others may prefer to spend a week or more hiking on Haleakala or diving off Molokini. However, there is no doubt that for the locals and many repeat visitors *Maui no ka oi*, "Maui is the best."

Approximate driving times from Kahului
- Haleakala: 1 hour 45 minutes
- Hana: 2 hours 30 minutes
- Kaanapali: 50 minutes
- Kapalua: 1 hour
- Lahaina: 45 minutes
- Wailea: 35 minutes

Loko O Mokuhinia
One of the most sacred sites of ancient Hawaii now lies buried beneath a baseball diamond in Lahaina's Maluulu O Lele Park. Once there was a sacred freshwater fishpond here, Loko O Mokuhinia, guarded by Princess Kihawahine (daughter of Maui's famous 16th-century chieftain, Piilani), who changed into a *moo* (giant lizard goddess) on her death. It was considered a place of the highest *mana* (spiritual power). Kamehameha III built himself a private retreat here, as well as a royal tomb for his mother, Queen Keopuolani, his sister, Nahienaena, and her child (later moved to Wainee churchyard).

Brig Carthaginian II

LAHAINA

A long, thin strip of a town stretched along the waterfront, the attractive old whaling port of Lahaina still seems a nugget of 19th-century New England in Paradise. Even though galleries and T-shirt shops replace the whaling era's grog shops and ships' chandlers, and a measure of rum at the Pioneer Inn now takes the form of a cocktail with a complimentary paper umbrella and half a fruit bowl floating on top, Front Street's clapboard buildings retain a distinctly old-fashioned, maritime air.

The 18th-century chieftain Kahekili held court in Lahaina and Kamehameha I, in the early days of his reign, built the "Brick Palace," the first Western-style structure erected in the Islands, down by the harbor. Set back from here, around the Reverend Baldwin's mission home, is the heart of old Lahaina, now a National Historic Landmark and well worth exploring on foot (see pages 130–1).

There is a helpful tourist information kiosk at the Wharf Cinema Center, 658 Front Street, where the free Lahaina Express bus service drops its passengers from Kaanapali. The kiosk is a handy place to make tour arrangments and to find out what price deals are available.

Traffic moves even more slowly than the pedestrians on Front Street, and parking in the town is a problem. There is a three-hour car park at the corner of Front and Prison Streets, and several of the shopping centers off Wainee Street (one block inland from Front Street) provide customer parking. The town's center meters give only one hour's parking.

►► Baldwin House 130B2

Front Street
Open: daily 10–4. Admission charge: moderate
This handsome green- and white-painted two-story house overlooks the harbor across the town square. The oldest existing building in Lahaina, the mission house was built in 1834. The Reverend Dwight Baldwin and his wife Charlotte moved here in 1838. Tours of the first floor reveal details of the life of a missionary-physician in the 1800s. Besides period furnishings, there are hand-crafted family heirlooms, and the Reverend Baldwin's gruesome medical instruments, also his antique passport, which, without the benefit of a photograph, lists his features: "Forehead—High, Nose—Aquiline, Chin—Obtuse."

►► Brig *Carthaginian II* 130A2

Off Wharf Street (next to the Small Boat Harbor)
Open: daily 9–4:30. Admission charge: moderate
The 93-foot steel-hulled *Carthaginian II* was built in the 1920s and is a replica of the fast, square-rigged brigs which brought the whalers and traders to Lahaina in the 19th century. It is now a whaling museum. Exhibits are augmented with audio-visual displays, including videos of whales in action and an original whaling boat that was recovered in Alaska and returned to Lahaina in 1973.

► Hale Pai 122A3

Lahainaluna High School (2 miles north of Front Street)
Open: Mon–Sat 10–4. Admission charge: inexpensive
In 1831, the missionaries established the Lahainaluna Seminary up in the hills behind town. Here they installed a printing house, the Hale Pai, where they produced text-books, religious tracts, dictionaries and teaching aids in the then newly devised Hawaiian alphabet.

The seminary is now a high school, with the printing house in its grounds respectively the oldest educational establishment and oldest printing works in the country west of the Rockies. The Hale Pai printed the first news-paper and paper currency in Hawaii, and printing demon-strations are given using a replica of the original Ramage press. One of the best reasons for coming here is the view over the town.

Front Street, Lahaina

Art comes to town
Friday night in downtown Lahaina is "Art Night," when many of the town's 40 or so art galleries throw open their doors and invite visitors to come in and watch demonstrations, talk to local artists about their work, nibble snacks, and enjoy free entertainment.

The Lahaina–
Kaanapali Sugar
Cane train

Luaus and *hula*
When it comes to finding a
good luau on Maui, the Old
Lahaina Luau, 505 Front
Street (tel: 808/667-1998)
has a long-standing
reputation for providing
one of the Islands' most
authentic Hawaiian feasts.
The site is great—right on
the beach front—numbers
are limited and the music
and dance truly traditional
Hawaiian. The Maui
Intercontinental Resort at
Wailea (tel: 808/879-1922)
has won awards for its
traditional *luau* and *hula*
show with an oceanfront
setting. The Hyatt Regency
Maui (tel: 808/661-1234) in
Kaanapali, and the Maui
Marriott (tel: 808/661-5828)
tend to put on a more
Polynesian-type experience.

► **Hawaii Experience**   130A3
Domed Theater, 824 Front Street (tel: 808/661-8314)
Open: daily 10–10, shows every hour. Admission charge:
moderate
A whistle-stop tour of the best scenery Hawaii has to
offer is provided courtesy of a giant three-story-high, 180-
degree movie screen. During the 40-minute film, spectators "swim" with reef fish and humpback whales, brave
close encounters with fiery fountains of volcanic lava, are
dazzled by sunrise over the Haleakala crater, and swoop
above Kauai's dramatic Waimea Canyon.

► **Lahaina Jodo Mission**   122A3
12 Ala Moana Street
Open: grounds only, daily. Admission free
Near the northern end of Lahaina's Front Street, against a
backdrop of the West Maui mountains, is the Buddhist
Jodo Mission. Its compound contains the largest Amida
Buddha statue outside Japan. The serene copper and
bronze figure of the Amida, worshipped by the Pure Land
Buddhists, stands 12½ feet tall, weighs around 3½ tons
and was brought here from Kyoto, Japan, in 1968 to
commemorate the arrival of the first Japanese immigrants in Hawaii 100 years before. (The pagoda and
temple within the compound are closed to the public.)

►►► **Lahaina–Kaanapali & Pacific**
      Railroad   122A3
Lahaina and Kaanapali depots inland of Honoapiilani
Highway (free bus to central Lahaina)
Open: daily 8:30–4:30, schedules tel: 808/661-0089.
Admission charge: one-way, moderate
A genuine 1890s locomotive known as the "Sugar Cane
Train" plies the 6-mile (30-minute) route between Lahaina
and Kaanapali. There are six round-trips a day, and the
conductor provides an entertaining history of the local
sugar industry along the way.

►►► **Molokini Excursions**   122B3
The marine preserve around the largely submerged,
crescent-shaped Molokini Crater, 11 miles out from
Maalaea harbor, is one of the world's best (and busiest)
snorkeling spots. There is a stunning array of brilliantly

colored reef fish in its warm, gin-clear waters, dolphins and sea turtles are frequently spotted, and from December to April the round-trip out to the crater becomes an unofficial whale-watching cruise.

Most cruises leave from Maalaea harbor (off HI-30 at the southwest corner of West Maui) or the Lahaina Small Boat Harbor. Two of the nicest ways to go are aboard Maui Classic Charters' *Lavengro* (tel: 808/879-8188), an elegant 1926 schooner; and the Coon family's comfortable 44-foot trimaran, *Trilogy IV* (tel: 808/661-4743). Snorkeling instruction and equipment, together with breakfast and lunch, are all part of the deal. Maui Classic Charters also operate morning and afternoon trips to the crater on the 53-foot, glass-bottomed catamaran *Four Winds,* which allows its passengers to admire the underwater scenery without getting wet (snorkelers are welcome too).

►► Pioneer Inn 130A2

658 Wharf Street
Admission free
Built in 1901 by a Royal Canadian Mountie who journeyed all the way to Maui but did not get his man (instead he fell in love with a local girl and stayed), the Pioneer Inn is the oldest hotel on Maui. The timber-framed, Victorian-style inn was too late to welcome the whalers, but the walls of the lobby and bar are decorated with whaling memorabilia and antique photographs, as well as a copy of the original house rules ("Women is not allow in you room... If you burn you bed you going out"). The inn still takes guests, and there is a selection of restaurants and shops arranged around its central courtyard.

►► Wo Hing Temple 130A3

858 Front Street (tel: 808/661-5553)
Open: daily 10–4:30. Admission charge: donations
Guarded by a pair of carved jade *fu* dogs, this former temple is now a modest museum devoted to Chinese history and culture in the Islands. It was built in 1912 by Chinese immigrants, but as the Chinese population in Maui declined so did the building, which was restored in 1983. Next door, in the old wooden cookhouse, among the pots, pans, woks and baskets, there is a continuous showing of flickering, black-and-white films shot in downtown Lahaina by Thomas Edison in 1898 and 1906.

Pioneer Inn

Buddhist tranquility at Lahaina Jodo Mission

Walk Around Old Lahaina

[Map of Old Lahaina showing streets and landmarks including Wo Hing Temple, Lahaina Whaling Museum, The Master's Reading Room, Hokoji Lahaina Shingon Mission, Hauola Stone, Baldwin House, Brick Palace, Brig Carthaginian II, Pioneer Inn, Hale Pa'ahao, Old Courthouse, Banyan Tree and Town Square, Waterfront Fort, Maluulu o Lele Park, Wainee Church; streets include Lahainaluna Road, Dickenson Street, Hale Street, Wainee Street, Luakini Street, Market Street, Hotel St, Canal Street, Prison Street, Front Street, Shaw Street, Honoapilani Highway; Auau Channel, Harbor, directions to Kaanapali, Kahului/Kihei]

130

The historic heart of Lahaina is ideally suited to a leisurely sightseeing stroll because of its compact size. Preface the walk by having breakfast at the Pioneer Inn, which overlooks the harbor and the brig *Carthaginian II*. The entire stroll should take around an hour without stops for sightseeing.

To the south of the Pioneer Inn is the **town square**. It is dominated by a massive **banyan tree,** which was a mere 8-foot sapling when it was planted in April 1873 to celebrate a half-century of missionary work in Lahaina. Now its spreading limbs, supported on 12 major trunks, shade over two-thirds of an acre, making it the largest banyan tree on the Islands. Behind the tree, the **Old Courthouse**, built in 1859, houses the Lahaina Arts Society gallery. In the far corner of the square, some coral blocks mark the site of an old harbor-front fort.

Still in the harbor area, have a look at the handsome square-rigged brig, the *Carthaginian II*, which now tells the town's maritime and whaling history in a small on-board museum (see page 127). A little farther on from the brig is the site of the **Brick Palace**. Kamehameha I commissioned two ex-convicts from Australia to build a Western-style "Brick Palace" for Queen Kaahumanu here on the waterfront. The queen, however, preferred a traditional grass hut to the two-story brick building with its stuffy glazed windows. All that now remains of the palace is the excavated foundation. Nearby, below the seawall, the flat **Hauola Stone** was venerated in ancient times for its healing powers.

Go up Market Street into Front Street, and turn left to find the Chinese **Wo Hing Temple** (see page 129). During the 19th century, successful Chinese merchants in

Hawaii set up friendly societies, one of which built this small temple, now a cultural museum. From here, cross the street to Crazy Shirts, 865 Front Street. Tucked in the back of this shop is the **Lahaina Whaling Museum**, which has a small, free display of whaling artifacts, from log-books to scrimshaw and harpoon guns.

Backtrack down Front Street to Lahainaluna Road; turn left for one block, then right onto quiet Luakini Street. Shaded by glossy breadfruit and mango trees, it is a welcome break from the bustling crowds in Front Street. Look for the **Hokoji Lahaina Shingon Mission**, a simple, green and yellow wooden mission building typical of many plantation-era Japanese temples. Take a left turn into Hale Street then right onto Wainee Street, passing the plumeria trees of the Episcopal Cemetery and the fanciful coral-rock garden of No 635, to Prison Street and the **Hale Pa'ahao (Old Prison)**. This was built in 1854 and, according to a contemporary report by one William Stetson, life was far from hard for the inmates of Lahiana's "stuck-in-irons-house." The single block of cells, constructed out of coral stone, is surrounded by a grassy yard, where male and female inmates "mingled promiscuously" and "any sedate individual could therefore lay back all day with a pipe in his mouth and enjoy himself...as

Harbor fortress ruins

well as though he was comfortably stowed away in a beer house."

Return to Wainee Street and walk as far as the **Wainee Church**. This is the site of Hawaii's oldest stone church, although the present edifice was built in the 1950s. The church-yard contains the tombs of several kings and queens who converted to Christianity: they include Queen Keopuolani, Princess Nahienaena, and the last king of Kauai, Kaumualii.

Turn right onto Shaw Street and return to Front Street. Drop in to the mall at **505 Front Street** before visiting the **Baldwin House** (see page 127).

131

Beneath the banyan

"Damming of the Waters" Park

In 1790, Kamehameha I scored a significant victory over his rival Kahekili in the Iao Valley. Though Kahekili himself was absent on Oahu, Kamehameha sailed across from Hawaii and engaged Kahekili's son, Kalanikupule, in battle. Armed with a Western cannon and assisted by two British seamen, Kamehameha's forces trounced the defending army and pushed it back into the mountains. The piles of bodies dammed the river, hence the name of Kepaniwai ("Damming of the Waters") Park, a mile or so downstream (see page 136).

Iao Needle

West Maui

►   **Honolua-Mokuleia Bay and the North Coast**   *122A4*

HI-30, just beyond Mile Marker 32
Open site. Admission free

Beyond Kapalua, HI-30 turns into a twisting corniche road which hugs the northern coast around to Nakalele Point (Mile Marker 38). There are panoramic views of the jagged black and red volcanic rocks crumbling into the ocean below, while Molokai looms large on the horizon across the Pailolo Channel.

Steep cliff paths lead down from the road to several secluded beaches. The sandy crescent of beach fronting the marine-life conservation district of Honolua-Mokuleia Bay is rarely crowded, and it is an excellent place for snorkeling and bodysurfing.

►►   **Iao Valley State Park**   *122B3*

HI-32, 3 miles west of Wailuku
Open: daily 7–7. Admission free

The inaccessible green buttresses and misty valleys of the West Maui mountains encircle Puu Kukui, the summit of Maui's oldest volcano. This is the second wettest spot in Hawaii (after Kauai's Mount Waialeale), receiving an average 400 inches of rain a year. Over millions of years, erosion has chiseled away the softer rock which connected the Iao Needle to neighboring ridges, leaving the 1,200-foot-tall, free-standing volcanic plug wedged into a valley between steep, green cliffs.

Honolua Bay surfer

Iao Needle is the centerpiece of the State Park, and there is a 133-step stairway winding up from the parking lot to a lookout platform. Below, other paths lead down to a boulder-strewn stream bed. (To avoid the crowds visit the park in the early morning or after 4:30PM.)

▶▶▶ Kaanapali-Kapalua   *122A3*

Kaanapali, about 5 miles north of Lahaina, was the first planned resort development in the state, and remains one of its most attractive vacation destinations. The long, sandy beach lining Kaanapali Bay stretches on either side of a volcanic outcrop known as Black Rock.

South of Black Rock, a 3-mile run of elegant, high-rise hotels and condominiums set in landscaped grounds offers hedonistic accommodations and fine restaurants. "Shop-'til-you-drop" vacationers have plenty of choice in the hotel boutiques and the classy Whalers Village shopping mall, which also offers two whaling museums (see below), while the temptations of downtown Lahaina are only ten minutes away.

Outdoor activities include tennis, watersports and great snorkeling around Black Rock, and golf courses with views. More than half a dozen nightclubs offer scope to night owls, and there are *luaus* and family entertainment in the form of children's programs put on by hotels.

Between Kaanapali and Kapalua to the north is Napili Bay where more moderately priced condominiums have gone up alongside a good swimming beach. Gracious living is restored within the 750-acre spread of the tasteful Kapalua Bay Resort, which has its own tennis courts, championship golf courses, and stores. Just north of Kapalua, D.T. Fleming Beach is definitely one of Maui's finest stretches of sandy shoreline.

For a riveting insight into the history of whaling in the Pacific region, do not miss the **Whalers Village Museum** and **Hale Kohola (House of the Whales)▶▶** (Whalers Village Mall, Kaanapali. *Open:* daily 9:30AM–10PM. *Admission free*). The museum's informative signboards, displays of whalers' weapons, scrimshaw items, and a replica of a claustrophobic forecastle where a crew of between 12 and 20 men would be cooped up for months on end cover the subject in an accessible and lively way.

In the Hale Kohala, opposite, attention is focused on live whales. More models and photographs tell you in detail about these amazing creatures, and there is a film theater for video presentations. The gift shop does a brisk trade in whale books, model kits, jewelry and art.

Light and scent
Did you know that the blubber of a single sperm whale could yield up to 2,000 gallons of high-quality oil? It was used in 19th-century lamps and for lubricating fine machinery. As well as oil, sperm whales yielded spermaceti, a thick white waxy substance which was made into candles, and ambergris, which was used in perfumes to make the fragrance last longer.

■ **Few mysteries run as deep as the enigmatic song of the humpback whale, and there are few sights as stirring as these magnificent creatures cavorting in their winter breeding and calving grounds off the coast of Maui. From November until April, Hawaii is one of the world's prime whale-watching spots.** ■

Whale-watching

Hemmed in by Lanai and Molokai, the quiet, sheltered waters off the west coast of Maui are the best whale-watching territory in Hawaii. In winter, charter-boat operators offer daily whale-watching excursions, though plenty of whales are sighted from the shore off Kaanapali, Wailea and, best of all, Maalaea Bay. Sometimes a whale may come in as close as 100 yards from the beach. Other good spots around the Neighbor Islands for whale-watching include Kilaueau Point and Poipu on Kauai; Hanauma Bay on Oahu; and the Big Island's Kona Coast.

A baby humpback whale in Maalaea Bay

Cetacean playground Humpbacks are not the only whales to be spotted in Hawaiian waters, since the Islands also play host to the occasional sperm whale or killer whale, not to mention such year-round residents as pilot whales, and fellow members of the cetacean family, spinner and bottlenose dolphins.

Cetaceans are warm-blooded, air-breathing mammals that nurse their young. The biggest is the 100-foot-long blue whale, while the smallest belong to the porpoise family. Humpbacks are the fifth largest of the cetaceans, a mature adult measuring between 40 and 50 feet and weighing around a ton per foot.

Feeding and moving Humpbacks, like blue and right whales, are baleen (toothless) whales (*Mysticetes*). Their mouths are lined with up to 600 rows of fringed baleen instead of teeth, and they feed by taking great mouthfuls of sea water—hundreds of gallons at a time assisted by expandable vents in the throat. The water is then filtered past the rows of baleen, which capture plankton, small fish and shrimp-like krill. Humpbacks can consume almost a ton of food a day, but can live for almost six months without feeding.

The humpback's scientific name is *Megaptera Novaeangliae*, meaning "great wing of New England," a reference to its enlarged pectoral fins. Each fin is between 15 and 16 feet long (the longest limb of any animal), and has a bone structure remarkably similar to that of a human hand. The whale uses its "pecs" to steer, but power is provided by the massive tail flukes. Although the humpback averages only 3–6m.p.h. when

on the move, its caudal muscles, which control the tail, are so well developed that speeds of up to 20m.p.h. can be achieved over short periods.

Whales need to breathe air, and the blow hole is placed on top of the head. When a whale "spouts," it ejects compresssed air from its lungs, which emerges in a fine mist. Whales' eyes are set low on either side of their heads, but their chief sensory mechanism is their ears. They have acute hearing and communicate using complex sequences of sounds known as "songs."

Migrations and breeding Hawaii's humpback whales are part of the North Pacific humpback population which spends the summer months feeding in the temperate waters off Alaska. At the onset of the arctic winter they journey south, some heading for California and Mexico or Japan, while around two-thirds aim for Hawaii.

Humpbacks come to Hawaii to breed and calve in the warm, shallow waters. The gestation period for a female is around 11 months, so having conceived one year the females return to calve the following winter. Whale calves are born tail first, measure between 12 and 14 feet and weigh about a ton. The minute they are born the mother must nudge her calf to the surface to breathe. The calf must also be taught to swim, and mother and calf are usually attended by a protective male "escort" at first. Later they will travel as part of an extended family group, or pod.

Humpback numbers At the turn of the century the world population of humpback whales was an estimated 100,000, about 15,000 of which belonged to the North Pacific. Commercial whaling had reduced the numbers to around 1,000 by the mid-1960s, but today that figure has increased to between 2,500 and 3,000, thanks to the international bans on whaling. Individual whales can be identified by the distinctive markings on their broad, flat tail flukes, which are as unique as a human fingerprint. Tracking individual whales has taught researchers a great deal about whale habits and migration patterns. Perhaps one day the experts may just unravel the mystery of whale song.

What's in a name?
The humpback whale gets its name from the way it arches its back before diving. In whale-watcher jargon this is called a "round out." Other key behavior patterns are the slow and stately "head rise," when the top third of the body rises out of the water; the "pec slap," when the humpback rolls over sideways and slaps its pectoral fin on the surface of the water; "head slaps;" "tail slaps;" and the breathtaking "breach," when all or most of the body is propelled vertically out of the water.

Spouting adults

Whale-watching

Tram tours at the
Maui Tropical
Plantation

Hawaii Nature Center
Located in Kepaniwai Park,
the Center offers guided
hikes into the 2,000-acre
Iao Valley forest preserve.
The hikes, which last
around 1½ hours, follow a
rocky trail along the valley
floor, and sensible
footwear and rain gear are
recommended. Children
under 8 are not allowed.
There are daily excursions
Monday to Saturday, with
additional hikes on
Wednesdays. Call for
schedules and reservations
(tel: 808/244-6500).

► **Kepaniwai Park**   122B3

Iao Valley Road (2 miles west of Wailuku)
Open site. Admission free
Visitors explore a series of pavilions built in the different
styles of Hawaii's main ethnic groups in this small cultural
park, on the road to Iao Valley State Park. Lion-dog gates
guard the Chinese pavilion, and there are Japanese
gardens with dwarf trees, pagodas and bridges around an
airy Japanese bamboo house. The Portuguese corner is
decorated with *azuelos* (hand-painted tiles), a white
picket fence encircles a New England cottage, and the
grass-roofed Polynesian hut has its own taro terrace.

► **Maui Arts & Cultural Center**   122B3

Maui Central Park, Kahului (tel: 808/242-2787)
Open: Gallery, Tue–Fri 10–4, Sat–Sun 12–4. Admission
free
On the outskirts of Kahului, a ten-minute drive from
Wailuku, this attractive modern arts complex features a
1,200-seat theater, an outdoor amphitheater and a gallery
hosting frequently changing exhibitions. The box office
doubles as a gift shop selling a small selection of
reasonably priced artists' prints and cards. Telephone for
details of the latest programs.

►► **Maui Tropical Plantation**   122B3

HI-30, south of Wailuku (tel: 808/244-7643)
Open: daily 9–5. Admission free; tram tours, moderate
A tropical plantation turned tourist trap, this is the most
popular attraction on the island. Not surprisingly, it has a
souvenir superstore piled high with all the usual T-shirts,
pineapple-motif beach bags and *aloha*-print fashions, but
it also does an impressive line in more upmarket Hawaiian
food items such as macadamia nut oil, exotic fruit
relishes, honeys and dried fruits, as well as fresh produce.

By day, tram tours (40 minutes) trundle around the 50
acres, which feature areas of plumeria orchard, heliconias
and gingers, as well as pineapple and coffee, passion-
fruit, papaya and guava orchards. Guides describe the
contribution sugar, fruits and macadamia nuts make to

the island's economy. A nursery sells exportable orchids, anthuriums and hibiscuses, and there are *lei*-makers on hand for demonstrations. Three times a week the Plantation puts on a Hawaiian Barbecue and dinner show.

▶▶ Wailuku   122B3

Guarding the access route to the sacred Iao Valley, the burial place of the highest Maui chieftains, Wailuku was an important site to the ancient Hawaiians. It became Maui's second town when Kamehameha I established the capital of the Islands at Lahaina. When missionaries arrived here in 1832, they founded a school for girls to complement Lahaina's boys-only Lahainaluna Seminary. Wailuku later became a sugar town and is now Maui's administrative seat.

The Reverend Jonathan Green founded the mission station and girls' school in Wailuku on lands donated by Maui's Governor Hoapili, who made education compulsory for the island's children. Edward Bailey, the school's first principal, enlarged the building, now the **Bailey House Museum▶▶** on the Iao Valley Road, Wailuku (*Open: Mon–Sat 10–4. Admission charge:* inexpensive), and plans show how the house grew over the years.

An upstairs bedroom and sitting-room have been fitted out with hefty Victorian furnishings, while on the first floor there are displays of Hawaiian artifacts, tools, crafts and archaeological finds, and an exhibition of Bailey's paintings, many of which were sold to fund the school. Bailey also raised money by milling flour and sugar, before going into the sugar industry full time when missionary funds were withdrawn in the 1850s. The museum gift shop sells a variety of Hawaiian crafts.

Below the Bailey House, on a slope above the main Iao Valley road, **Kaahumanu Church ▶** was named in honor of Kamehameha I's favorite wife, who was born on Maui and became an ardent convert to Christianity. The spotlessly clean 19th-century church, with its lofty wooden steeple, was founded on top of a *heiau* associated with Kahekili in what was no doubt a deliberate show of religious one-upmanship. In a corner of the churchyard there is an early Hawaiian Christian burial plot.

Missions on Maui
Governor Hoapili played an important role in the success of the missions on Maui. Determined that his people should be educated, Hoapili made available land grants to set up mission schools in Lahaina and Wailuku. Though born Ulumaheihei, the future governor was renamed Hoapili or "Close Companion," for his friendship with Kamehameha I. After the king's death, Hoapili married Kamehameha's sacred wife, Keopuolani.

137

The Bailey House grew in several stages

Drive The road to Hana

See map on pages 122–123.

The twisting road to Hana down the windward coast of East Maui is one of the island's, indeed Hawaii's, great excursions. It is also something of an endurance test, as on the last 30 miles or so of the route there are around 600 curves and 54 small bridges to negotiate. Leave three hours to drive from Kahului to Hana (54 miles) with a couple of stops, and another 30 minutes from Hana to reach the Oheo Gulch.

The first stretch of road on HI-36 through **Paia** (see page 142) is straightforward. The "Hana Highway"

Keanae Arboretum

itself begins after Paia, when the road becomes HI-360, and the speed limit drops to a maximum 35m.p.h. About ¾ mile past Mile Marker 16 is the **Keanae Arboretum**, with 6 acres of towering trees, magnificent stands of bamboo, moss-covered tree trunks sprouting ferns, eucalyptus trees, palms, heliconias, hibiscus and plumeria. At the top of the gardens, there is a series of terraced taro patches irrigated by a stream.

Continue as far as Mile Marker 19 and the **Wailua Valley State Wayside Lookout**. Park the car and take the steps to the lookout with panoramic views out to sea across the farmlands and taro fields of the Wailua Valley, and inland to the Keanae Valley and mist-wreathed Koolau Gap, a breach in the rim of the Haleakala crater.

Just short of Hana, at Mile Marker 32, **Waianapanapa State Park** is a good place to stretch car-cramped legs, have a picnic, take a dip (beware of rough surf), or hike along the shore to a series of ancient caves. The wild and beautiful volcanic coastline has been sculpted by centuries of wind and waves into sea stacks and arches tufted with beach *naupaka* plants. There is a small black-sand beach, and a screwpine grove on the cliff.

Hana, the birthplace of Queen Kaahumanu, is a quiet, down-to-earth ranch and fishing town with one very fancy hotel (the Hotel Hana-Maui). In addition to its clutch of timber-framed houses, there is a 19th-century church, a couple of general stores and a horse-riding center. The small museum of Hawaiiana and local history in the **Hana Cultural Center** is worth a stop (follow the signs) and is housed in a plantation-era cottage next door to the diminutive 1871 police station-cum-courthouse. This is also the place to pick up local information from the friendly staff.

Beyond Hana the road changes its name again (to HI-31), and gets more narrow and twisty and even more beautiful, winding along the cliffs and ravines and through a deep green tunnel of overhanging mango and guava trees *en route* to Kipahulu. Ten miles farther on from Hana, the **Oheo Gulch** is often referred to as the "Seven Sacred Pools" on maps. In fact, some 20 un-sacred but impressive pools fed by the Oheo Stream drop down the last mile of the gulch in the shadow of Haleakala. The lowest of these are apt to turn into a series of municipal swimming pools full of hot, sticky tourists. The Pipiwai Trail (2 miles) cuts a rough track up through the rainforest to the base of the 400-foot Waimoku Falls (a two-hour roundtrip; sturdy shoes and mosquito repellent needed), or there is the short (half-mile, 20-minute) Kuloa Loop trail from the parking lot, along the coast and around to the gulch pools.

A mile beyond Oheo Gulch, look for the modest sign to Palapala Hoomau on the left and turn down the track to **Palapala Hoomau Congregational Church**. Flanked by drooping banyan trees, this tiny, pretty coral-rock and wood church was built on the clifftop in 1857. It is the last resting place of famous aviator Charles A. Lindbergh (1902–74), who is buried in the flower-filled country churchyard.

Pools at Oheo Gulch

139

The rare silversword plant (see panel opposite)

Sunrise at Haleakala

East Maui

▶   **Alexander & Baldwin Sugar Museum**   *122B3*
Puunene Mill, 3957 Hansen Road (tel: 808/871-8058)
Open: Mon–Sat 9:30–4:30. Admission charge: inexpensive

The cloying smell of molasses greets visitors to this small museum nestling in the shadow of the state's largest sugar factory. Displays in the old Superintendent's Residence tell the story of A&B, from its small beginnings as a 12-acre plantation founded by missionary children Samuel Alexander and Henry Baldwin in 1869, to one of Hawaii's "Big Five" companies. Detailed scale models, broad-ranging storyboards and photographs illustrate plantation-era life, and there is an interactive sugar exhibit as well as a gift store selling Maui brown sugar.

▶▶▶   **Haleakala National Park**   *123D2*
Haleakala Crater Road (HI-378), off HI-377 south of Makawao (tel: 808/572-9306).
Open: daily. Admission charge: inexpensive

The road up to the summit of Haleakala is festooned with signs warning drivers to look out for cattle, bicyclists (see panel opposite) and, as the treeline is surmounted, clouds. However hot it may be down on the beach, bring warm clothes for an ascent of the world's largest dormant volcano, as the rarified air at 10,000 feet can be extremely nippy. Above the sunny upcountry pastures, the upper reaches of Haleakala are subalpine desert. In winter, fog and freezing rain are not unusual, so it is advisable to call ahead for a weather report. That said, Haleakala is not to be missed.

Haleakala's vast crater is a geological masterpiece. In reality a giant depression formed by erosion, rather than a true crater made by volcanic explosion or the collapse of a

Cyclists with altitude

magma chamber, it plunges 3,000 feet down from the mountain rim and measures 7½ miles by 2½ miles. The surreal, multicolored landscape of volcanic ash and cinders, in dozens of different tones of red, brown, gray and green, is dotted with cinder cone hillocks.

There are several viewpoints and a Visitor Center with interpretive displays and information by the Puu Ulaula Overlook. For serious hikers, there are 36 miles of trails which descend into the crater area plus backcountry campsites. In summer, visitors to the crater rim can join the free ranger-guided walks which last between 30 minutes and a couple of hours.

▶▶ **Kula** *122C2*

Kula's botanical gardens (see below), surrounded by vegetable and flower farms, lie to the south of the Haleakala access road and make an interesting detour on a trip to the volcano. Another diversion is the 1894 **Holy Ghost Mission Church** on Lower Kula Road, built in three tiers and topped with a fancy tower and silver roofs. The pretty, octagonal interior is painted seashell pink and was decorated with Stations of the Cross by Portuguese migrants who came to the island to ranch or farm.

The 8-acre **Enchanting Floral Gardens of Kula▶** (HI-37, Mile Marker 10. *Open:* daily 9–5. *Admission charge:* inexpensive), tucked behind a magnificent bougainvillea hedge, is a formal affair featuring more than 500 species of plants and flowers from around the world. Unusual exotics and tropical fruit trees, scented *pikake* (jasmine) and plumeria are planted around the flower beds. Bromeliads and vines clamber around arches that straddle the paths, and there are strategically placed gazebos at the best viewpoints.

The **Kula Botanical Gardens▶▶** (HI-377. *Open:* daily 9–4. *Admission charge:* inexpensive) range over a 5-acre hillside site with outstanding views. The lava-rock terraces overflow with colorful bedding plants, shrubs and exotics, and more than 1,700 different plants, from proteas to hydrangeas, flourish in the mild, damp climate at some 3,300 feet above sea-level. There are strange little "pig-tail" anthuriums with curling fingers, decorative red pineapples, scented honeysuckle, and banks of lilies and ferns. Look for oddities such as the "touchy-feely" velvet leaf from Madagascar, but do not touch anything in the toxic-plant section, where a deadly mature datura hangs over the *koi* pond.

Freewheeling in Paradise
For a 38-mile bike ride that tests the wrists not the legs, try coasting down Haleakala. Only about 400 yards of the switchback road down from the volcano summit to the coast require any pedaling, the rest is brake work. Operators such as Cruiser Bob's (tel: 808/579-8444), Maui Downhill (tel: 808/871-2155), Maui Mountain Cruisers (tel: 808/871-6014) and Mountain Riders (tel: 808/242-9739) supply bikes, helmets, gloves, guides, escort vans and a free hotel pick-up service, plus onward tour options.

Silverswords
"Their cold frosted silver gleam made the hillside look like winter or moonlight," wrote Isabella Bird, who was a visitor to Hawaii in 1873. She was describing the rare Haleakala silversword plant (*Argyroxiphium sandwicense*), which the Hawaiians call *ahinahina* after Hina, the moon goddess. It grows only on Maui and the Big Island at elevations between 6,000 and 10,000 feet. The plant can live for up to 20 years, but blooms only once, producing a single tall spike with red-purple flowers, after which it dies.

Windsurfers off Wailea

Upcountry arts center
A couple of miles north of Makawao on the Paia road is Kaluanui, a villa built in 1917 for sugar magnate Harry Baldwin. The house is now home to the Hui No'eau Visual Arts Center, and the first floor has been turned into a gallery shop and exhibition space for local and visiting artists.

Protea bloom

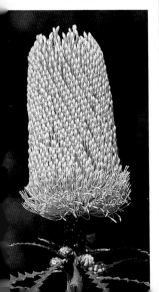

▶ **Makawao** 122C3

Makawao's 19th-century antecedents are still visible in the Old-West-style, false-fronted stores leading downhill along Baldwin Avenue in the direction of Paia. But behind the freshly painted façades of this upcountry ranch town, old-time country stores have been hijacked by boutiques and designer household-goods emporia selling everything from Provençal-herb salad dressing to linen skirts and straw hats for that expensively contrived ranch-chic look.

Old-style Makawao still lingers in the no-nonsense (and "No Loitering," according to the sign) Komodo Store & Bakery, and Makawao Feed, Garden and Hardware Store, with its crate of day-old chicks on the floor and aisles overflowing with nuts and bolts, nails and rat poison. And the town still goes back to its ranching roots for the annual Fourth of July rodeo.

▶▶ **Paia** 122C3

On the road to Hana, Paia is a good place to buy a picnic or breakfast at the Wunderbar, 89 Hana Highway (*Open:* from 7:30AM). Many of the false-fronted stores have been turned into boutiques and galleries selling arts and crafts, and antiques. One of the best is the excellent Maui Crafts Guild, 34 Hana Highway, at the entrance to town. This local artists' co-operative displays pottery, prints, wood and stone carvings, jewelry and "fiber sculpture"— basketry woven from native plants (*Open:* daily 9–6).

West of town, Baldwin Beach is a good bodysurfing and windsurfing spot. To the east, Hookipa Beach Park offers world-class surfing conditions.

▶ **Sunrise Protea Farm** 122C2

Haleakala Crater Road (HI-378)
Open: daily 8–4. Admission free
Sunny days and cool nights are ideal for cultivating protea flowers, natives of South Africa and Australia. Proteas were first grown commercially on Maui in 1975, and Sunrise is one of the island's major producers, with more than a dozen varieties on show in a small walk-through garden. Bouquets and arrangements of fresh or dried flowers can be bought or shipped to the mainland U.S. from the on-site shop.

►► Tedeschi Winery 122C2

HI-37/31
Open: daily 9–5 (tours 9:30–2:30). Admission free

A lovely upcountry drive leads through rolling pastures and small settlements to the Tedeschi vineyards at the Ulupalakua Ranch on the southwestern slopes of Haleakala. During spring the roadside is adrift with the lilac-colored blossoms from dozens of jacaranda trees.

Perched at a cool elevation of 2,000 feet, the 22-acre Tedeschi vineyard was established in 1974. Its first vintage, however, was not a grape wine but Maui Blanc Pineapple Wine. Since then three red wines, a white, a rosé and two sparkling wines (all made with grapes) have appeared. The *méthode champenoise* Maui Brut-Blanc de Noirs has even been served at the White House. There are free tours of the winery and King's Cottage, where King David Kalakaua came to stay, as well as a wine shop and all-important tasting room.

Just down the road, the Ulupalakua Ranch Store sells snacks as well as genuine cattleman hats, bandanas, and Ulupalakua Ranch souvenirs.

► Wailea and Makena 122B2

The quiet, upmarket resort areas of Wailea and Makena lie to the south of the bustling Kihei shopping mall and condominium complex on a series of crescent-shaped beaches that stretch along the shore. It is so quiet here that migrating whales love it; and this is one of the best shoreline whale-watching spots on Maui.

Wailea has been nicknamed "Wimbledon West" for its tennis facilities, and it can also boast three championship golf courses as well as a small shopping mall. At the end of the coast road is Makena with a further 36 holes of golf laid out by Robert Trent Jones Jr., and Makena Beach (in reality two adjoining beaches called Big Beach and Little Beach), a huge expanse of glittering sand with a beach activities center.

The southern ranchlands
For those who like their landscapes rugged and unpopulated, HI-31 runs into the open ranchlands above the south coast. Between the towering mountains and fractured black talons of rock clawing at the surf, the only signs of life amidst the acres of billowing, flaxen grass are cattle and game birds. The first Western visitors to Maui landed at La Pérouse Bay, down on the scrubby southwest tip of the island. North of here, the red volcanic cone of Puu Olai rises to a height of 360 feet, and there are sea views off to Molokini, Kahoolawe and Lanai.

143

The rolling hills of upcountry Ulupalakua

Hawaii's paniolo cowboys

■ The upcountry ranchlands of Maui, the Waimea-Kamuela district of Hawaii's Big Island, and the West End of Molokai offer not only a change of scenery but a change of style. Perhaps it is some miraculous property of the upcountry air which has preserved an old Hawaiian lifestyle that has altered little in 50 years or more. ■

Riding out on the range
Makena Stables (tel: 808/879-0244) offers morning or evening rides, and an optional visit to the Ulupalakua Ranch's Tedeschi Winery (see page 143). On the Big Island, Paniolo Riding Adventures (tel: 808/889-5354) head out across the Ponoholo Ranch in the Kohala Mountains. (For details of Molokai Ranch Trail Rides, see panel on page 118.)

Rodeo skills

The upcountry ranchlands are Hawaii's *paniolo* country, where third- and fourth-generation cowboys still round up the herd on horseback and demonstrate their skills in the rodeo ring. Things have changed dramatically since those early days, but it seems not even the arrival of motorized "Japanese quarter horses" (all-terrain vehicles) is going to part the Hawaiian *paniolo* from his trusty hoss.

A gift of cattle The British explorer Captain George Vancouver, who had sailed with Cook, introduced the first pair of cattle to the Islands in 1793. They were a gift to Kamehameha I. The king loosed the beasts on Hawaii, and pronounced a *kapu* (taboo) on them so they could roam free and unmolested for ten years. At the end of that time, herds of wild and unapproachable longhorn cattle were roving throughout the mountains and tearing up the native vegetation.

Hawaii's paniolo cowboys

In 1803, Captain Richard Cleveland presented Kamehameha with a mare and her foal, and before long wild mustangs were also making themselves at home on the slopes of Mauna Kea. The chief ingredients for ranching were now in place, and there was a ready market for meat, hides and tallow anchored in the increasingly busy ports of Lahaina and Honolulu.

A young New England adventurer, John Palmer Parker, and a former whaler, Irishman Jack Purdy, were charged with the task of bringing the king's herds under some sort of control. Together with Spanish-Mexican *vaqueros* (cattlemen) brought over from California, they taught the Hawaiians the ropes.

The *paniolos* The newcomers were known as *Espanols*, from the Spanish, or "*espaniolos*," which in turn became the pidgin Hawaiian *paniolo* for cowboy. Later they were joined by Portuguese immigrants from the Azores, who introduced the *braguinha*, or ukelele, this swiftly taking over from the Spanish guitar as the *paniolos'* favorite accompaniment to "home-on-the-range" ditties.

The first organized move toward the establishment of Hawaii's great ranches came with Kamehameha III's Great Mahele land division in 1848. John Parker's *alii* wife, Kipikane, received 640 acres at Waimea, which under her husband's management increased with the purchase of additional pockets of land. Today, the vast 225,000-acre Parker spread is the fourth biggest (and the largest family-owned) ranch in the nation.

By the turn of the century, cattle ranching was Hawaii's third biggest industry (after sugar and pineapples), and the *paniolos* were hard at work. One of the toughest jobs was loading live cattle for transportation to Honolulu. Maui's Ulupalakua Ranch would send a thousand head of steer across to Oahu every year, which entailed driving the cattle down to the shore at Makena and forcing the terrified animals into the surf. Here, they were loaded onto waiting longboats, tethered by their horns, and ferried out to the steamboat transport, where they were winched on board for the trip up the Islands.

Hawaii's *paniolos* could play as hard as they worked. Not for nothing was the ranch town of Makawao once known as "Macho-wao." Back in 1908, Ikua Purdy, the Ulupalakua Ranch's head cowboy, stripped the five-times world champion roper, Angus MacPhee, of his title at the World's Steer Roping Championship held in Wyoming. Today's Hawaiian *paniolos* can still steal a march on any visiting cowboy at the rodeos held at the Parker Ranch Arena and Makawao's Oskie Rice Arena, named for a famous Maui ranch manager who helped found the Maui Roping Club in 1955.

Eyeing up the competition

Rodeos
The Oskie Rice Arena at Makawao is the centerpiece for the town's Fourth of July Rodeo Parade, as well as November's Maui County Rodeo Finals (for information tel: 808/572-9928). July sees the Parker Ranch Rodeo and Horse Races at the Parker Ranch Arena in Waimea-Kamuela (tel: 808/885-7655); and August has the annual Molokai Ranch Rodeo (tel: 808/552-2767).

Breaking-in

LANAI

Map labels:

Kalohi Channel
Auau Channel
Kealaikahiki Channel

Polihua Beach
Hale o Lono
Lapaiki
Kahua
Shipwreck Beach
Kaena Point
Kaena Heiau
Polihua Trail
Halulu
Kahokunui
Keanapapa Point
Garden of the Gods
1,797ft
Mt Kanepuu
Lapaiki
Kahua
Maunalei
Hauola
Keomuku Beach
Keomuku Village
Kakaalani Gun Range
Hookio Battleground (1778)
Malamalama Church and Sugar Mill Ruins
Kahea Heiau
Koele
Cavendish Golf Course
Lanai City
Munro Trail
3,369ft
Mt Lanaihale
Japanese Cemetery
Halepalaoa Landing
Honopu
Ana Puka Cave
Luahiwa Petroglyphs
Waiopa
Lopa
Kaumalapau Harbor
440
Lanai Airport
Palawai Basin
Miki Basin
2,073ft
Mt Puu Manu
440
Kahobo
Naha
Kabolo
Pali
Kahekili's Leap
Ancient Village
Palaoa Point
Kaunolu
Hulopoe Beach
Manele Bay
Hulopoe Bay
Puupehe
Manele-Hulopoe Marine Life Conservation Area
Lahaina, Maui

0 5 km
0 5 miles

A B C
1 2 3

Pineapple island Some 9 miles across the Auau Channel from Lahaina on Maui's resort-lined northwest coast, the "Private Island" of Lanai offers a radically different vacation destination for the discriminating visitor. This small island was once the world's largest pineapple plantation and was virtually a tourist-free zone until the early 1990s.

When the bottom fell out of Hawaii's pineapple market in the 1980s, the Dole Food Co. Inc., which owns 98 percent of Lanai, turned to tourism in an effort to diversify. In a bid for the exclusive top end of the market, the company built not one but two superbly elegant resort hotels, and equipped them with designer golf courses, fine restaurants and every conceivable luxury. The Manele Bay Hotel, surrounded by glorious gardens, sits down by the ocean on a sandy bay while the manor-house-style Lodge at Koele nestles on the slopes of Mount Lanaihale, at 1,700 feet above sea-level.

Lanai, at 18 miles by 13 miles, is the smallest of the main Hawaiian Islands, with a coastline ringed by sea cliffs and beaches. Along the east side of the island, a north–south ridge of mountains planted with Norfolk pines brings down some moisture, but Lanai is basically dry. Mormon missionaries introduced cattle-ranching in the 1850s, and at the end of the 19th century unsuccessful attempts were made to grow sugar cane in the dusty red earth of the Palawai Basin. It was not until James Dole bought the island in 1922 that a successful crop of any kind was grown. That crop was pineapples, which were to become the mainstay of the island's economy.

LANAI

Left: near the Garden of the Gods looking over to Molokai

LANAI

"The Cathedrals" offer some of the best scuba-diving in the Islands

148

Kanepuu dryland forest
Off the Polihua Trail, just south of the Garden of the Gods, another jeep track heads west to Kanepuu. Here, the Nature Conservancy preserves 462 acres of rare dryland forest which contains 48 native Hawaiian species. Among the protected plants are *olopua*, native olive trees; *lama*, persimmon; *iliahi*, sandalwood; and several varieties of *nanu*, gardenia. The preserve is a restricted area, but interested visitors can contact the Nature Conservancy offices in Honolulu (tel: 808/537-4508) for details of guided tours.

The bizarre and mysterious Garden of the Gods

Lanai City, founded by James Dole in 1924, is home to 2,500 of the island's total resident population of 2,800. Their ethnic diversity—Filipino, Japanese, Korean, Puerto Rican, and Hawaiian—is a reminder of the island's plantation heritage. At the end of the plantation era, Lanai's population dwindled as young people left in droves to find work elsewhere, but the burgeoning tourist industry is now bringing them home.

Attractions Lanai's twin resorts are a hedonist's heaven and a golfer's paradise, but for those who are interested to explore beyond the 18th hole, there is a whole host of activities. Landlubbers can take their pick from *hula* and horse-riding classes, mountain biking, tennis, or hunting for pheasant, partridge, wild turkey, quail, mouflon sheep and axis deer in season. On the water there are ocean-raft tours, whale-watching cruises to the humpback whale calving grounds (November–April), deep-sea fishing for *mahimahi* and *wahoo*, and snorkeling and scuba-diving. For the historically minded, there are petroglyphs and a few interesting archaeological sites, while botanists may be interested in Lanai's unique dryland forest, now under the protection of the Nature Conservancy (see panel).

Transportation on Lanai is limited, but then there are only 30 miles of paved road. A hotel shuttle, which links Manele Bay and Koele via Lanai City, also serves the airport; and there are five daily round-trip boat crossings to Lahaina. Four-wheel-drive vehicles can be rented in which to explore the island's dozens of jeep tracks that strike out cross-country to isolated beaches and abandoned fishing villages or to traverse the mountainous and muddy 7-mile Munro Trail along the ridge running behind Lanai City and up Mount Lanaihale.

►► Garden of the Gods 146A2

Lying 6 miles to the northwest of Lanai City on the Polihua Trail, this dusty "garden" of volcanic pinnacles, giant boulders, and teetering rocks is an eerie place. Viewed in the middle of the day, it is not at its most impressive. Instead, the bizarre rock formations, said to house the spirits of Hawaiian warriors, are best seen at sunset (or sunrise), when the rays of shifting light accentuate the desert colors and cast long shadows.

►►► Hulopoe Beach 146B1

Road access from Manele Bay

This sandy crescent on Lanai's south shore is a favorite swimming and fishing beach. It is a marine conservation area, and has been voted one of the ten best snorkel and dive sites in the world. Spinner dolphins are a common sight in the early morning, and whales appear off shore in the winter calving season. There are picnicking facilities and even a small campground.

► Kaunolu 146B1

Southwest coast; jeep trail from Kaumalapau Harbor

Kaunolu, a former fishing village, was abandoned in the 18th century. Now a National Historic Landmark, it is one of the finest collections of ancient Hawaiian ruins in the Islands. Just up the coast at the sea cliff known as Kahekili's Leap, warriors would test their strength and courage by jumping out over a treacherous rock outcrop into the ocean 60 feet below.

►►► Lanai City 146B2

At the center of the island, in the lee of Mount Lanaihale, the neat plantation town of Lanai City is built on a grid of broad streets lined with tin-roofed, timber-framed houses and flower-filled gardens. Around a spacious village common planted with Norfolk pines, there is a period playhouse, galleries, and a couple of Lanai-style mom-and-pop stores, shelves laden with bottles of *kim chee*, *adabo* sauce, packs of instant *saimin* and *poi* as well as more Americanized staples. A small museum is due to open shortly in a plantation-era building next to the S & T diner.

To the north of the common, the Hotel Lanai was built by Dole in 1923 as a clubhouse to accommodate guests of the pineapple company. It now offers alternative accommodations to the two fancy resorts on the island.

To the south, at 8th Street and Gay, the police station boasts three little blue and white painted lock-up cells with padlocks on the doors; quite sufficient for coping with Lanai's virtually non-existent criminal element.

Legend of Makakehau

A trail leads up from Hulopoe Beach onto the rugged headland that divides Hulopoe from Manele Bay. Off shore is a huge black rock known as Puupehe ("Pehe's Hill"). Local legend tells of a fisherman, Makakehau, who had a beautiful wife called Pehe, whom he loved dearly and kept hidden away in a sea cave. One day when he was out collecting fresh water in the mountains, a storm blew up and surf submerged the cave, drowning Pehe. With the gods' help, Makakehau buried her on top of the rock, and then threw himself off to his death.

149

Keomuku village ruins

Keomuku, on the east coast, had a population of 2,000 around the turn of the century, but this former sugar town was abandoned for good in 1954. Today, there is little to see aside from a coconut grove and the 1903 Kalanakila O Ka Malamalama church. A couple of miles down the track, near the old wharf site of Halepalaoa, is an ancient *heiau* (temple) site.

Dozy Lanai City

LANAI

On the Munro Trail

Jeep rental
Ordinary cars are available to rent on Lanai, but they really are a waste of money as the island has just 30 miles of paved road to explore. The only way to get off the beaten track by vehicle is to rent a jeep, which is not cheap. The rudiments of four-wheel drive can be learned in a few minutes. Be sure to pack essentials such as water, suntan lotion, and picnic materials before setting out for the day. And don't wear white! That red dust gets everywhere.

Shipwreck Beach

▶▶ **Munro Trail**   146B2

Trail from behind the Lodge at Koele
Open site. Admission free
This 7-mile jeep trail extends along the sharp ridge of mountains behind Lanai City and scales Mount Lanaihale, the island's highest point at 3,370 feet. Viewed from the Palawai Basin, the island's mountainous backbone is feathered with matchstick-sized Norfolk pines planted by George Munro, a New Zealand naturalist and ranch manager who lived on Lanai from 1911 to 1935. The pines were designed to draw down the clouds and release moisture on the arid island, and the ridge is frequently cloaked in drizzle. Although this can render the trail a muddy morass, it makes a great if strenuous two-hour drive or day's hike. On a crisp, clear day the views from Mount Lanaihale stretch over five islands—Maui, Molokai, Kahoolawe, Hawaii, and even distant Oahu.

▶▶ **Polihua Beach**   146A3

North coast; Polihua Trail from Lanai City
Open site. Admission free
Windswept Polihua lies a dusty drive across the island to the north shore, and was once famous for the sea-turtles that came ashore to lay their eggs on the sandy beach here. Its name literally means "Bay of Eggs." Picnic and sunbathe by all means, but do not swim—strong currents make it very dangerous.

▶▶▶ **Shipwreck Beach**   146B3

Northeast coast (north from the road head)
Open site. Admission free
The aptly named Shipwreck Beach, known in Hawaiian as Kaiolohia, meaning "choppy" or "changing sea," is a beautiful and isolated 8-mile stretch of sandy beach and rocky outcrops, punctuated with the hulks of wrecked ships that have come to grief in the stormy Kalohi Channel. Although dangerous for swimming, it is a good place to beachcomb for driftwood and Japanese fishing floats. Just inland from the beach are rocks carved with ancient but well-preserved petroglyphs (rock carvings).

Pineapples

■ When Christopher Columbus introduced pineapples to the West, gourmets and royalty were so smitten with the exotic delicacy it was nicknamed the "King of Fruit." During the 16th and 17th centuries, colonists helped spread the pineapple throughout South America, India, and Asia. By the 18th century, pineapples were even grown in George Washington's hothouse at Mount Vernon. ■

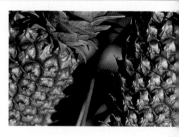

Father of the pineapple Hawaii's pineapple industry was founded by Captain John Kidwell in the 1880s, but the true "Father of the Hawaiian Pineapple" was Boston-born James Drummond Dole. The 22-year-old horticulturist arrived in the Islands in 1877, acquired a 61-acre plot of land on Oahu and experimented with growing various types of fruit plants. Pineapples above all others thrived in Hawaii's mineral-rich soil.

Dole founded the Hawaiian Pineapple Co. in 1901, and by the 1930s Hawaii provided two-thirds of the world's canned and fresh pineapple. Dole's biggest plantation was on Lanai (which he bought in 1922), with some 16,000 acres under cultivation for the fruit until 1992, when the plantation finally closed.

Commercial pineapple-growing is backbreaking work. Encumbered with broad-brimmed sun-hats, wearing canvas aprons and gloves to ward off cuts and scratches, and with faces covered with bandanas and goggles to keep out the dust, thousands of Asian immigrant laborers toiled in the hot, dusty fields, bent double from dawn to dusk. A skilled laborer could plant 1,000 plants daily (one-third of an acre). At harvest time he or she might be expected to pick a ton of fruit a day.

Tourism replaces pineapples Though many regret the demise of the Hawaiian pineapple industry in the face of low-priced competition from Asia, few who actually worked the fields are nostalgic. In Lanai there is cautious optimism that strictly controlled tourism will provide a better standard of living for the next generation, and that the island's community spirit will survive intact.

"Excellent fruit"
Pineapples are believed to have originated in Paraguay. Their scientific name, *Ananas comosus*, is derived from the Paraguayan *ananas* meaning "excellent fruit" in the Guarani Indian dialect, but the Spanish explorers called them *piña de Indias* for their resemblance to pine cones. Later the pineapple became a symbol of hospitality, its unmistakable form frequently used to decorate colonial furniture and even to adorn gateposts as an advance welcome for guests.

151

When pineapples were king

HAWAII

152

Alenuihaha *Channel*

Mookini Heiau &
Kamehameha Birthsite
Upolu Point
Kapaau
Hawi
Kapaa Beach Park
Kamehameha
Statue
Pololu Valley
Lapakahi State
Historical Park
250
Kohala
*Waipio
Bay*
Kukuihaele
Kahua
Ranch
Malae Point
270
*Kohala
Forest
Reserve*
5,501ft
Waipio Valley Overlook
Kawaihae
Kobala Mountains
Waimanu
Waipio
Honokaa
5
Kawaihae
19
Waimea-Kamuela
Hamakua
*Kalopa State
Recreation Area*
Paauilo
Kawaihae Bay
Mailekini Heiau
Puukohala Heiau
National Historic Site
Kamuela
Museum
Parker Ranch
Historic Homes
*Hamakua
Forest
Reserve*
Kalopa
*Manowaialee
Forest Reserve*
Hapuna
Beach
Kamakoa
Haleplula
Mauna Lani
Resort
Anaehoomalu
Beach
Kibolo Bay
Waikoloa
Resort
190
Coast
Kohala
Kiholo
Keamuku
Mauna Kea
Observatory *13,792ft*
Mauna Kea
19
Kona Village
Puuanahula
Forest Reserve
Hale Pohooku
4
Maliaiula
Huehue
3,867ft
Puu Waawae
Pohakuloa
Mauna Kea State
Recreation Area
Keahole Point
Kalaoa
SADDLE ROAD
Honokohau
8,233ft
Hualalai
Kaupulehu
Forest Reserve
6,757ft
Puu Hulubulu
Kona Marina
Honokohau Bay
Kailua-Kona
Ahuena Heiau
Hulihee Palace
Mokuaikaua Church
Holualoa
Waiaha Springs Forest Reserve
**Mauna Loa
Forest Reserve**
3
Keauhou
Kealakekua
Observatory
Mokuaweoweo
Crater
13,671ft
Mauna Loa
Mauna Loa Trail
Kilauea
Forest
Rese
Kip
Pua
Captain Cook
Monument
Captain Cook
Kona Historical Society
Museum
**Hawaii Volcanoes
National Park**
MAUNA LOA ROAD
Napoopoo Beach Park
Kealakekua Bay
State Underwater Park
Mauna Loa Royal
Kona Coffee Mill
Keokea
Puuhonua O Honaunau
National Historical Park
St Benedict's Painted Church
11,326ft
*Sulphur
Cone*
**Kapapala
Forest Reserve**
TA Jagg
Muse
Halemau
Overlo
Hookena
11
2
Kauluca
Point
**South Kona
Forest
Reserve**
Kau
Wood Valley
Forest
11
*Kau
Deser*
Papa
6,872ft
Puu o Keokeo
Milolii
Kapua-Manuka
Forest
Reserve
Pahala
Reserve
Kuee
Ruins
Okoe Bay
Punaluu
Punaluu Beach Park
Manuka State
Park
Waiohinu
Honuapo
Honuapo Bay
Kauna Point
Kahuku Ranch
Naalehu
Waikapuna
1
Heiau o Malino
*Pohue
Bay*
Petroglyphs
SOUTH POINT ROAD
South Point
(Ka Lae)
Mahana Beach
Petroglyphs and
Ancient Canoe Moorings

A   B   C

See drive pages 174-5

HAWAII

Ookala
Laupahoehoe

Hilo
Iaokoa
19 Kahuka
Hakalau
Forest
Akaka Falls
State Park
Honomu
Reserve
Pepeekeo Point
Maukaloa
Hawaii Tropical
Botanical Garden
Kapue
Papaikou
Onomea Bay
Rainbow *Hilo*
Falls *Bay*
Liliuokalani Gardens
Hilo
Wailuku
Boiling
Pots
Hilo Tropical Gardens
Forest Lyman Mission
House and Museum
Hilo
Hilo International Airport
Reserve
Nani Mau Gardens
Mauna Loa Macadamia
Panaewa
Rainforest Zoo
11 Nut Farm and Visitor Center
Upper
Waiakea
orest Reserve
Waiakea
Forest
Reserve
Keaau
Haena
Kaloli Point
Oloa
Forest Reserve
Anthurium
Nurseries
130
Nanawale
Cape
Kumukahi
Lighthouse
Hawaii
Volcanoes
National Park
Pahoa
Forest
Lava Tree State Park
sitor
enter
Winery
Akatsuka
Orchid Gardens
Reserve
Malama-Ki
Isaac Hale
Beach Park
Volcano
Puna
Forest Reserve
Kauleau
CRATER
I DRIVE
Kilauea
Crater 4,090ft
CHAIN OF CRATERS
Keauohana
Forest
Reserve
Mackenzie
State Park
Puu Oo
Hawaii Volcanoes
Kehena
Kalapana
Hokuma Point
Hawaii
National
Park
ge Trail
ROAD
Kupaahu
Wahaula Heiau
Puu Loa
Petroglyphs
Apua
Point

| 0 | | 10 | | 20 | | 30 km |
| 0 | 5 | | 10 | | 15 | 20 miles |

D   E

HAWAII

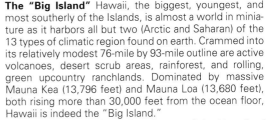

Approximate driving times from Hilo
- Hapuna: 1 hour 45 minutes
- Kailua-Kona (via Waimea): 2 hours 15 minutes
- Volcanoes National Park: 45 minutes
- Waimea-Kamuela: 1 hour 15 minutes

Approximate driving times from Kailua-Kona
- Hapuna: 45 minutes
- Kealakekua Bay: 45 minutes
- Volcanoes National Park: 2 hours 30 minutes
- Waimea-Kamuela: 1 hour

The "Big Island" Hawaii, the biggest, youngest, and most southerly of the Islands, is almost a world in miniature as it harbors all but two (Arctic and Saharan) of the 13 types of climatic region found on earth. Crammed into its relatively modest 76-mile by 93-mile outline are active volcanoes, desert scrub areas, rainforest, and rolling, green upcountry ranchlands. Dominated by massive Mauna Kea (13,796 feet) and Mauna Loa (13,680 feet), both rising more than 30,000 feet from the ocean floor, Hawaii is indeed the "Big Island."

Sixty-five percent bigger than the rest of the *Hawaii nei* (Hawaiian Island group) combined, and still growing, the "Big Island" is also rural, relaxed, and full of heart.

Historical background The first Polynesian immigrants probably landed at the Big Island's South Point as early as AD 500 and spread throughout the Islands. Under the Tahitians the island witnessed the first human sacrifices, in the 13th century, and there are numerous ancient sites and petroglyphs which remain as a testament to Hawaii's importance over the centuries.

When Captain Cook died in Kealakekua Bay in 1779 (see pages 36–7), there were around 80,000 Hawaiians living on the Big Island under the rule of Kalaniopuu. On his death, the old chief bequeathed guardianship of Kukailimoku, the family war god, to his nephew, Kamehameha. The young warrior built a great temple on the north Kohala coast, the Puukohala Heiau, dedicated to Kukailimoku, and united the Islands into a single kingdom, which he called Hawaii after his island birthplace.

During Kamehameha I's reign, cattle and horses were introduced into the Big Island and laid the foundations for large-scale ranching. The New England adventurer, John Palmer Parker, was appointed to manage the herds, and was allocated a small plot of land as a reward. He married Kamehameha's granddaughter and built up the vast Parker Ranch at Waimea, one of the largest in the U.S.

Surf's up on the Big Island of Hawaii

Within a year of Kamehameha's death in 1819, the first missionaries arrived in "Owhyhee," and missions were soon established in Hilo, Kailua, and Waimea. From the mid-19th century, immigrant workers arrived to work Hawaii's sugar plantations, and the very first tourists began to make their way to the island. Mark Twain was bowled over by a night visit to Kilauea in 1866, where he saw lava flows that "looked like a colossal railroad map of the State of Massachusetts done in chain lightning on a midnight sky."

Big Island round-up Kilauea is currently the world's most active volcano, and is top draw at the Hawaii Volcanoes National Park. But this is by no means all that the Big Island has to offer. Each of the six ancient districts, linked by the Hawaiian Belt Road which encircles the island, has its own individual character and charms.

The island has two natural starting-points (and airports): Hilo, on the damp windward coast; and Kailua-Kona, focus of the Kona and Kohala coast resorts. Hilo is better placed for the volcano park, but despite its attractive bayfront position, it will never be a favored tourist destination. It rains too much here, a fact which also keeps the lush Puna district to the south rural and unspoiled.

The Belt Road around the island runs southwest from the volcano park through the sparsely populated Kua region to the Kona coast and coffee groves on the drier leeward shore. Kailua-Kona is a seaside town at the southern end of the barren lava fields which border the Kohala coast. Along the white-sand shoreline, the Big Island's top resorts have sculpted amazing gardens and golf courses from the black rock. To the north, the Kohala Mountains rise behind the ranch town of Waimea-Kamuela, and fall down to Hamakua, the green, rainswept northeast. Sometimes known as the "Scottish Coast," Hamakua's valleys and cane fields have a backcloth of towering Mauna Kea, rainforest and waterfalls.

It does take time to explore the Big Island, but its fans return again and again.

Snow-boarding on Mauna Kea

Hele-On bus
Hawaii's public transportation system, the Hele-On bus, is one of the best travel bargains in the Islands. Buses cover just about every corner of the island, stopping at most major attractions and resorts. They operate from Monday to Saturday (for information and times, tel: 808/935-8241).

A cast net fisherman tries his luck in Hilo Bay

Hilo and surroundings

The Big Island's county seat and chief seaport is Hilo, which skirts the rim of lovely Hilo Bay. Situated on the lush, rainforested windward coast, it has the reputation for being the wettest city in the country. Try to visit in the morning when there is a better-than-average chance of hitting a dry spell.

Behind the parks, which replaced the waterfront area wiped out by a destructive *tsunami* (tidal wave) in 1960, downtown Hilo's remaining Western-style false-fronted shops and plantation-era buildings clamber up the hillside past missionary churches and the Lyman House Museum. The Hawaii Visitors Bureau office on the corner of Haili and Keawe streets is the place to pick up a map showing historic sites, and other local information (tel: 808/961-5797. *Open:* Mon–Fri 8–12, 1–4:30).

▶▶ Hilo Tropical Gardens 153D3

1477 Kalanianaole Avenue (2 miles off HI-11)
Open: daily 9–5. Admission charge: inexpensive
Just south of town, these colorful tropical gardens have been open to view for 50 years. Narrow paths weave past fern trees and crotons, bushy azaleas and orchids galore. There are canopies of passion fruit vines and plumeria, grottoes full of impatiens, bizarre ornamental pineapples that look like horticultural hand-grenades, and an interesting section devoted to Hawaiian food and medicinal plants. Make liberal use of the free mosquito repellent posted by the entrance.

▶ Liliuokalani Gardens 153D3

Banyan Drive
Open site. Admission free
The centerpiece of this park is the Japanese-style gardens laid out around a series of lava outcrops and small lagoons spanned by picturesque bridges. Dwarf palms and miniature stone pagodas dot the shore, and there are stands of bamboo and mango trees. At the top of the gardens, a bridge links Coconut Island (Moku Ola), a popular weekend picnic haunt, to the mainland.

Market days

On Wednesdays and Saturdays, Hilo's colorful Farmers Market spills out over the corner of Kamehameha Avenue and Mamo Street. Dozens of stalls are piled high with local produce, from glossy aubergines and peppers to Chinese greens and avocados, fat bunches of radishes, stacks of yams, sweet Maui onions, cherry tomatoes, baby bananas, papayas, guavas and gourds galore, as well as gorgeous cut flowers. Extravagant sprays of orchids, parrot's-beak and lobster-claw heliconias, bird-of-paradise flowers, proteas, red ginger and anthuriums grown in nurseries and back gardens all over the Hilo and Puna districts, erupt exuberantly out of massed plastic buckets.

▶▶▶ Lyman Mission House and Museum 153D3

276 Haili Street (tel: 808/935-5021)
Open: Mon–Sat 9–5, Sun 1–4; guided tours of the
Mission House, every half hour 9:30–11:30, every hour
1–4. Admission charge: inexpensive

The Reverend David Belden Lyman and his wife Sarah arrived in Hawaii in 1832, and became the mainstays of the Hilo mission for half a century. Their single-story mission home, thatched with *ti*-leaves, was built in 1839. Later, a second story was added to accommodate their eight children. Beautifully restored, the house has been furnished throughout with antiques, many of them Lyman family heirlooms, and re-creates the mid-19th-century mission lifestyle in fascinating detail.

Next door is the Lyman Museum, devoted to Hawaiiana. Chronological displays on the first floor cover every aspect of local history and culture, from native basketwork and royal regalia to the story of Captain Cook and Hawaii's immigrant past. Upstairs, the Earth Heritage Gallery gives the low-down on volcanoes, and in the seashell section, shell-collectors can have a field day down amongst the bivalves, frilly murex shells, and conches amassed by Frederick Lyman.

▶ Mauna Loa Macadamia Nut Factory and Visitor Center 153D3

5 miles south of Hilo on HI-11, then 3 miles east following signs
Open: daily 8:30–5. Admission free

The Big Island produces 90 percent of the world's crop of macadamia nuts and celebrates this fact with an annual Macadamia Nut Festival every August. One of the biggest players in the mac nut field is the Mauna Loa company, which processes some 32 million pounds of the delicious sweet, white nuts a year.

The road to the farm's Visitor Center passes right through the heart of the 2,500-acre, 225,000-tree Keaau Orchard. If one of the five or six annual harvestings is taking place, you can watch the action from viewing windows overlooking the processing plant. An on-site shop sells macadamia nuts in various guises, from the straight unsalted nuts to chocolate-covered macadamia nut cookies and macadamia nut-flavored coffees.

Liliuokalani Gardens

Merrie Monarch Festival
The week-long Merrie Monarch Festival is held in Hilo each spring. This is the most prestigious *hula* festival in the Islands, and draws *hula* troops from throughout the state as well as from overseas. There are two types of *hula* on show: the *kahiko*, or traditional interpretation of Hawaiian stories accompanied by drumming and chanting; and the *auana*, or modern style, in which competitors are judged on their elaborate costumes and adornment as well as for style and movement. The town is booked up months in advance for the festival. For further information tel: 808/935-9168.

Macadamia nuts

Nani Mau views

▶▶　　**Nani Mau Gardens**　　153D3

421 Makalika Street (4 miles south of Hilo, off HI-11)
Open: daily 8–5. Admission charge: moderate

This stunning 20-acre spread of formal gardens is a must for plant lovers. The first section is divided up into groupings of related plants such as the Bromeliad Garden, the wonderfully scented Gardenia and Jasmine Garden, and a fruit orchard. An interesting small, modern museum examines the role of plants in nature, culture and agriculture, and has a well-stocked reference library.

From the glories of the Orchid Walkway, a path leads to the Makalapua Lookout for an overview of the 6-acre Annual Garden, with its colorful massed beds laid out around sweeping lawns.

▶▶　　**Panaewa Rainforest Zoo**　　153D3

Off Mamaki Street (4 miles south of Hilo via HI-11)
Open: daily 9–4. Admission free

A great outing for children, this well laid out, 12-acre zoo is home to 150 animals from 50 species, including tigers, monkeys, and native birds. Rain shelters dotted about its grounds are well used, as the park has around 125 inches of precipitation a year, but the zoo is still a favorite picnic spot and there is plenty to enjoy.

▶　　**Rainbow Falls**　　153D3

Follow signs off Waianuenue Avenue (1½ miles from Hilo)
Open site. Admission free

Waianuenue Avenue leads up from the Hilo waterfront to the popular Rainbow Falls. *Waianuenue* means "Rainbow-Seen-in-Water," and as the 80-foot cascade plummets down a lava-rock cliff, it sends up a fine mist of white spray frequently shot through with rainbows.

A path leads through the woods from the parking lot to a viewpoint overlooking the Boiling Pots, a series of pools linked by smaller falls. The smell of fermenting mangoes pervades the wood (the rotting fruits make the path slippery in season), while a massive banyan tree looks like an open invitation to the Swiss Family Robinson.

Fishy business
Early risers looking for some local color should make tracks for the Suisan Fish Auction. This is held between 7:30 and 8:30 every morning except Sunday at the fish market by the mouth of the Wailoa River, next to the Liliuokalani Gardens. Local chefs and housewives inspect the morning's catch, and everyone discusses the price of fish.

Mauna Kea and the Saddle

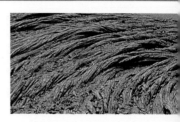

■ The world's tallest sea mountain, 32,000 feet from the ocean floor to its snow-capped peak, Mauna Kea reaches a height of 13,796 feet above sea-level. A shield volcano shaped alternately by fire and ice, the "White Mountain" last erupted over 3,600 years ago; since then its peaks and troughs have been honed by glacial action. ■

The "White Mountain" From December to March or April Mauna Kea's higher levels are capped with virgin snow, so while it is a blistering 90 degrees on the beach, visitors with a taste for adventure can actually ski Mauna Kea with **Ski Guides Hawaii** (tel: 808/885-4188). Full-day ski packages include transportation and ski shuttles (there are no lifts), experienced guides (no marked trails either) and lunch. Equipment is also available to rent, and the best snow months are January and February.

Star-gazing Mauna Kea is also a mecca for astronomers. Nowhere else on earth offers the same combination of altitude, clear air, absence of artifical light and accessibility. By the year 2000, some 14 international observatories will have been established here, along with the world's largest telescope for viewing both the northern and southern skies.

Observatory tours are available from Friday to Sunday, but to get there it is better to join an excursion with Paradise Safaris, who operate from Kailua-Kona (tel: 808/322-2366), or with the Waipo Valley Shuttle out of Waimea-Kamuela (tel: 808/775-7121). The latter also offers straightforward summit tours. Both companies issue warnings about the dangers of high altitude to sufferers of heart and respiratory conditions, and will not take young children.

Saddle Road Access to Mauna Kea is via the Saddle Road (HI-200), a four-wheel-drive route which links Hilo to HI-190 just south of Waimea-Kamuela. Ordinary cars are not permitted on the Saddle Road. Drivers with four-wheel-drive vehicles should check weather conditions with the Visitor Center in advance (tel: 808/969-3218).

Observation point

Star-gazers gather on Mauna Kea's summit

Molten pahoehoe *lava*

Madame Pele reigns
Madame Pele's presence in the Halemaumau Crater means that this region has always held a special spiritual significance for Hawaiians. Priests performed important religious rites here, and even today many visitors leave small gifts of coins, food and flowers to placate the goddess. However, Madame Pele guards her firepit home jealously, and it is unlucky to remove so much as a pebble. Every day, park rangers receive packages of pilfered lava fragments accompanied by tales of the bad luck they have brought upon the senders.

Thurston Lava Tube

The South

▶▶▶ Hawaii Volcanoes National Park   *153C/D2/3*
HI-11 near Volcano, 30 miles south of Hilo/95 miles east of Kailua-Kona (general information, tel: 808/967-7311; eruption update, tel: 808/967-7977)
Open: daily. Park, 24 hours; Visitor Center, 7:45–5; Museum, 8:30–5. Admission charge: inexpensive; tickets are valid for seven days

The sprawling 229,177-acre park comprises part of the state's two active volcanoes, Mauna Loa and Kilauea. It is the safest and most accessible place in the world to watch volcanic activity, and the park's various facilities include scenic drives, 150 miles of hiking trails, a visitor center, a museum, an observatory, campsites and a hotel right on a crater rim.

Kilauea, the youngest and most active volcano in the Hawaiian Islands, is the central focus of the park. Measuring a mere 4,093 feet above sea-level at its peak, Kilauea is small compared with neighboring Mauna Loa (13,677 feet). However, Kilauea's vast 2-mile by 2½-mile, 400-foot-deep summit caldera, caused by the collapse of a subterranean magma chamber, is as impressive as any, and the Puu Oo vent in the volcano's flank has been erupting continuously since 1983.

To orient yourself, pick up maps and information from the **Kilauea Visitor Center**, which also provides updates on volcanic activity and a short introductory film to the park shown every hour. Opposite the Center, a path cuts through to the Volcano House hotel and a crater-rim lookout with a panoramic view across the caldera to Madame Pole's firepit home, Halemaumau, a 500-foot-deep secondary crater which oozes wisps of sulfurous steam from fissures in its lava floor.

The 11-mile **Crater Rim Drive** is a must. It takes about an hour, but leave plenty of time for stops along the way. This loop drive encircles the caldera, passing through a great variety of terrains, and provides access to the 23-mile **Chain of Craters Road** which winds its way down to the coast. Here, lava-flows from the active Puu Oo vent have added over 400 acres of new land since 1986.

Heading counterclockwise around the caldera, you come to areas of odoriferous sulfur banks and hissing steam vents, where groundwater seeps through cracks in the earth and vaporizes in temperatures which can reach 100–150°C just a few feet beneath the surface.

The **Thomas A. Jaggar Museum**, named for the founder of the Hawaiian Volcano Observatory, covers vulcanism in general but with particular emphasis on Hawaii. Dramatic action videos show live footage of volcanic eruptions, meanwhile working seismographs measure minute earth movements.

Leaving the *lehua* scrublands behind, the road runs across the southwest rift zone's blackened lava flows stretching like a sea of cracked and crumpled tarmac away from the crater rim. Here, the **Halemaumau Overlook**, just a few minutes' walk from the road, is worth a stop.

Other popular side trips include the eerie **Devastation Trail**, a boardwalk across pumice-cinder dunes scattered with the bleached wood bones of a former forest. Also the **Thurston Lava Tube**, a 450-foot-long tunnel created as molten lava continued to flow beneath a cooled and set crust, all but buried in the mossy, green *hapuu* (tree-fern) forest on the windward side of the caldera.

Giant **Mauna Loa** ("Long Mountain"), quiet since 1984, is a textbook example of a shield volcano. From the ocean floor to its 3-mile by 1½-mile, 600-foot-deep summit caldera, Mauna Loa's massive barrow-shaped form measures 10,000 cubic miles. Few visitors actually tackle Mauna Loa, which towers almost 2 miles higher than Kilauea. Its summit lies 33 miles northwest of the park headquarters, and a two-day hike from the top of the Mauna Loa Strip Road. However one excellent detour from the Strip Road is **Kipuka Puaulu**, an island of mature forest amidst the lava flows which acts as a bird reserve.

Lava from Kilauea's Puu Oo vent builds a new coastline

Volcanoes National Park trails
Those exploring the park on foot have several options. The challenging four-day Mauna Loa Trail, two-day Halape Trail down to the coast, and full-day Napau Crater Trail with fine views of the Puu Oo vent, are for serious hikers. But the Crater Rim Trail is a relatively straightforward seven hours, and it can be shortened by taking in parts of the Halemaumau or Byron Ledge trails across the central lava fields of the Kilauea crater, or the Kilauea Iki Trail, which descends through lush jungle to a young secondary crater.

HAWAII: THE SOUTH

En route stops
Just east of South Point Road, a handful of small villages offers a convenient break in the 100-mile journey between Kailua-Kona and Volcano. Half-pint-sized Waiohinu, the southernmost community in the U.S., boasts the Mark Twain Monkeypod Tree, which shoots from the roots of a long-toppled tree planted by the author in 1866. At Naalehu, a couple of miles east, the Punaluu Bake Shop serves its own recipe sweet bread, sandwiches, snacks and cold drinks. Punaluu itself has a beach park, and a rocky beach with a picnic pavilion overlooking Ninole Cove.

Volcano Golf Course, in sight of the Kilauea Caldera

▶ **Isaac Hale Beach Park**   153E3

HI-137, south Puna
Open site. Admission free

Highway 137 divides just beyond Lava Tree State Park (see below), and the right fork to the Isaac Hale Beach Park makes a pretty drive to the coast. For the last few miles the single-track country road runs through a dense tunnel of mango trees and, in season, the air is heavy with the scent of squashed and fermented fruit.

The waterfront park does not have much of a beach, but the rocky shore is a popular weekend picnic spot. Local families come here to fish, surf and launch boats from the ramp. To the north (off HI-137), there is a road out to Cape Kumukahi, the easternmost cape in the state, with an old lighthouse that narrowly avoided the lava flows of Kilauea's 1960 eruption.

▶▶ **Lava Tree State Park**   153E3

HI-132, 2½ miles east of HI-130 at Pahoa
Open site. Admission free

Once upon a time, deep in the rainforest jungle, a lava river flowed, engulfing all in its wake and turning trees to stone. It sounds like a fairy tale, but a river of molten lava from Kilauea did pass this way in 1790 and engulfed an *ohia* grove. Moisture contained within the tree trunks was sufficient to set a solid lava coating, leaving casts of the trees behind when the lava flow receded. Dozens of lava stumps and tubes are now dotted around amongst the ferns and new *ohia* forest. Along the 20-minute trail, look for wild orchids in the woodland clearings.

▶ **South Point**   152B1

Almost halfway between Volcano and Kailua-Kona, South Point Road strikes off HI-11 at Mile Marker 69 and travels down to South Point, the southernmost point in the U.S.

The Hawaiians call it Ka Lae, and it is thought that this is where the first Polynesians came ashore. Archaeological remains include petroglyphs (see page 170) and canoe moorings set in solid rock.

Local fishermen take advantage of the excellent fishing off the coast by lowering their boats into the sea using ropes, then reaching them on cliffside ladders. A 3-mile hike to the north leads to green-sand Papakolea Beach, created by the collapse of an olivine cinder cone.

►► Volcano 153D2

Just east of the volcano park, bypassed by HI-11, the little village of Volcano offers a couple of stores, a pleasant inn (Kilauea Lodge), and several friendly bed-and-breakfast establishments tucked discreetly behind hedges of hydrangeas and tree ferns in the cool, damp rainforest. In addition to the national park, there are a couple of minor local attractions and the Volcano Golf & Country Club (tel: 808/967-7331), where players can enjoy 18 holes of golf with volcano views.

In operation since 1974, **Akatsuka Orchid Gardens** ► (HI-11 at Mile Marker 22.5. *Open:* daily 8:30–5. *Admission free*) have one of the largest orchid collections in Hawaii. The greenhouse garden contains a profusion of rare and colorful blooms, some fragrant, some bizarre. There are also dozens of waxy anthuriums, fiery red ginger flowers and massed bougainvillea in several shades. Cut flowers and plants are available for sale and can be shipped direct to the mainland.

The southernmost winery in the U.S., the **Volcano Winery** (Golf Course Road, Volcano, off HI-11. *Open:* daily *10–5. Admission free*) specializes in a brace of white wines from the relatively new Symphony grape variety, and there is also a selection of exotic wines flavored with tropical fruits such as guava and passion fruit, as well as a grape-free honey wine. Production is around 1,500 cases a month, and all of it is sold within the Islands. Tastings are offered in the gift shop, which sells souvenirs with a vinous theme.

Mahana Beach

Pollination tricks
Strange but true, the yellow and brown "dancing doll" orchid (*Oncidium*) relies on an elaborate hoax to ensure its pollination. It attracts the attention of naive young centris bees by masquerading as an enemy insect. The bees challenge the "intruder" bloom with head butts and wind up carrying the pollen on their brows. The bees will then pollinate several plants.

Petrified lava trees

Captain Cook monument at Kealakekua Bay

The Kona Coast

▶▶   Kealakekua Bay   *152A3*

Napoopoo Road, off HI-11 at Captain Cook (12 miles south of Kailua-Kona), or HI-160 north from Honaunau
Open site. Admission free

The laid-back country town of Kealakekua straddles the Belt Road (HI-11) high above broad Kealakekua Bay. At the southern end of town, near the village of Captain Cook, signposts indicate the twisting 4-mile road that leads down to the shore past gardens dripping with fruit and tropical flowers, roadside stalls selling bargain-priced mangoes and papayas, coffee groves, and the massed yellow blooms of a commercial plumeria orchard.

When Captain Cook sailed into Kealakekua Bay on January 17, 1779, almost a year to the day since he had first set foot in the Hawaiian Islands at Kauai, the British explorer was greeted as an incarnation of Lono, the peaceable Hawaiian god of agriculture and fertility. Cook and his ships, HMS *Resolution* and HMS *Discovery*, stayed in Kealakekua for three weeks enjoying Hawaiian hospitality and entertaining the chieftain Kalaniopuu and his entourage in return.

A week after the ships set sail again, Cook was forced to return when the *Resolution*'s mast was snapped in a squall. This merely served to confirm the Hawaiians' growing doubts about the visitors' godliness, and, during a dispute over a stolen boat, Cook was killed in a skirmish on the north shore of the bay.

Because of its clear water and variety of marine life, the bay is now protected as a Marine Life Conservation District, one of the state's two underwater parks. It is one of the few places in the world where spinner dolphins swim close to the shore (they use the protected waters for resting and breeding). Kealakekua's reefs offer superb snorkeling and diving with excellent visibility. Snorkeling equipment and canoes are available to rent, and there are trips in glass-bottomed boats.

▶   Kona Historical Society Museum   *152A3*

HI-11 (Mile Marker 112.5), Captain Cook
Open: Mon–Fri 9–3. Admission charge: inexpensive

Housed in the old Greenwell Store at Captain Cook, this local history museum displays a modest collection of period photographs, antiques and memorabilia, much of it related to the Greenwell family. Businessman and rancher Henry Greenwell built the store next door to the family home (now in ruins) in the mid-19th century from volcanic rock and lime mortar made from crushed coral. It served as a travelers' watering post, dry goods store and post office, and the Greenwells were among the first to export Kona coffee to Europe in the 1870s.

▶   Mauna Loa Royal Kona Coffee Mill   *152A3*

Napoopoo Road, south of Captain Cook
Open: daily 9–5. Admission free

Mauna Loa is the largest macadamia nut grower in the world, and also brews a mean cup of coffee. Here at its Kona Coast operation, viewing windows open onto the factory floor and visitors can sample a selection of Kona coffees. Coffee blends run the gamut, from relatively

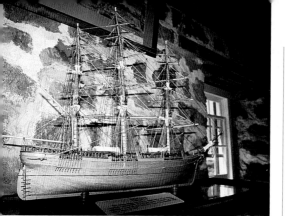

NAPOOPOO BEACH

Model ship at the Kona Historical Society

Naupaka
The indigenous beach *naupaka*, with its strange half-formed white flower, is a common sight along Hawaii's shores. Another type of *naupaka* grows in the mountains, and when the two half-flowers are placed together they make a whole. So the story goes, there were two lovers whom the goddess Pele wished to part. When she failed to win the young man's love, she hurled fiery lava after him, but the youth was rescued by Pele's sisters and turned into mountain *naupaka*. Pele then chased the girl into the sea until again the sisters intervened, transforming her into beach *naupaka*.

straightforward French, Viennese or espresso-style roasts to more exotic concoctions flavored with vanilla, chocolate macadamia nut, or cinnamon. There is a short video presentation and a store crammed full of Mauna Loa products, from chocolate-dipped coffee beans to macadamia nut brittle.

▶ **Napoopoo Beach Park** *152A3*
Kealakekua Bay
There is good swimming from this rocky stretch of shore, which borders onto Kealakekua Bay. Boogie boards can be rented here, as well as snorkeling equipment, and there are changing rooms.

In a small park by the boat ramp, the stone platform of Hikiau Heiau was an important ancient Hawaiian shrine dedicated to the god Lono. Captain Cook's auspicious appearance at this sacred site during the winter-time Makahiki festival celebrations (see page 35) guaranteed him and his men a warm welcome.

A plaque records the burial of seaman William Whatman performed by Captain Cook here on January 28, 1779. This funeral was the first recorded Christian service to be held in the Islands.

The ancient Hikiau Heiau at Napoopoo

Coffee and chocolate

■ **Throughout the world, the name Kona has become synonymous with coffee. Above the sunny South Kona coast more than 600 coffee farms crowd into a narrow belt stretching along the leeward slopes of the Mauna Loa and Hualalai mountains. Between them they produce 2 million pounds of the world's finest coffee every year.** ■

Plantations in action
Numerous coffee farms along the Belt Road (HI-11) offer tastings, farm and mill tours. Visitors are welcome to drop in on the Langenstein Farm (Mile Marker 104.5), where Kona coffee is grown, picked, milled and roasted on the property. Another good place to see a working plantation is family-owned Bay View Farm, near St. Benedict's Painted Church (off HI-160; see opposite).

King of coffee Kona's coffee farms flourish in elevations between 800 and 2,000 feet above sea-level, where the combination of rich volcanic soil, wind shelter, rainfall and all-important cloud-shade in the hot afternoon produces ideal conditions for coffee-growing.

The first coffee bushes were introduced to the Islands in 1828. Hawaii is the only place in the U.S. where coffee can be grown commercially, and the Big Island is by far the biggest producer. Gourmets particularly prize Kona coffee's delicious aroma and mellow, full-bodied flavor.

Harvesting of the bright-red coffee berries, known as "cherries," takes place in the autumn and winter, generally between August and February. The hand-picked cherries are then milled to extract the coffee beans, which are sun-dried on racks, then sorted, roasted and packaged for the market.

An average plant produces 5 pounds of cherries a year, which converts to about a pound of processed beans. The highest-grade coffees are made from pea berries, single beans from the cherry, which normally produces two.

A chocoholic's Paradise Another U.S. commercial first for the Big Island is Hawaiian Vintage Chocolate, the nation's only chocolate producer. In 1986, Jim Walsh planted 18,000 cocoa trees and his first "vintage" went on sale in 1992. Since then, Hawaii's top chefs, and restaurateurs and delicatessens as far away as New York, have been clamoring for his top-quality product, made from fragrant and flavorful criollo cocoa.

Bags of flavor from the Kona Coast

▶▶▶ Puuhonua O Honaunau National Historical Park   152A2

HI-160 (off HI-11), 22 miles south of Kailua-Kona
Open: daily 7:30–midnight; Visitor Center until 5:30.
Admission charge: inexpensive

Up until 1819, every aspect of Hawaiian life was regulated by *kapu*, a system of taboos designed to protect society and natural resources (see page 33). The punishment for breaking any *kapu* was death, and the only possibility of absolution for a *kapu*-breaker was to reach a *puuhonua*, or place of refuge. In the mass destruction of religious sites which followed the abolition of the *kapu* system, the Puuhonua O Honaunau ("Place of Refuge at Honaunau") escaped by virtue of its importance. A former royal village as well as a refuge, it was one of the most sacred sites in Hawaii.

Reconstructions of traditional timber-framed buildings have been built in the former royal palace grounds. These are still divided from the *puuhonua* by a tremendous 1,000-foot-long, 10-foot-high and 17-foot-thick L-shaped drystone wall. At its northern end, the thatched Hale O Keawe mausoleum-temple, which was rebuilt in 1968 on mid-17th-century foundations, is guarded by ferocious *kii* idols. Raised platforms around the enclosure, known as *lele*, were used for offerings to placate the gods.

Take plenty of time to explore the park. Picnicking is permitted and the grounds stay open until late.

▶▶ St. Benedict's Painted Church   152B2

Signposted off HI-160, east of Puuhonua O Honaunau
Open: daily. Admission free

This small church makes a popular detour from the Puuhonua O Honaunau (above) and Kealakekua Bay. The interior has been decorated from head to toe: biblical scenes and grandiose *trompe-l'oeil* vistas cover the walls, while Hawaiian-language quotations from the scriptures wind around the pillars.

Sanctuary

Both land and sea routes to the *puuhonua* were fraught with dangers, but if a *kapu*-breaker made it to the refuge, he or she could return home safely after a ceremony of absolution. Sanctuary was also offered to those too young, old or disabled to fight in times of war. Defeated warriors could seek sanctuary as well; when the fight was over they then owed allegiance to the victor.

Hale O Keawe

The *heiau* (temple) of Hale O Keawe in the *puuhonua* was built around 1650 in honor of Chief Keawe, whose bones were later stored there, carefully wrapped in cloth. Hawaiians believe that *mana,* or spiritual power, remains in the bones after death, so Hale o Keawe became a place of spiritual force. Over the years, the remains of 23 other chieftains, forebears of Kamehameha I, were also interred there, but all the bones were removed to a secret hiding place in 1829.

A trompe-l'oeil masterpiece

Kailua-Kona

Kailua Pier

Kailua Pier is always bustling. It is a great place for a stroll, or to just sit and watch the pleasure boats and fishing vessels coming and going, outrigger crews practicing their paddle work, and kids cavorting on the murky beach after school. Captain Bob's Glass Bottom Boat Cruises (tel: 808/332-3102) leave from the pier daily except Monday for one-hour reef jaunts. There are also snorkel cruises with Body Glove (tel: 808/326-7122) or Captain Zodiac (tel: 808/329-3199), amongst others; and submarine adventures with *Atlantis* (tel: 808/329-6626) and *Nautilus II* (tel: 808/326-2003).

Located midway down the Big Island's drier, sunnier leeward side, Kailua sits on the boundary between the Kona coast to the south and the Kohala coast to the north. It was a Hawaiian gathering place for centuries, and in the early 19th century became the capital of the Hawaiian kingdom for the last few years of Kamehameha I's reign. This was also the spot where the first missionaries put ashore in the Islands in 1820.

Kailua is sandwiched between the luxury resorts of the south Kohala coast and a long strip of condominiums and hotels stretching down to Keauhou. All the main sights and stores are found on Alii Drive, which parallels the shore. Here, the touristy Kona Inn Shopping Village is a good place to pick up local information and book boat trips. The Hawaiian Visitors Bureau also has an office in the Kona Plaza Shopping Arcade, next to Mokuaikaua Church (tel: 808/329-7787. *Open:* Mon–Fri 8–12, 1–4:30).

▶▶▶ Ahuena Heiau 152A3

In the grounds of King Kamehameha's Kona Beach Hotel, Palani Road
Open site. Admission free

In 1812, his kingdom secured, the aging Kamehameha I returned to his home island of Hawaii and established the royal court at Kamakahonu ("Eye of the Turtle"), an oceanfront site just north of the present-day Kailua Pier. Here, he rebuilt an ancient *heiau*, which had once been a sacrificial site, re-dedicated it to peace-loving Lono, and lived out his days in a traditional compound of thatched buildings, several of which have been reconstructed overlooking the bay.

Dominating the Hale Pahu ("House of the Drum") and Hale Mana, where the king prayed and consulted with his ministers, is a tall Anuu, or oracle tower, used by the high priest to commune with the gods and proclaim their will.

Offerings at the reconstructed Ahuena Heiau temple complex

Placed around the compound are *lele* (raised platforms) used for offerings, and protective *kii akua* (carved temple images). When Kamehameha died in 1819, his body was prepared for burial at the *heiau* before being taken to a secret burial place.

▶▶▶ Hulihee Palace   152A3
5718 Alii Drive
Open: Mon–Fri 9–4, Sat–Sun 10–3. Admission charge: inexpensive

The Iolani Palace in Honolulu claims to be the only true palace in the U.S., but as far as the locals are concerned this modest residence also qualifies. Built for Governor John Adams Kuakini in 1838, the fine seafront house became a favored royal summer retreat and contains plenty of regal memorabilia.

Governor Kuakini stood 6 foot 6 inches tall and the Hulihee's imposing *koa*-wood doors were built to accommodate his height. The 3-foot-thick walls keep the high-ceilinged rooms cool in summer, and the splendid furnishings include a four-poster bed adorned with carved crowns and a custom-built chair made for the 6-foot 4-inch Princess Ruth Keelikolani.

The palace gardens lead down to a tiny beach with good snorkeling. On weekday afternoons, visitors may be treated to an impromptu show if a *hula halau* (hula school) is practicing in the garden.

▶▶ Mokuaikaua Church   152A3
Alii Drive
Open daily. Admission free

Edged by colorful plumeria and hibiscus blossoms, the church is set back from the road opposite the Hulihee Palace. The very first Christian church in the Hawaiian Islands was established on this site in 1820, and several simple thatched buildings followed before the present lava-rock structure was built in 1835.

Native *ohia* and *koa* woods were used for the interior, and the body of the church is ringed by a wooden gallery. Behind a *koa*-wood screen at the rear is a small historical display with views of Kailua-Kona and its group of thatched huts as it was *circa* 1845, plus a model of the brig *Thaddeus* which brought the first New England missionaries to the Islands.

The spire of Mokuaikaua Church rises behind the waterfront and Hulihee Palace

King Kamehameha's Kona Beach Hotel
En route to the Ahuena Heiau, take time to inspect the various exhibits on display in the lobby of King Kamehameha's Kona Beach Hotel. In amongst the artifacts and portraits of Hawaiian royalty, actual-size models of World Record Pacific Blue Marlin leap out from between the trophies and assorted memorabilia relating to the annual Hawaiian International Billfish Tournament, and there is also a collection of Hawaiian musical instruments.

■ **The ancient Hawaiians did not have a written language, but they could record detailed messages through petroglyphs, symbolic carvings etched in the smooth lava rock. Called *kii phaku*, "stone images," in Hawaiian, many thousands of petroglyphs are scattered throughout the Islands, but the greatest concentration is found on Hawaii, in the Hawaiian Volcanoes National Park.** ■

Watch your feet
When visiting petroglyph areas, take care not to step on the dozens of ancient carvings underfoot. It is also forbidden to take rubbings of the images except at specially designated areas such as at the Puako Petroglyph Preserve in the Mauna Lani resort.
Early morning or evening is the best time to see petroglyphs and to take photographs, as the light is at the right angle.

Rock-carvings The word "petroglyph" comes from the Greek *petros* for "rock," and *glyphe* "to carve." Though often described as rock art, petroglyphs were more important than mere decoration, since they were used to record special festivities, religious beliefs, and ancestor genealogies. Other images described day-to-day activities such as hunting, fishing and journeys, and important events including pregnancy, birth and death.

On the Hawaiian Islands, petroglyphs occur most commonly on smooth expanses of *pahoehoe* lava or on cliff faces and inside caves. Most were made with a sharp rock acting as a chisel and struck repeatedly with a heavy hammer stone, or by rubbing a blunt stone against the lava surface to break the natural glaze.

Carved messages

Petroglyph sites There is a good chance that sites where ancient Hawaiians gathered, or which were the focus of their journeys, will yield up petroglyphs. The historic 175-mile Ala Kahakai Trail from the northern tip of the Big Island at Upolu Point to the Volcano area passes through the bleak lava flows spreading down to the Kohala coast. Here, tucked in amongst the resorts and golf courses, are two important sites. At the petroglyph field near the King's Shops mall at the Waikoloa Beach Resort there are more than 9,000 carved images, some dating from as early as the 10th century. In the grounds of the Mauna Lani resort, interpretive signboards guide visitors around 3,000-plus stickmen, shapes and symbols at the Puako Petroglyph Preserve. But by far the greatest concentration of petroglyphs is found at the Puu Loa site in the Hawaii Volcanoes National Park, where a 2-mile trail takes in some 15,000 carvings dating from many different ages, with the greatest concentration of them at the Hill of Long Life.

Kohala Coast and the North

▶▶ **Anaehoomalu Beach** 152B4

Waikoloa Beach Resort, off HI-19 (23.8 miles north of Kailua-Kona)
Open site. Admission free

The sandy sweep of coconut-palm-fringed Anaehoomalu, bordering the Waikoloa resort complex, is an excellent family beach with calm water and good snorkeling. Helpful signboards list the various marine species that swim about in the bay, and there are rock pools to poke around in, too. Windsurfing equipment and sail boats can be rented here, and full rest-room and changing facilities are provided.

Visitors are welcome to explore several historic sites in the area. A series of ancient Hawaiian fishponds borders the beach, while there are dozens of mysterious petroglyphs spread over a lava area near the Waikoloa Beach Resort's King's Shops mall (see opposite).

▶▶▶ **Hapuna Beach** 152B4

Off HI-19 (31 miles north of Kailua-Kona)
Open site. Admission free

This is one of the Big Island's finest beaches (and so is often crowded), with a broad crescent of dazzling soft white sand backed by palm trees. It is also a renowned surfing spot when the waves are on form. At other times, the exceptionally clear water makes for interesting snorkeling around a rocky outcrop near the center of the beach, but watch out for boogie-boarders. The beach park facilities include a snack concession, barbecue grills, picnic tables, and showers.

▶▶▶ **Kona Village** *Luau* 152A4

Kona Village Resort, off HI-19 (15 miles north of Kailua-Kona)
Open: Friday only; reservations, tel: 808/325-5555
Admission charge: expensive

The Kona Village Resort hosts one of the state's best *luaus* (see pages 16–17). Make reservations in advance, and arrive in plenty of time to explore the grounds with their Polynesian-style accommodations. Visitors can check out the petroglyphs, or take a wander on the beach and generally work up a serious appetite for the feasting ahead. Do not miss the moment when the steaming *imu* (underground oven) is unwrapped. It is pure theater!

Kona Marina
Want to charter a boat, rent a kayak, book sail, snorkel and dive adventures, or organize a day or half-day's deep-sea sport fishing? Then drop by the Kona Marina at Honokohau harbor, just north of Kailua-Kona on the road to the airport, where all these activities can be arranged. The complex is a popular anchorage for yachts and also contains the Harbor House bar-restaurant, fishing and diving supply shops.

Body-boarding at Hapuna

Sailing on Anaehoomalu Bay

Parker Ranch Store

Next door to the Parker Ranch Visitor Center, would-be cowboys and girls can get kitted out *paniolo*-style from a selection of western clothes on sale in the Parker Ranch Store. Western-style shirts, hats, boots and belts come in all shapes and sizes, and there is the complete young person's gunfighter outfit in chic but impractical (unwashable) suede.

John Palmer Parker

Parker first came to Hawaii in 1809 aboard a whaling ship from Massachusetts. Glad to escape the ship's stench, he spent some time in the Islands, when he befriended Kamehameha I, before going back to sea. He returned to Hawaii for good in 1814, and worked for the king rounding up wild cattle (see pages 144–5) before ranching on lands leased from the crown. Parker was over 50 before he owned a single acre in his own right.

Parker Ranch, Mana Hale

▶▶▶ Waimea-Kamuela 152B4

Usually known as Kamuela (Hawaiian for "Samuel") to distinguish it from the town of Waimea on Kauai, this pleasant upcountry town is "Parker Ranch Central." A Western-style town, it lies at the heart of Hawaii's *paniolo* (cowboy) country, surrounded by lush pastures, rolling ranchlands and patches of forest. Its location in the foothills of the Kohala Mountains at a cool and comfortable 2,500 feet above sea-level makes it a delightful escape from the broiling coast, and there are several worthwhile attractions as well as the landscape.

The history of ranching on the Big Island is really the story of the Parker Ranch and is told in the **Parker Ranch Visitor Center▶▶▶** (Parker Ranch Shopping Center, HI-190. *Open:* daily 9–5. *Admission charge:* moderate; joint tickets with Parker Ranch Historic Homes, see below). From a 2-acre parcel of land allocated to John Palmer Parker for the sum of $10 in 1847, the Palmer spread has grown to 225,000 acres and is now one of the largest ranches in the U.S., stretching from the mountains to the ocean.

Artifacts, photographs and a short film explain both family and Big Island history. Informative signboards impart all sorts of anecdotes and descriptions of life on the ranch, and there is even a reconstructed back country *paniolo*'s hut made of weathered *koa*-wood shingles.

There are two very different family houses at the **Parker Ranch Historic Homes▶▶** (HI-190, half a mile south of town. *Open:* daily 10–5. *Admission charge:* moderate; joint tickets with Parker Ranch Visitor Center), each offering an intriguing slice of Parker family history. On the one hand is a reconstruction of John Palmer Parker's humble New-England-style wooden saltbox house, Mana Hale; on the other is gracious Puuopelu ("Rolling Hills"), the home of his son and heirs.

Visits begin at Puuopelu, founded by John Parker II in the mid-19th century. The single-story exterior is deceptively modest, for the spacious interior has inherited a theatrical elegance from its last owner, the actor-singer Richard Smart, a sixth-generation Parker who died in 1992. French and Italian furnishings and Asian porcelain set the stage for his art collection, which includes works by Degas, Renoir, and Dufy.

When John Palmer Parker Sr died, he left the ranch to his son, John II and grandson Samuel, who were total opposites. While John moved from the original Mana Hale homestead to Puuopelu and undertook the serious business of ranching, Sam stayed on at Mana Hale and had a thoroughly good time. Sam Parker was a friend of King David Kalakaua, and had a reputation for being a lavish and hospitable host. His cozy, four-room *koa*-wood cabin is now adorned with 19th-century photographs of the ranch-owner with his family and cronies (including the king), framed royal warrants bestowing legions of honors and titles, and family papers as well as solid, old-fashioned furniture.

John Palmer Parker's great-great-granddaughter, Harriet Solomon, and her husband, Albert, have been amassing artifacts and antiques for over 60 years, and the fruits of

The Kamuela Museum is full of surprises

their labors have taken over most of the first floor of their home. The resulting **Kamuela Museum**▶▶ (2 miles west of Kamuela on HI-19 at HI-250. *Open:* daily 8–5. *Admission charge:* inexpensive) is wonderfully eclectic and somewhat eccentric.

After stepping carefully past the giant stuffed bear that guards the reception hall, you may feel as if you have been let loose in an Aladdin's cave where dinosaur bones and ancient Hawaiian strangling cords jostle for attention with a gate key from the Iolani Palace and a pen filled with volcanic ash from Mount St. Helen's. There are Hawaiian hammer stones for smashing holes in war canoes, an 18th-century silver muffineer for sprinkling sugar on muffins, and then there is the tale of the Japanese pilot's sister who tracked down the machine-gun salvaged from her kamikaze brother's plane.

Mexican sun screen

Drive **North Kohala**

See map on pages 152–153.

A terrific trip, this 75-mile drive encompasses ancient Hawaiian sites, a beautiful north coast valley and a memorable upcountry excursion. You might stop in Waimea-Kamuela (see pages 172–3), and if you really want to get a feel for the Big Island's *paniolo* country, call Paniolo Riding Adventures (tel: 808/889-5354) in advance, and book a couple of hours' horseback-riding on an 11,000-acre mountain ranch.

Start at the intersection of HI-19 and HI-270, 10 miles west of Waimea-Kamuela, and take HI-270 north for half-a-mile to the **Puukohola Heiau** (*Open*: daily 7:30–4. *Admission charge*: donations). In response to a prophecy that he would rule the Islands if he constructed a mighty *luakini heiau* (sacrificial temple) dedicated to Kukailimoku, his ancestral war god, Kamehameha I had this huge lava stone platform built within a year. The inaugural sacrificial victim was his cousin and rival, Keoua. Continue north on HI-270 for 13 miles.

The **Lapakahi State Historical Park** (*Open*: daily 8–4. *Admission free*) is set amongst rocks and boulders, sun-bleached grasses and twisted-trunk *keiwe* trees on the sea shore. This old Hawaiian fishing village dates back around 600 years, and a self-guided tour leads around house sites and shrines, and past boulders that were used for salt-drying or covered in little holes to make *konane* "boards" for playing a Hawaiian version of Chinese checkers.

Another 6 miles north on the HI-270, there is a left turn for Upolu Airport and something of an offroad detour. At the entrance to the airfield turn left again and follow a graded dirt track for 2 miles along this rugged and remote stretch of coast, buffeted by wind and surf, until you come to the **Mookini Heiau**, one of the most complete and imposing of the ancient Hawaiian sites. Founded in the 13th century, it is believed to be one of the first *luakini* (sacrificial sites) in the Islands.

The stone-walled compound of **Akahi Aina Hanau** nearby was specifically chosen for its isolation when Kekuiapoiwa, Kamehameha's mother, gave birth to her child in

Beachfront Lapakahi

secret in the mid-1700s. Prophecies of the child's future power and success put his life in danger from his own father, and the child grew up in hiding in the Waipio Valley beyond the reach of the court. He was later named Kamehameha, the "Lonely One." Return to HI-270.

As the road continues north it enters the luxuriant north shore rainbelt, and there is an explosion of greenery, fruit trees and flowering plants along the roadside. Drive through the quiet plantation town of Hawi to the village of Kapaau (3½ miles), where the original of the famous **Kamehameha Statue** in Honolulu stands outside Kapaau's Kohala District Courthouse. Cast in Italy in 1880, the bronze statue was lost at sea on its way to the Islands, and was then rediscovered in the Falkland Islands years later, after a second cast had already been installed in Honolulu.

From Kapaau, continue east to Pololu Point at the end of the road

Puukohala Heiau

(5½ miles). There is a marvelous view from the lookout across the **Pololu Valley**, which cuts back into the interior from the north-coast sea cliffs. A steep (often muddy) trail leads down through screwpine and ironwood trees to the shore.

Retrace the road to Hawi and, just beyond Mile Marker 23, turn left onto HI-250. This wonderful upcountry route through the horse and cattle pastures of the **North Kohala Mountains** is a highlight of the drive. The rolling green landscape, full of peaks and knolls, patches of ironwood forest and not infrequent rainbows, becomes positively alpine as the road reaches its 3,564-foot crest before descending towards Waimea-Kamuela. From the intersection of HI-250 and HI-19 it is 10 miles back to where you started.

Pololu Valley pali

175

*Enigmatic stone
stacks on the shore*

Scenic detour
There is a pretty detour off
the main Belt Road (HI-19)
up the Hamakua Coast
north of Hilo.
Approximately 7 miles
north of Hilo, just beyond a
pedestrian overpass, look
for a blue sign' on the right
marked "Scenic Route 4
miles long." Exit from HI-19
here and follow the coastal
loop road as it winds over a
series of streams and
through lush tropical
jungle, past the Old Yellow
Church and Hawaii
Tropical Botanical Garden
until it rejoins HI-19.

*Giant bamboo in the
Hawaiian Tropical
Botanical Gardens*

Hamakua Coast

▶▶ Akaka Falls State Park   153D4
*13 miles north of Hilo on HI-19, then 5 miles west on
HI-220, Akaka Falls Road*
Open: daily. Admission free

Tucked into the rainforest behind the coast, the Akaka's
combination of gorgeous tropical plants and plashing
waterfalls exemplifies picture-postcard Hawaii. A circular
trail (20 minutes) plunges down into a valley planted with
philodendrons, heliconias and torch gingers, orchids and
great stands of bamboo. From the 100-foot Kahuna Falls,
the path winds on to Akaka, a white-water cascade which
thunders more than 420 feet down the rock face to a caul-
dron of black volcanic rock below. It is particularly impressive after heavy rains. The village of Akaka Falls, with an
assortment of shops and places to eat, and a flea market,
is just below the park, its torpor somehow undisturbed by
the streams of tourists.

▶▶▶ Hawaii Tropical Botanical Garden   153D4
Off HI-19, 8 miles north of Hilo
Open: daily 9–4:30. Admission charge: moderate

These magnificent tropical gardens carpet 45 acres of a
lush valley stretching back from the ocean's edge at
Onomea Bay. Within the rainforest, native birds and
brightly plumed South American macaws add a flash of
color. More than 2,000 different plant species contribute
to the eye-catching array of heliconias, bromeliads,
mango trees, coconut groves and tropical fruits. Special
features include medicinal plants, a water-lily lake and
Japanese *koi* ponds.

Visitors park at the reception center in the converted
yellow church building on the Scenic Route (see panel);
transportation is provided to the gardens. Bring mosquito
repellent; umbrellas are provided on rainy days.

▶ Honokaa   152C5

At one time the old plantation town of Honokaa looked
like a spent force, but efforts to pull Mamane Street, the
main street, back into shape are paying off. Behind
Western-style raised pavements, old-fashioned, false-
fronted shops have been occupied by small businesses.
Browsers can while away a half-hour or so in a handful of
curio shops, and the Bad Ass Macadamia Nut Company
(which also produces coffee) welcomes visitors to its
local candy factory.

▶▶ **Waipio Valley** 152C5

HI-240, 10 miles northwest of Honokaa
Open site. Tours, Mon–Sat 8 or 9–4 (reservations
advised). Admission free. Tours: expensive

The verdant and fertile Waipio ("Curving Water") Valley, inhabited for over 1,000 years, is a classic ancient Hawaiian *ahupua*, a triangular wedge of land which contained all the elements needed to sustain viable communities—arable land, timber forest, fresh water from the mountains and fish from the sea.

From a mile-wide black-sand beach, the valley floor stretches back 6 miles into the 2,000-foot-high *pali* (cliffs), between towering green walls streaked with waterfalls. Once the most cultivated valley on the island, it was home to several thousand Hawaiian villagers who planted taro patches, yams, bananas, breadfruit and coconut groves here. There was an abundance of wild game and good fishing, and fishponds were constructed to farm *opae* (shrimp) and mullet. Today, only a very few families remain, still cultivating taro and tending gardens lush with mangoes and guavas. No traces of the original settlement site are visible.

There is a valley lookout just north of Kukuihaele, at the head of a twisting track (suitable for four-wheel drives only) to the valley floor. Waipio Valley Shuttle (tel: 808/775-7121) offers mini-bus tours down to the valley, and there are mule-drawn wagon rides with Waipio Valley Wagon Tours (tel: 808/775-9518); both tours last 1½ hours. It is also possible to hike down the steep trail (about 25 minutes), but the journey back is tough.

Trail to the Waimanu Valley
One of the finest hikes in the Islands is the 12-mile round-trip trek from Waipio to the neighboring uninhabited Waimanu Valley. It crosses the floor of the Waipio Valley and then there is an arduous climb up the 1,200-foot cliffs on a winding, switchback path, which continues up and down numerous ravines to Waimanu. There are fabulous views, and wild, "Jurassic Park" landscape but only experienced and well-equipped hikers should attempt the trek.

177

Lush Waipio Valley

■ **Hawaii offers some of the best deep-sea sport fishing in the world, and nothing can compete with the Big Island's Kona coast for magnificent Pacific blue marlin. Kailua-Kona is host to the prestigious annual Hawaiian International Billfish Tournament, the father of amateur sport-fishing competitions in the Pacific, attracting anglers from far and wide every summer.** ■

Neighbor Islands' sport fishing

Kona may boast the biggest tournament fishing, but all the Islands offer sport fishing, mainly off their leeward shores. The rich fishing grounds off Oahu's Waianae Coast have been popular with the Hawaiians for centuries; charter boats are available from Pokai Bay and from Honolulu's Kewalo Basin. Kauai's charter fleet puts out year-round from Nawiliwili and reels in spectacular yellowfin in spring. Penguin Banks, off Molokai's West End, is legendary; and from Maui, boats head out from Lahaina and Maalaea Bay for the waters around Kahoolawe.

Fishing for ahi

Ideal conditions The Kona coast has two of the prime ingredients for great deep-sea fishing: it has the calm seas that are generally found on the sheltered leeward sides of the Islands; and there is easy access to deep water—anglers can reach deep-water fishing grounds at 1,000–2,000 fathoms a relatively short distance off shore. Hawaii's main sport-fishing season lasts from spring to autumn, hitting a peak at the July/August tournament time. Marlin fishing is possible year-round, but the sea can be pretty rough during the winter months.

A wealth of fish Pacific blue marlin, called *ahu* by the Hawaiians, is the king of catches, with record-breaking billfish weighing in at over 1,000 pounds, but several other game fish are also up for grabs in local waters. Yellowfin tuna (*ahi*) average between 25 and 100 pounds; a 300-pound individual is not impossible. Dolphinfish (*mahi-mahi*), not to be confused with true dolphins which are mammals not fish, can weigh around 70 pounds. There are also swordfish, skipjack tuna (*aku*), jack crevelle (*ulua*), and the wahoo (*ono*).

Boats and tackle Plenty of professional deep-sea fishing charter boats operate out of the Big Island's Honokohau harbor, north of Kailua-Kona. They offer full-day (eight-hour) and half-day (four-hour) charters for individuals, or "share boats" for an average of four to six anglers. Tackle is provided, but not necessarily lunch. The catch is generally left for the crew, but any potentially record-breaking fish will be taken to Kailua Pier for a ceremonial weighing-in at the tournament fish scale, which will record weights of up to one ton!

178

TRAVEL FACTS

By air
The major gateways to Hawaii include the following:

● Oahu
Hawaii's major airport is **Honolulu International** (tel: 808/836-6411), about a five-hour flight from West Coast cities and a 20-minute drive from Waikiki. If you're flying from Honolulu to another island, you'll need to locate one of the separate inter-island terminals (one for Aloha Airlines and Hawaiian Airlines and one for Island Air and Mahalo Airlines) to the left of the main terminal as you come out of the exit. There is a free WikiWiki Shuttle bus to take you to and from the inter-island terminals; however, it is only an easy five-minute walk between the international and the inter-island terminals.

● Maui
Maui's efficient **Kahului Airport** (tel: 808/872-3803), in Maui's central town of Kahului, has a new modern terminal. Maui's other airport, the **Kapalua–West Maui Airport** (call either Island Air or Hawaiian Airlines) capably handles the traffic it gets. For visitors to West Maui, landing at the Kapalua facility is the easiest way to arrive. It saves about an hour's drive from the Kahului airport. The tiny town of **Hana** in East Maui also has

Frequent flights to the Hawaiian Islands from several U.S. cities

an airstrip (tel: 808/248-8208), but it is only serviced by one commuter airline and one charter airline.

● Kauai
On Kauai, visitors have a choice between the recently expanded **Lihue Airport** (tel: 808/246-1400) on the east side of the island, and **Princeville Airport** (tel: 808/826-3040) near the north shore.

● The Big Island of Hawaii
Those flying to the Big Island generally land at one of two fields. Kona's **Keahole Airport** (tel: 808/329-2484), on the west side, best serves Kailua-Kona, Keauhou and the Kohala Coast. **Hilo International Airport** (tel: 808/933-4782), formerly General Lyman Field, is also a large, new airport but is more appropriate for those going to the east side.

● Lanai and Molokai
I anai (tel: 808/565-6757) and **Molokai** (tel: 808/567-6140) airports are centrally located on those islands. Both are small rural airports that can handle only a limited number of flights and planes per day.

Carriers Carriers serving the Honolulu International Airport include **America West** (tel: 800/235-9292); **American** (tel: 800/433-73000; **Continental** (tel: 800/525-0280); **Delta** (tel: 800/221-1212); **Hawaiian** (tel: 800/221-1212); **Northwest** (tel: 800/225-2525);

181

TWA (tel: 800/221-2000); and **United** (tel: 800/241-6522). Many flights origi- nate in Los Angeles and San Francisco, but it is also possible to fly direct from Dallas, Chicago, St. Louis, New York, Seattle, Minneapolis, San Diego, and other gateways. United Airlines—which handles some 50 percent of the airline traffic to Hawaii—flies directly into the Big Island's Keahole Airport, Maui's Kahului Airport, and Kauai's Lihue Airport.

By sea
Aside from working a passage to the islands on a cargo ship or crewing for an ocean-going yacht, the only way to get to Hawaii by sea is with a cruise ship, although in practice the number of Hawaii-bound cruises is limited. The San Francisco-based Royal Cruise Line (tel: 415/956-7200) operates winter cruises lasting between eight and 16 days which visit the islands of Maui, Kauai, and Hawaii. Cunard (tel: 800/221-4770) and Holland America (tel: 800/426- 0327) include stops in Hawaii on their longer Pacific cruises. Another cruise line that visits the Hawaiian Islands is the Royal Caribbean

An aloha *welcome*

Cruise Line (tel: 800/327-6700). Within the islands, American Hawaii Cruises operates loop cruises lasting seven days and calling at several islands within the group (see By boat, pages 184).

Customs
The State Department of Agriculture maintains strict regulations on the import of live plants and animals to Hawaii by visitors. Dogs and cats must undergo a 120-day quarantine period. For more information, contact the **Plant Quarantine 'Branch** (tel: 808/586-0844) or **Animal Quarantine Station** (tel: 808/483-7171).

Help with directions

Climate and when to go

The main Hawaiian Islands all lie within the tropics, so temperature variations are slight from season to season. The charts below show some of the variations between islands.Average summer (May–September) temperatures range from 73°F to 88°F. In winter (October–April), expect an average of 65°F to 83°F and snow on the 13,000-foot peaks of the Big Island.

Even in the height of summer, the islands are generally fanned by cooling northeastern trade winds. Occasionally the wind direction shifts to the south, bringing muggy "Kona conditions" and the possibility of tropical storms.

Hawaii's wet season lasts from December to February, though rain showers on the sheltered leeward coasts tend to be fairly short-lived. Throughout the year, the islands' windward coasts (north and east) are wetter and greener than those on the south and west.

There is sunbathing weather in Hawaii year-round, especially on the sunnier, drier leeward sides of the islands, where most of the major resort areas are situated. Golf is played all year, too.

Diving and snorkeling are best in the summer when the ocean is calm and the water clear, while surfers are likely to find the biggest waves in winter. Winter is also the whale-watching season, when humpback whales from Alaska venture south to breed and calve in Hawaiian waters between November and March.

Public holidays

Hawaii observes all the major public holidays, plus it has a few special ones of its own:

- **New Year's Day** January 1
- **Martin Luther King Day** 3rd Monday in January
- **President's Day** 3rd Monday in February
- **Prince Kuhio Day (Hawaii)** March 26
- **Lei Day (Hawaii)** May 1
- **Memorial Day** Last Monday in May
- **Kamehameha Day (Hawaii)** June 11

- **Independence Day** July 4
- **Admission Day (Hawaii)** 3rd Friday in August
- **Labor Day** 1st Monday in September
- **Veterans' Day** November 11
- **Thanksgiving Day** 4th Thursday in November
- **Christmas Day** December 25

Time differences

Hawaii observes Hawaiian Standard Time, which is two hours behind Pacific Standard Time and five hours behind Eastern Standard Time. However, Hawaii does not observe daylight saving time, so you should add an extra hour to all the above time differences between April and October

Money matters

All the major credit cards (American Express, Carte Blanche, Diners Club, Discover, MasterCard and Visa) are widely accepted throughout the state. But if you plan to visit the more remote parts of the islands, it is a good idea to carry a certain amount of cash for purchases in small, upcountry towns as well as for out-of-the-way bed-and-breakfast establishments.

Local taxes

A 4½ percent sales tax is added on to many "luxury" items including some foodstuffs for sale in supermarkets.

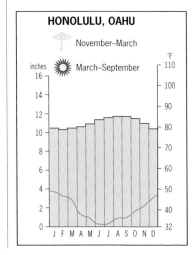

HONOLULU, OAHU

Local taxes are also added to car-rental bills and accommodations charges.

Souvenirs to bring home

The most popular souvenir of Hawaii is probably the Aloha shirt, on sale everywhere.

High-quality genuine Hawaiian-made articles of the arts and crafts variety are available throughout the Islands. Museum gift shops are often a good place to look for items such as *kukui*-nut jewelry, quilting kits and koa-wood carvings The Mission Houses Museum also has inexpen-

Regatta racing off Diamond Head, Oahu

sive prints produced from period plates on the original mission press.

Food from afar makes a good souvenir. Macadamia nuts are a Hawaiian specialty, and come in many guises, both sweet and savory. Jams, jellies and preserves made from exotic fruits such as guavas, pineapples and mangoes are another idea, while coffee blends grown on the Big Island's Kona Coast are light to pack and will bring back many memories.

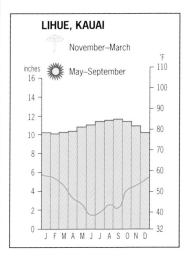

LIHUE, KAUAI

November–March

May–September

inches / °F

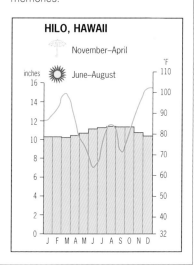

HILO, HAWAII

November–April

June–August

inches / °F

By air

Island-hopping by air is a way of life in Hawaii. It is quick and easy, and most flights take only between 20 and 30 minutes.

Hawaiian Airlines (U.S. mainland, tel: 1-800/367-5320) and **Aloha Air** (U.S. mainland, tel: 1-800/367-5250) each offer more than 200 jet services daily to and from all the main islands.

Mahalo Air (tel: 808/833-5555) flies to Oahu, Kauai, Maui and Hawaii with twin-engined prop planes;

Air Molokai (tel: 808/553-3636) has daily flights from Oahu to Kaunakakai and Kaluapapa on Molokai, and to both Kahului and Hana on Maui; while Aloha Airlines subsidiary **Island Air** (tel: 808/484-2222) serves smaller commuter airports such as Kapalua on Maui and Kauai's Princeville, as well as Molokai and Lanai.

Oahu
- Main airport: Honolulu International.
- Hawaiian Airlines (tel: 808/838-1555).
- Aloha Airlines (tel: 808/484-1111).

Kauai
- Main airport: Lihue.
- Commuter airport: Princeville.
- Hawaiian Airlines (tel: 808/245-1813).
- Aloha Airlines (tel: 808/245-3691).

Molokai
- Main airport: Hoolehua (Kaunakakai).
- Commuter airport: Kalaupapa.
- Hawaiian Airlines (tel: 808/553-3644).

Taking to the water

Maui
- Main airport: Kahului.
- Commuter airports: Hana (East Maui) and Kapalua (West Maui).
- Hawaiian Airlines (tel: 808/871-6132).
- Aloha Airlines (tel: 808/244-9071).

Lanai
- Main airport: Lanai City.
- Hawaiian Airlines (tel: 808/565-7281).

Hawaii
- Main airports: Hilo International and Keahole-Kona (Kailua-Kona).
- Commuter airport: Waimea-Kohala.
- Hawaiian Airlines (tel: 808/326-5615).
- Aloha Airlines (tel: 808/935-5771).

By boat

The rough seas of the open ocean around the Islands are not conducive to ferry traffic. However, two boat services ply the relatively sheltered waters between Lahaina on the West Maui coast and the islands of Molokai and Lanai.

Cruise ships are better suited to the conditions. **American Hawaii Cruises** (tel: 1-800/765-7000 or on the mainland, 1-800/944-5988) offers regular seven-day loop cruises out of Honolulu which visit four ports in Maui, Hawaii and Kauai.

Car rental

The best way to explore the islands is by car. Charges for rental cars on Hawaii are higher than those available on the mainland. Fly-drive deals, and some hotel packages that combine

accommodations with car rental, offer good value.

All the major rental agencies are represented on the larger islands; on Molokai the choice is limited to Budget and Dollar, and on Lanai only Dollar operates.

To rent a car in advance, contact:
- **Alamo** (tel: 1-800/327-9633)
- **Avis** (tel: 1-800/331-1212)
- **Budget** (tel: 1-800/527-7000)
- **Dollar** (tel: 1-800/800-4000)
- **Hertz** (tel: 1-800/654-3131)
- **National** (tel: 1-800/2327-7368)

Documentation Drivers must be over 21 and have held a full, valid license for a minimum of one year. Some form of Collision Damage Waiver (CDW) is required when renting a vehicle, and visitors should read the insurance stipulations very carefully. If you do not have a major credit card, a sizeable cash deposit will be required.

Rules, regulations and road conditions The maximum speed limit is 55 m.p.h. unless otherwise stated. Speed limits in urban areas vary between 20 and 40 m.p.h., and they are also kept deliberately low in some country areas even when the road conditions are good. The local police set speed traps on long, straight stretches of road a short distance out of town.

Throughout the state, the main highway system is well-maintained and as efficient as the constraints of local geography will allow. However, the roads are largely two-lane, and local drivers like to take their time, so leave plenty of leeway when planning a trip.

There are certain stretches of road in the Hawaiian Islands that are off-limits to drivers of rental cars. Whatever the local map says, check and follow the details on the map supplied by the rental compay before setting out on an island drive. For instance, a section of the marked "road" shown on some maps west of Hana on Maui's south coast is actually a rocky and narrow dirt-track out of bounds to drivers of rental cars, and any accidents or damages incurred in such an area are not covered by the rental companies' insurance policies.

Public transportation
Local bus services provided by Oahu's The Bus and the Big Island's Hele-On bus are cheap, efficient and offer a comprehensive network of routes covering most of the two islands' important towns, attractions and resort destinations.

The other islands are less well served. Kauai has a peak-hour service, the Iniki Bus, which runs up the east coast from Lihue, and west to Waimea. Maui has airport and local resort shuttles, but no integrated island-wide transport system. Neither Molokai nor Lanai has any public transport at all. (See individual island entries for further details.)

Tours
Tour companies abound in Hawaii, and transportation comes in all shapes and sizes, ranging from air-conditioned coaches or minibuses to glass-bottomed boats, helicopters and even bicycles. Hotels and activity desks in main resort areas are a good place to check out the options available.

For the most extensive range of full- or half-day bus tours, try **Polynesian Adventure Tours** (tel: 808/833-3000). Based in Oahu, the company has local island branches in Kauai, Maui and Hawaii and also organizes day trips to the Neighbor Islands.

Sightseeing, snorkel and dive cruises are a specialty of Maui, Lanai and the Big Island. On Kauai, boat trips offer stunning views of the Na Pali coast. And in winter, do not miss the opportunity to go whale-watching.

The best islands for **helicopter tours** are Kauai, Maui and Hawaii. There is eye-popping scenery along Kauai's Na Pali coast and Waimea Canyon; Maui boasts the world's largest dormant volcano, Haleakala; and the Big Island's volcanoes offer both fire and ice.

Local cycle operators on Maui and Hawaii have perfected the almost effortless **bicycle tour.** They specialize in downhill excursions, delivering safety-kitted clients and mountain bikes to upcountry locations, then shepherding them back down.

185

Floral phones

Media

The state's top-selling daily papers are *The Honolulu Advertiser* and *The Honolulu Star Bulletin*. Mainland U.S. papers are available on newsstands, as are current domestic and international magazines and periodicals.

Free tourist publications are everywhere and jam-packed with discount vouchers for attractions, activities and restaurants. *This Week* has individual Oahu, Maui, Kauai and Hawaii editions covering local events, attractions, entertainments and dining, plus maps, tour suggestions and short local-interest features.

Post

Post offices, found in all major towns, are generally open Monday–Friday 8:30–5, and Saturday 8–noon. Stamps can also be bought in hotels.

Mail boxes on parade

Telephones and faxes

Public pay phones are found on many streets and public areas, and also in restaurants, bars and hotel lobbies. The area code for the state of Hawaii is 808. It is not needed if you are dialing a local number on the same island, but use it when making inter-island calls or calls to Hawaii from outside the state.

Telephone calls made from hotel rooms are generally subject to a service charge, which can add considerably to the basic cost. Some hotels levy a small daily room charge that covers any local calls.

It is cheaper to make calls in the evening and on weekends. Inter-island calls are considered long distance.

Most hotels offer fax service; charges are determined according to the length of the document. Incoming faxes are cheaper, if not free.

Language

English and Hawaiian are the two official state languages, though you are unlikely to hear much Hawaiian being spoken, except perhaps at a traditional church service or a local festival. It is a soft rolling language, both interesting and refreshing to the ear. Pidgin (see page 28) is much used by the *kamaainas* (locals), who do not necessarily welcome any attempts by *malihini* (newcomers) to mimic them. Japanese is widely spoken, and it is not unusual to hear Vietnamese and Chinese being spoken around town, or Filipino in rural areas.

Emergencies

Crime

Hawaii is the land of *aloha*, but like anywhere else in the world it is not crime-free. The greatest problem for tourists is petty theft. Car break-ins are fairly common, and visitors should be on their guard. Cars parked at attractions or beaches are popular targets, so remove all valuables before locking up.

It pays to take a few elementary and commonsense precautions:
• always carry money and valuables in an inside pocket or in a bag with a secure strap
• never carry your money and travel documents in the same wallet or bag
• never leave valuables visible in a parked car or unattended on a beach
• do not flaunt valuable jewelry
• pay particular attention to expensive cameras and video cameras

Violent crime directed at tourists is relatively rare, but Waikiki has had its problems. After dark, there is a fair amount of street prostitution here. Avoid unlit streets and alleyways, and do not walk alone.

Despite the determined efforts of the state authorities to stamp out local marijuana-growing, visitors, especially the young, may be approached by drug dealers hawking *pakalolo* (pot). Buying and smoking it is illegal.

Emergency telephone numbers

• Dial: 911 for police, ambulance or fire service.

Lost property

Report lost or stolen traveler's checks and credit cards to the police as well as to a bank displaying the logo of the issuing company or direct to the credit card company's emergency telephone number.

If items have been left on a plane or bus, report the loss to the airline company or bus operator as soon as possible. If the item has been found, it will be held at the appropriate lost and found property office for collection.

Any lost or stolen valuables covered by insurance should be reported to the police and a copy of the report obtained for insurance purposes.

State patrol

Medical treatment

Hotel reception desks will be able to help with a list of local doctors, or look under "Physicians" in the telephone directory, where you will also be able to find dentists and hospitals listed.

In a real emergency, call 911.

Life's a beach

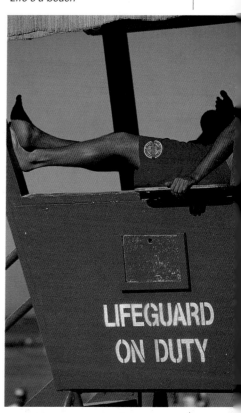

LIFEGUARD
ON DUTY

Camping

The majority of Hawaii's camping facilities are operated by the federal, state and county park services, and camping permits are required.

Visitors planning a camping vacation, or even a couple of nights under canvas in a state or national park, should contact the local offices listed below for full details of the camping facilities available and the necessary permits.

State parks do not charge a fee for camping permits, but there is a charge for tent camping at some county parks. In general, the length of a stay is limited; the maximum period allowed is between three and seven days.

In addition to campgrounds, both Maui's Haleakala National Park and the Hawaii Volcanoes National Park on the Big Island also offer cabin accommodations for visitors, as does Kokee State Park on Kauai, all three with spectacular scenery.

Oahu
● Division of State Parks, Oahu District P.O. Box 621, Punchbowl Street, Honolulu HI 96809 (tel: 808/587-0300).
● Honolulu City & County Department of Parks and Recreation 650 S. King Street, Honolulu HI 96813 (tel: 808/523-4525).

Kauai
● Division of State Parks, Kauai District 3060 Eiwa Street, Lihue HI 96766 (tel: 808/241-3444).
● Kauai County Division of Parks & Recreation 4193 Hardy Street, Lihue HI 96766 (tel: 808/241-6670).

Molokai
● State Parks (see Maui below).
● Maui County Department of Parks and Recreation P.O. Box 1055, Kaunakakai HI 96748 (tel: 808/553-3204).

Maui
● Division of State Parks, Maui District 54 S. High Street, Wailuku HI 96793 (tel: 808/243-5354).

Hawaii
● Division of State Parks, Hawaii District P.O. Box 936, 75 Aupuni Street, Hilo HI 96721-0936 (tel: 808/961-7200).
● Hawaii County Department of Parks and Recreation 25 Aupuni Street, Hilo HI 96720 (tel: 808/933-4200).

Warning signs

STRONG CURRENT

Beaches

Ask people why they vacation in Hawaii and most of them will tell you they go there for the beaches. The 50th state has some of the most beautiful stretches of sand and surf in the world. What can be found in the way of facilities, however, will very greatly from place to place. Most areas have fresh running water, bath and changing rooms and outside showers. Picnic tables are less common. Popular areas offer equipment rental for windsurfing, snorkeling, sailing and para-sailing. Hawaii's beaches are clean compared to many coastal areas and visitors are asked to help keep them that way. All beaches are open to the public.

Oahu's Waikiki beach is nearly synonymous with Hawaii. Stretching from the Hilton Hawaiian Village to the foot of Diamond Head, the strip still ranks as the premier place to soak up the sun. Oahu's other sandy seashores include the north shore's Sunset Beach, famous in the surfing world, Kailua Beach Park, home to international windsurfing competitions, and Makapuu Beach near Sea Life Park with some of the best bodysurfing to be found in the state.

On **Hawaii Island**, Hapuna Beach has sparkling white sand, while near the southeastern town of Kalapana, there are green- and black-sand beaches. Newest beaches in the state are stretches of black sand formed by the lava from the active Kilauea volcano flowing into the sea.

Maui's Kaanapali Beach, close to a number of luxury hotels, is a fine place to spot movie stars and other celebrities. Hookipa Beach Park, near the town of Paia, is a windsurfing mecca.

Molokai has the sensational 3-mile long Popohaku Beach, the largest white-sand beach in the state. On **Lanai**, Hulopoe Beach offers excellent snorkeling.

Kauai's south shore has Poipu Beach Park, popular with bodysurfers as well as sunbathers. On the opposite side of the island is Lumahai, a small beach rimmed with black lava and vegetation that proved the perfect setting for the movie *South Pacific*.

Keep off the reefs

Health

The Hawaiian sun is hot, hot, hot, so be sure to take it easy, spending only a short time on the beach in the first few days. Use a high-factor sun-protection lotion, and make especially sure that children are well protected.

Mosquitoes are a nuisance, and although less active in the cooler winter months, they can still prove a major irritant in rain forests. This is a warning not just for hikers, but also for anyone visiting rain forest gardens, waterfalls and other warm, damp beauty spots. Keep a supply of mosquito repellent handy, and remember to use it before you set out.

In the water, beware of the coral; cuts can become infected. Also, you can easily damage the coral of the reefs by walking on them.

Occasionally, Portuguese men-of-war jellyfish drift into the shallows. They can deliver a nasty sting. Vinegar is one of the most effective neutralizers for mild attacks, although more serious stings should be treated by a doctor.

Pharmacies Drugstores are normally open 9–9.

Hiking

Hawaii offers marvelous hiking in some of the most spectacular landscapes in the world. Trails (many of which are demanding and strenuous) are usually well maintained and

marked, but it is important to be prepared for weather conditions and to give the park rangers an itinerary if you are trekking into back-country.

Maps and hiking information are available from the **Department of Land and Natural Resources, Division of Forestry and Wildlife,** 1151 Punchbowl Street, Honolulu, HI 96813 (tel: 808/548-2861; Public Information office, tel: 808/587-0320), or from the state parks information

Stock up on film to capture the moment

centers (see Camping, page 188).

Always carry sunscreen, drinking water and mosquito repellent. Wet weather gear is a must for overnight campers, and take warm clothing for the high altitudes of the Hawaii Volcanoes National Park, Mauna Kea,

Treat the Hawaiian sun with respect

and Haleakala, where it may snow.

Opening times
- **Banks** Mon–Thur 10–3, Fri 10–5.30.
- **Pharmacies** Daily 9–9 (some 24 hours).
- **Offices** Mon–Fri 8 or 8:30–5:30 or 6.
- **Post offices** Mon–Fri 8:30–5, Sat 8–noon.
- **Shops** Supermarkets, Mon–Sat 8 or 9–9, Sun 9–7; shopping malls and tourist areas, Mon–Sat 10–9, Sun 10–6; country areas, Mon–Sat 8 or 8:30–6, Sun closed.

Places of worship
Hawaii's multicultural society means that most local communities are served by churches of several denominations including Protestant, Catholic and Buddhist places of worship.

Visitors with disabilities
The **Hawaii State Commission on Persons with Disabilities** distributes a guide to accommodations and facilities for travelers who use wheelchairs. The guide also lists beaches and shopping malls offering reasonable access and restrooms for people with disabilities. The guide is available free (small charge if sent by mail) from the Commission at 919 Ala Moana Boulevard, Suite 101, Honolulu, HI 96813 (tel: 808/586-8121).

Books on Hawaii
Hawaii by James A. Michener gives a historical perspective of the Islands as the background to a novel. *Hawaii: An Uncommon History,* by Edward Joesting, gives a behind-the-scenes look at the factual side of some of the same events in the Michener novel. Captain James Cook's *A Voyage to the Pacific Ocean* could be considered the first guidebook to the Islands. More recent history comes to life in Robert Louis Stevenson's *Travels in Hawaii,* while *A Residency of Twenty-one Years in the Sandwich Islands* by Hiram Bingham records the details of missionary life in the early years. *Chanting the Universe,* by John Charlot, examines Hawaiian culture through its poetry and chants, and the ancient Hawaiians gods and goddesses are discussed in *Hawaiian Mythology* by Martha Warren Beckwith. *Hawaii's Birds* by the Hawaii Audubon Society is perfect for the bird-watcher.

The balloon goes up at Oahu's Aloha stadium

The head office of the Hawaii Visitors Bureau in Waikiki is open to visitors Mon–Fri 8–4:30. The HVB also maintains local representative offices on most of the main islands, as well as regional offices on the U.S. mainland and many countries overseas.

The bureau publishes an official state travel guide, *The Islands of Aloha,* as well as various brochures, a comprehensive calendar of events, an accommodations guide (which includes everything from the distance of a property from the beach to its amenities), and a restaurant-listing containing one-line descriptions.

There are more than 3,000 members of the bureau, including hotels, car-rental companies, restaurants, cafés and a number of tourist attractions.

Members can easily be identified by the distinctive Hawaiian Visitor Bureau logo, a Hawaiian warrior wearing the traditional red and yellow feather cape and helmet.

- **Oahu** Hawaii Visitors Bureau Main Office, 2270 Kalakaua Avenue, 7th Floor, Honolulu HI 96815, tel: 808/923-1811; fax 808/922-8991.

- **Kauai** Hawaii Visitors Bureau, Lihue Plaza Building, Suite 207, 3016 Umi Street, Lihue HI 96766, tel: 808/245-3971; fax 808/246-9235.

- **Molokai** Molokai Visitors Association, P.O. Box 960, Kaunakakai HI 96748, tel: 808/553-3876; fax 808/553-5288.

- **Maui** Maui Visitors Bureau, P.O. Box 580, 1727 Wili Pa Loop, Wailuku HI 96793 tel: 808/244-3530; fax 808/244-1337.

- **Hawaii**
Hilo: Hawaii Visitors Bureau, 250 Keawe Street, Hilo HI 96720, tel: 808/961-5797; fax 808/961-2126.
Kona: Hawaii Visitors Bureau, 75-5719 West Alii Drive, Kailua-Kona HI 96740, tel: 808/329-7787; fax 808/326-7563.

Hawaii Visitors Bureau on the Mainland
- **New York** Empire State Building, Room 1827, 350 Fifth Avenue, New York NY 10118 tel: 212/947-0717; fax 212/947-0725.
For information about other Hawaii Visitors Bureau offices on the mainland, contact the New York office.

Festival finery

ACCOMMODATIONS

From beachfront condominiums to golf-course resorts, and from chic little downtown boutique hotels to upcountry bed and breakfasts, Hawaii offers visitors a wealth of choice for accommodations. Room rates are adjusted according to season, hitting a peak from mid-December to March (high season), and dropping around 30 (sometimes even 50) percent at other times. Always check for discounted rates (particularly at weekends) and packages that include car rental, discounts on meals, entertainments and sightseeing tours. The local Outrigger hotel chain, for instance, offers a special Fifty-Plus program which cuts 20 percent off room rates for senior citizens.

Many hotels have rooms in several price ranges. In the lists below, accommodations have been classified according to price categories based on a daily double occupancy rate for a standard room:

- **budget ($) = up to $85**
- **moderate ($$) = $85–$160**
- **expensive ($$$) = over $160**

Double rooms often sleep more than two people, so children can easily be accommodated with their parents at no extra cost. A Hawaiian State tax of 4.17 percent and a 6 percent room tax are added to hotel bills.

Bed and breakfast accommodations are becoming increasingly popular in the Islands. Several agencies provide a centralized booking facility for bed and breakfast operators throughout the state. These include:

- **All Islands Bed & Breakfast** 823 Kainui Drive, Kailua HI 96734 (tel: 808/263-2342; fax 808/263-0308).
- **Bed & Breakfast – Hawaii** P.O. Box 449, Kapaa HI 96746 (tel: 808/822-7771 or 1-800/733-1632; fax 808/822-2723).
- **Hawaii's Best Bed & Breakfasts** P.O. Box 563, Kamuela HI 96743 (tel: 808/885-4550 or 1-800/262-9912; fax 808/885-0559).

OAHU

Honolulu and Waikiki

Aston at the Waikiki Banyan ($$) 201 Ohua Avenue, Honolulu HI 96815 (tel: 808/922-0555). Condominium with 300 spacious family-style units in an 860-unit complex just five minutes' walk from the beach. Pool, tennis courts, barbecue facilities and a children's playground.

Aston Waikiki Beach Tower ($$$) 2470 Kalakaua Avenue, Honolulu HI 96815 (tel: 808/926-6400). Luxurious condominium resort with 140 spacious and comfortable suites. Full kitchens and *lanais* (verandas). Pool, jet spa, sauna.

Aston Waikiki Beachside ($$–$$$) 2452 Kalakaua Avenue, Honolulu HI 96815 (tel: 808/931-2100). Attractive boutique hotel with 79 rooms across the street from the beach. Welcoming atmosphere.

Aston Waikiki Circle ($$) 2464 Kalakaua Avenue, Honolulu HI 96815 (tel: 808/923-1571). At the heart of Waikiki, with 104 compact but comfortable rooms across from the beach (yet only just out of $-bracket).

Colony Surf Hotel ($$–$$$) 2895 Kalakaua Avenue, Honolulu HI 96815 (tel: 808/923-5751). At the Diamond Head end of Waikiki. Beachfront condominium of 90 units with views, and home to the excellent Michel's restaurant.

Halekulani ($$$) 2199 Kalia Road, Honolulu HI 96815-1988 (tel: 808/923-2311). One of the original Waikiki beach hotels founded at the turn of the century, graciously rebuilt in the 1930s, and massively expanded to 456 luxurious rooms and suites in the 1980s. Still elegant and much sought-after. Fabulous restaurants, rarified atmosphere; pool, tennis, spa.

Hawaii Prince Hotel Waikiki ($$$) 100 Holomoana Street, Honolulu HI 96815 (tel: 808/956-1111). Ultra-modern hotel at the city end of Waikiki, next to the Ala Wai marina; 521 rooms with ocean views. Pool, tennis, spa, shuttle to hotel golf course.

Hilton Hawaiian Village ($$–$$$) 2005 Kalia Road, Honolulu HI 96815 (tel: 808/949-4321). An oceanfront resort within a resort, the 20-acre Village complex offers 2,542 rooms in four high-rise towers, ten restaurants, a pool, stores, children's programs and nightly entertainment.

Hyatt Regency Waikiki ($$$) 2424 Kalakaua Avenue, Honolulu HI 96815 (tel: 808/923-1234). Twin towers containing 1,230 well-appointed rooms and suites flank a ten-story atrium. Four restaurants, pool, shopping.

Ilikai Hotel Nikko Waikiki ($–$$) 1777 Ala Moana Boulevard, Honolulu HI 96815 (tel: 808/949-3811). Spacious rooms and condominium units overlooking the Ala Wai marina and Waikiki Beach. Restaurant, pool, terrace, tennis, spa.

Manoa Valley Inn ($$) 2011 Vancouver Drive, Honolulu HI 96822 (tel: 808/947-6019). Lovely old inn with eight rooms tucked away in the Manoa Valley near the university. Antique furnishings and ceiling fans. Continental breakfast; wine and nibbles in the evening.

New Otani Kaimana Beach Hotel ($$) 2368 Kalakaua Avenue, Honolulu HI 96815 (tel: 808/923-1555). Small (for Waikiki), well-priced hotel with 124 rooms between Sans Souci Beach and Kapiolani Park. Good restaurant.

Outrigger Reef on the Beach ($$–$$$) 2169 Kalia Road, Honolulu HI 96815 (tel: 808/923-3111). One of the Outrigger chain's "Royal" properties, with 885 rooms, restaurants, shops, pool and, of course, beach access. Diamond Head-facing *lanais* are worth the extra cost.

Outrigger Reef Towers ($$) 227 Lewers Street, Honolulu HI 96815 (tel: 808/924-8844). Budget accommodations in the heart of downtown Waikiki offering 479 rooms/studios, some with kitchenettes. Restaurant, pool, showroom.

Royal Hawaiian ($$$) 2259 Kalakaua Avenue, Honolulu HI 96815 (tel: 808/923-7311). Waikiki's famous "Pink Palace" (see panel pages 76–7) has its own private beach; 526 luxurious rooms in the elegant old-style main building or modern tower. Restaurants, pool, entertainment.

Sheraton Moana Surfrider ($$$) 2365 Kalakaua Avenue, Honolulu HI 96815-2943 (tel: 808/922-3111). Gracious colonial-style beachfront hotel dating from the turn of the century; 791 rooms, restaurant, pool. Do not miss tea or cocktails in the Banyan Court.

Waikiki Joy Hotel ($$) 320 Lewers Street, Honolulu HI 96815 (tel: 808/923-2300). Waikiki's leading boutique hotel. Every room boasts a superb stereo and Jacuzzi tub; options include kitchenettes and bars. Restaurant, pool, and a karaoke studio for all those would-be Elvises.

Waikiki Parc Hotel ($$$) 2233 Helumoa Road, Honolulu HI 96815 (tel: 808/921-7171). A more affordable offshoot of the Halekulani across the street, with 298 attractively decorated rooms. Attentive service; good restaurant.

The South

Kahala Hilton ($$$) 5000 Kahala Avenue, Honolulu HI 96816 (tel: 808/734-2211). Perennial favorite on the south coast beyond Waikiki, popular with celebrities. Completely renovated in 1995; 369 well-appointed rooms, attractive landscaped grounds, restaurants, pool, beach, spa.

North Shore

Backpackers Vacation Inn & Plantation Village ($) 59-788 Kamehameha Highway, Haleiwa HI 96712 (tel: 808/638-7838). Budget accommodations near the north coast surfing beaches with a choice of dormitories, private rooms and cottages for groups.

Turtle Bay Hilton & Country Club ($$–$$$) P.O. Box 187, Kahuku HI 96763 (tel: 808/293-8811). Dramatically sited on the northeast coast at Kuilima Point, the 800-acre resort has great sports facilities including world-class golf and tennis, 485 rooms with ocean views, and children's activities.

West—Waianae Coast

Ihilani Resort & Spa ($$$) Ko Olina Resort, 92-1001 Olani Street, Kapolei HI 96707 (tel: 808/679-0079). Forty minutes west of Honolulu, yet light years away from the hustle and bustle, with 387 deluxe rooms and suites operated at the touch of an electronic bedside button. Restaurants, pools, Thalasso spa, golf, tennis.

195

Sheraton Makaha Resort and Country Club ($$) 84-626 Makaha Valley, Waianae HI 96792 (tel: 808/695-9511). Beyond Ko Olina, this get-away-from-it-all country resort offers golf, tennis, horse-riding and jogging, and has 185 rooms, a restaurant, and a pool. Beach nearby.

KAUAI

East Coast

Aston Kauai Beach Villas ($$) 4330 Kauai Beach Drive, Lihue HI 96766 (tel: 808/931-1400). Oceanfront condominium resort next door to the excellent Wailua Golf Course; 150 units with full kitchens, washer/driers and private *lanais*. Pool, tennis courts, barbecues.

Aston Kauai Beachboy Hotel ($$) 4-484 Kuhio Highway, Kapaa HI 96766 (tel: 808/822-3441). Affordable beach-front property next to Coconut Market Place; 243 rooms; pool, tennis, activities desk.

Coco Palms Resort ($$–$$$) 4-241 Kuhio Highway, Kapaa HI 96746 (tel: 808/822-4921). The classic Garden Isle hotel has been completely renovated. Lovely landscaped grounds, pools, tennis courts, wedding chapel.

Garden Island Inn ($) 3445 Wilcox Road, Lihue HI 96766 (tel: 808/245-7227). A handy budget option close to the airport and across the street from Kalapaki Beach; 21 simple rooms.

Kauai Coconut Beach Resort ($$) Coconut Plantation (P.O. Box 830), Kapaa HI 96746 (tel: 808/822-3455). An attractive full-service resort with 300 rooms set in a coconut grove alongside Waipouli Beach. Pools, tennis, children's summer programs, Hawaiian activities, and a *luau* six nights a week.

Kauai Marriott on Kalapaki Beach ($$–$$$) Kalapaki Beach, Lihue HI 96766 (tel: 808/245-5050). The island's largest and only truly highrise hotel resort has undergone a complete facelift. Elegant and refurbished, with 355 rooms, it sits on a pretty beach. Shops, pool, tennis and golf nearby.

Kauai Resort Hotel ($–$$) 3-5920 Kuhio Highway, Wailua (tel: 808/245-3931). Near the beach at the mouth of the Wailua River with 228 comfortable and well-priced rooms and cottages. Attractive landscaped grounds, restaurant, pool, tennis.

North Shore

Hanalei Bay Resort/Embassy Suites Kauai ($$–$$$) 5380 Honoiki Road, Princeville HI 96722 (tel: 808/826-6522). A choice of one-, two- and three-bed condominium units in a chic resort set amongst the Princeville golf courses. Fine hillside location overlooking Hanalei Bay.

Hanalei Colony Resort ($$) 5-7130 Kuhio Highway, Haena HI 96714 (tel: 808/826-6253). Condominium offering 52 light and airy two-bed units with huge picture windows and *lanais*. Quiet location on the shore between Hanalei and Kee Beach. Friendly staff; adjacent restaurant.

Pali Ke Kua ($–$$) Bali Hai Treasures, 5300 Ka Haku Road, Princeville HI 96714 (tel: 1-800/688-2254). Well-equipped and affordable condominium property with 62 brand-new units in the Princeville resort. Ocean views, *lanais*.

Princeville Hotel ($$$) 5520 Kahaku Road, Princeville HI 96722 (tel: 808/826-9644). The palatial, marbled, gilded and plumply upholstered lap of luxury; 252 rooms, beach, pool, spa, stores, gourmet dining and serious golf.

The South

Garden Isle Cottages ($–$$) 2666 Puuholo Road, Koloa HI 96756 (tel: 808/742-6717). Eleven pretty studios and cottages, some with kitchenettes, close to Poipu Beach. Pool. Shopping, tennis, and golf nearby.

Hyatt Regency Kauai Resort & Spa ($$$) 1571 Poipu Road, Koloa HI 96756 (tel: 808/742-1234). Relaxing Hawaiian ambience combined with superb service. Some 598 thoughtfully appointed rooms

placed in landscaped gardens. Excellent dining, fresh- and salt-water pools, spa and Jacuzzis, tennis, golf, Hawaiian cultural program, and entertainment.

Kiahuna Plantation ($$) 2253 Poipu Road, Koloa HI 96756 (tel: 808/742-6411). Attractive low-rise beachfront condominium complex; 333 one- and two- bed units with full kitchens. Restaurant, pool, tennis, Hawaiiana and children's programs; shopping, dining, and golf nearby.

Kokee Lodge ($) 3600 Kokee Road, P.O. Box 819, Waimea HI 96796 (tel: 808/335-6061). Basic cabins in Kokee State Park (12 altogether—the largest sleeps seven). Hot showers, stoves, linen and towels provided. Bring warm clothes for the evening.

Poipu Kai Resort ($$) 1941 Poipu Road, Koloa HI 96756 (tel: 808/742-7400). A 350-unit condominium complex reaching down to the ocean. Comfortable and well-equipped accommodations. Pools, spa, tennis courts.

Waimea Plantation Cottages ($–$$) 367-9400 Kaumualii Highway, Waimea HI 96796 (tel: 808/338-1625). Forty-seven enchanting one- to five-bedroom cottages set in a coconut grove by the beach. Kitchens, claw-foot baths, tin roofs and wooden *lanais*. Pool, restaurant.

Whaler's Cove ($$$) 2640 Puuholo Road, Poipu, HI 96756 (tel: 808/742-7571). Luxury oceanfront condominium units with terrific sea views, lots of space. Shopping, restaurants, golf, and tennis nearby. Good snorkeling.

MOLOKAI

Colony's Kaluakoi Hotel & Golf Club ($$) P.O. Box 1977, Kepuhi Beach HI 96770 (tel: 808/552-2555). Surrounded by manicured fairways on the ocean's edge, 114 spacious, high-ceilinged rooms and suites (some with kitchenettes) with *lanais* in low-rise "Polynesian"-style buildings. Restaurant, shops, lovely beaches, pool, watersports and activities.

Kaluakoi Villas ($$) 1131 Kaluakoi Road, Maunaloa HI 96770 (tel: 808/552-2721). Within the Kaluakoi Hotel complex, 50 condominium units with access to all the same facilities.

Wavecrest Resort ($$) HC01 Box 541, Kamehameha Highway, Kaunakakai HI 96748 (tel: 808/558-8103). A small number of condominium units available to rent in a secluded resort on the road out to the East End. Pool, tennis, shuffleboard; good swimming nearby.

MAUI
West Maui
Hyatt Regency Maui ($$$) 200 Nohea Kai Drive, Lahaina HI 96761 (tel: 808/661-1234). A truly superb property on the beach at Kaanapali, with luxurious rooms and grounds landscaped to resemble a South Seas amusement park; 815 rooms and every facility.

Kaanapali Beach Hotel ($$) 2525 Kaanapali Parkway, Lahaina HI 96761 (tel: 808/661-0011). Affordable beachfront hotel, old-fashioned and friendly with 430 rooms, restaurant, pool, golf. Special emphasis on things Hawaiian.

Kapalua Bay Hotel & Villas ($$$) 1 Bay Drive, Lahaina HI 96761 (tel: 808/669-5656). Sensitively designed and beautifully executed resort 30 minutes north of Lahaina; 294 spacious and attractive rooms and suites; excellent facilities including three championship golf courses; lovely beach; excellent restaurant.

Maui Park ($–$$) 3626 Lower Honoapiilani, Lahaina HI 96761 (tel: 808/669-6622). Across the street from the beach between Kaanapali and Kapalua, 288 budget condominium units with full kitchens, barbecues, guest activities desk. Stores and dining nearby.

Pioneer Inn ($–$$) 658 Wharf Street, Lahaina HI 96761 (tel: 808/661-3636). Historic inn that is part-attraction and part-B&B; 48 simple rooms with *lanais*. Bar and restaurant downstairs.

Plantation Inn ($$) 174 Lahainaluna Road, Lahaina HI 96761 (tel: 808/667-9225). Just a step away from bustling Front Street, with 18 individually decorated rooms furnished with antiques. Bed and breakfast; pool.

Royal Lahaina Resort ($$) 2780 Kekaa Drive, Lahaina HI 96761 (tel: 808/661-3611). At the quiet northern end of Kaanapali Beach, with 592 rooms and cottages. Tennis, golf nearby, pools, restaurants, and popular *luau* with Polynesian revue.

Sheraton Maui ($$$) 2605 Kaanapali Parkway, Lahaina HI 96761 (tel: 808/661-0031). Due to reopen in 1996 after a massive renovation program, the highly regarded Sheraton occupies a prime position on Kaanapali Beach.

Westin Maui ($$$) 2365 Kaanapali Parkway, Lahaina HI 96761 (tel: 808/667-2525). Sleek beachfront hotel with the island's largest swimming-pool, water gardens, children's camp, ocean activities, even a "director of romance" for wedding arrangements; 761 elegant rooms and suites; fabulous dining.

Whaler at Kaanapali Beach ($$) 2481 Kaanapali Parkway, Lahaina HI 96761 (tel: 808/854-8843). Oceanfront condominium with 340 attractive units in separate buildings. Stores, pool, tennis, spa.

East Maui
Destination Resorts Wailea ($$) 3750 Wailea Alanui Drive, Kihei HI 96753 (tel: 808/879-1595). Central reservations service for over 900 condominium units in Wailea-Makena area. Also golf course villas ($$$).

Grand Wailea Resort, Hotel & Spa ($$$) 3850 Wailea Alanui Drive, Wailea HI 96753 (tel: 808/875-1234). Grand by name and grand by nature. Impressive reception areas; 761 lovely rooms and suites; golf, tennis, spa, program of children's activities.

Hana Bay Vacation Rentals ($–$$) P.O. Box 318, Hana HI 96713 (tel: 808/248-7727). For town and country cottage rentals in the quiet Hana area.

Hotel Hana-Maui ($$$) P.O. Box 9, Hana HI 96713 (tel: 808/248-8211). Low-key but luxurious country resort with 97 rooms and suites in cottages dotted around beautiful gardens. Ceiling fans and pretty tropical décor; Hawaiian regional cuisine. Tennis, horseback-riding, spa, beach.

Kula Lodge ($–$$) RRI, P.O. Box 475, Kula HI 96790 (tel: 808/878-1535). Simple accommodations in wood cabins on the slopes of Haleakala (ask for a log fire). Terrific breakfasts to restore the circulation after watching sunrise atop the volcano.

Maui Inter-Continental Resort ($$$) 3700 Wailea Alanui Drive, Wailea HI 96753 (tel: 808/879-1922). Resort with 516 spacious and airy rooms and suites leading down to the ocean. Restaurants, pool, children's activities, award-winning Hawaiian culture program, and fine *luau*.

Maui Lu Resort ($–$$) 575 S Kihei Road, Kihei HI 96753 (tel: 808/879-5881). Resort complex offering 120 well-priced rooms on a 28-acre beachfront site. Restaurant, pool, tennis, activities desk, barbecues.

Maui Prince Hotel ($$$) 5400 Makena Alanui, Kihei HI 96753 (tel: 808/874-1111). In marvelous landscaped grounds at the end of the road, 310 rooms and suites with *lanais* and views of the Neighbor Islands. Restaurants, swimming, tennis, golf.

Silver Cloud Upcountry Guest Ranch ($–$$) RR2 Box 201, Old Thompson Road, Kula HI 96790 (tel: 808/878-6101). Nine comfortable rooms or studios plus a cottage with glorious upcountry views. Bed and breakfast; peace and quiet.

HOTELS AND RESTAURANTS

LANAI

Hotel Lanai ($$) P.O. Box A-199, Lanai City HI 96763 (tel: 808/565-4700). A former plantation guest house, this pretty 1920s hotel offers affordable, small but pretty rooms with bleached pine furniture, patchwork quilts, and Hawaiian prints. Good restaurant.

The Lodge at Koele ($$$) P.O. Box L, Lanai City HI 96763 (tel: 808/565-3800). Manor-house-style upcountry hotel with 102 charming and thoughtfully appointed rooms. Roaring fires and huge sofas; superb dining; exemplary service; great golf, pool, hiking, shuttle to the beach.

Manele Bay Hotel ($$$) P.O. Box L, Lanai City HI 96763 (tel: 808/565-7700). Oceanfront hedonism with 250 rooms and suites with Mediterranean and Asian influences laid out around tropical gardens. Excellent restaurant; golf course designed by Jack Niklaus; hot-spring spa, pool, snorkeling in the bay.

HAWAII

Hilo

Arnott's Lodge and Hiking Adventures ($) 98 Apapane Road, Hilo HI 96720 (tel: 808/969-7097). Ideal for backpackers on a budget; 58 rooms and bunks in dormitories, kitchen and laundry, barbecues, and amazing value hiking/4WD adventures around the island.

Hawaii Naniloa Hotel ($$) 93 Banyan Drive, Hilo HI 96720 (tel: 808/969-3333). Great position on the bay, and 325 recently renovated rooms. Restaurant, pool, spa, stores, and golf course.

Volcano

Kilauea Lodge ($$) P.O. Box 116, Volcano HI 96785 (tel: 808/967-7366). A welcoming upcountry inn popular with volcano visitors, so reserve well in advance; 12 rooms, some in a modern annex, others in the original building with lots of polished wood and fireplaces. Good food.

Volcano House ($–$$) Hawaii Volcanoes National Park, Volcano HI 96718 (tel: 808/967-7321). A 42-room inn with restaurant on the edge of the Kilauea caldera. Some rooms have spectacular crater views; hordes of people.

The Kona Coast

Aston Royal Sea Cliff Resort ($$) 75-6040 Alii Drive, Kailua-Kona HI 96740 (tel: 808/329-8021). A terraced oceanfront condominium resort with 154 large units. Full kitchens and *lanais*. No beach, but

fresh- and salt-water pools; tennis courts.

Kanaloa at Kona Resort ($$) 78-261 Manukai Street, Keauhou HI 96740 (tel: 808/322-9625). Resort with 166 one-, two-, and three-bed deluxe condominium units with ocean or golf-course views. Beach and good snorkeling, pools, tennis, activities desk; shopping and dining nearby. One of the Big Island's best deals.

King Kamehameha's Kona Beach Hotel ($$) 75-5660 Palani Road, Kailua-Kona HI 96740 (tel: 808/329-2911). Large hotel bordering a small beach close to Kailua Pier with 460 rooms, restaurants, pool, tennis, guest activities desk.

Kona Tiki Hotel ($) 75-5968 Alii Drive, Kailua-Kona HI 96740 (tel: 808/329-1425). A budget bargain just out of town with 178 rooms, some kitchens. Oceanfront position; pool.

Manago Hotel ($) P.O. Box 145, Captain Cook HI 96704 (tel: 808/323-2642). Low, low prices close to Kealakekua Bay in Kona coffee country; 64 rooms in old-style family-owned hotel with a restaurant serving local food. No children.

Three Bears' Bed & Breakfast ($) 72-1001 Puukala Street, Kailua-Kona HI 96740 (tel: 808/325-7563). Two pretty rooms with *lanais* in a cedar-wood home at a cool 1,600 feet above sea-level (ten minutes from town). Great views; generous breakfasts; all-islands B&B reservations.

Kohala

Hapuna Beach Prince Hotel ($$$) 62-100 Kaunaoa Drive, Kamuela HI 96743 (tel: 808/880-1111). Large and luxurious 1994 hotel overlooking Hapuna Beach, all 350 rooms have ocean views and every convenience. Restaurants, watersports, pool, tennis, golf; horseback-riding nearby.

Hilton Waikoloa Village ($$$) 425 Waikoloa Beach Drive, Kamuela HI 96743 (tel: 808/885-1234). A 62-acre South Seas fantasy carved out of the lava fields, featuring a lagoon, tropical gardens, waterways, golf courses and a mile-long Museum Walkway flanked by Polynesian and Asian artworks; 1,241 rooms with every facility. Dolphin encounter program.

Kona Village Resort ($$$) P.O. Box 1299, Kailua-Kona HI 96745 (tel: 808/325-5555). Voted the "Best Tropical Resort in the World" by Conde Nast "Traveler" readers, Kona Village offers 125 luxurious Robinson Crusoe/Polynesian-style thatched *hales* (cottages) dotted around an oceanfront grove and lagoon. No phone, no T.V. Restaurants, watersports, tennis, children's programs, terrific Friday night *luau*.

Mauna Kea Beach Hotel ($$$) 62–100 Mauna Kea Beach Drive, Kamuela HI 96743-9706 (tel: 808/882-7222). One of Hawaii's classiest and most luxurious resorts, decorated with antiques and artifacts; 310 deluxe rooms, great food, lovely beach, pools, championship golf.

Mauna Lani Bay Hotel and Bungalows ($$$) 1 Mauna Lani Drive, Kohala HI 96743 (tel: 808/885-6622). Superb beachfront resort with 372 rooms, bungalows and villas. Golf courses fashioned out of lava fields, spa, tennis, watersports.

Royal Waikoloan ($$) 69-275 Waikoloa Beach Drive, Kamuela HI 96743 (tel: 808/ 885-6789). Rather dated but beautifully situated right on Anaehoomalu Beach; 547 comfortable rooms, restaurants, pool, spa, tennis, golf, island activities. All-inclusive vacation-package option.

RESTAURANTS

Hawaii offers dining opportunities in a wide range of culinary styles and price brackets. While the all-American hamburger is everywhere and the Japanese influence is strong, the choices do not end there. The latest gastronomic craze is Hawaiian Regional cuisine, a sometimes inspired (at its best) combination of the best and freshest local ingredients with Asian and a hint of Mediterranean cooking styles, and it is well worth seeking out. (See also pages 74–5.)

The restaurants listed below have been classified into price categories as follows:

- budget ($) = under $15
- moderate ($$) = $15–$30
- expensive ($$$) = over $30

OAHU

Honolulu and Waikiki

Bali by the Sea ($$$) Hilton Hawaiian Village, 2005 Kalia Road, Honolulu HI 96815 (tel: 808/941-2254). An elegant oceanside dining-room providing excellent Continental cuisine with Hawaiian Regional accents: shrimp and scallops with ginger; seared *ahi* (tuna) with hot *wasabi* sauce. Good value.

California Pizza Kitchen ($) 1910 Ala Moana Boulevard, Honolulu HI 96815 (tel: 808/955-5161). Designer pizzas cooked over wood fires and served with enormous salads big enough for two.

Ciao Mein ($$) Hyatt Regency Waikiki, 2424 Kalakaua Avenue, Honolulu HI 96815 (tel: 808/923-2426). A suitably schizophrenic name for a Chinese-Italian restaurant. But there is no faulting the tastebud-tingling Szechuan eggplant or the *tiramisu*. (Dinner only, except Sunday brunch.)

Duke's Canoe Club – Waikiki ($$) Outrigger Waikiki Hotel, 2335 Kalakaua Avenue, Honolulu HI 96815 (tel: 808/922-2268). Casual beachfront eatery full of surfing memorabilia. Steaks and fresh seafood in the dining room; burgers and pizzas at the outdoor Barefoot Bar. Entertainment.

Gordon Biersch Brewery Restaurant ($–$$) Unit 1123, Aloha Tower Marketplace, 101 Ala Moana Road, Honolulu HI 96813 (tel: 808/599-4877). Eclectic menu running the gamut from Pacific Rim style pan-fried scallops with mango vinaigrette to innovative pizzas and hamburgers with garlic fries. Home-brewed beers.

Hau Tree Lanai ($$$) New Otani Kaimana Beach Hotel, 2863 Kalakaua Avenue, Honolulu HI 96815 (tel: 808/921-7066). Fresh seafood and Pacific Rim-influenced dishes served under a giant *hau* tree by the beach.

House Without a Key ($$) Halekulani Hotel, 2199 Kalia Road, Honolulu HI 96815 (tel: 808/923-2311). Beneath a spreading *kiawe* tree in the grounds of Waikiki's finest hotel, great for sunset drinks accompanied by old-style Hawaiian steel guitar music. Light and fresh Continental-cum-Hawaiian Regional cooking.

Keo's Thai Cuisine ($$) Ward Center, 1200 Ala Moana Boulevard, Honolulu HI 96814 (tel: 808/596-0020). Consistently good Thai curries, spicy fish, barbecued chicken and other dishes using freshly grown herbs and vegetables from North Shore farms. Also branches at 625 Kapahulu Avenue (tel: 808/737-8240) and 1486 S. King Street (tel: 808/947-9988).

La Mer ($$$) Halekulani Hotel, 2199 Kalia Road, Honolulu HI 96815 (tel: 808/923-2311). A beautiful dining-room with romantic views out over the ocean. Hawaiian Regional cuisine, here with a Provençal accent: *bouillabaisse* of local fish and *onaga* (red snapper) baked with a rosemary-salt crust. Try the killer surprise dessert made from the Big Island's home-grown Hawaiian Vintage Chocolate.

Monterey Bay Canners ($$) Outrigger Waikiki Hotel, 2335 Kalakaua Avenue, Honolulu HI 96815 (tel: 808/922-5761). Good family atmosphere with old favorites, from seafood and steaks to pasta and barbecued fresh fish.

Ono Hawaiian Foods ($) 726 Kapahulu Avenue, Honolulu HI 96815 (tel: 808/737-2275). No-frills neighborhood restaurant in Waikiki serving inexpensive plate lunches piled high with traditional Hawaiian favorites.

Parc Cafe ($$) Waikiki Parc Hotel, 2233 Helumoa Road, Honolulu HI 96815 (tel: 808/921-7272). Renowned for its elaborate buffets which are both generous and very good. One of the best is the excellent Hawaiian buffet. Call in advance to check schedules.

Singha Thai Cuisine ($$) 1910 Ala Moana Boulevard, Honolulu HI 96815 (tel: 808/941-2898). Thai dancers accompany dinner here. Spicy beef salad, curries, enormous hot chicken and cashew stir-fry.

Wo Fat ($) 115 N. Hotel Street, Honolulu HI 96817 (tel: 808/533-6393). Chinatown's most touristy restaurant, founded in 1882, serves good seafood and a long menu of classic Chinese dishes.

The South

Roy's Restaurant ($$$) Hawaii Kai Corporate Plaza, 6600 Kalanianaole Highway (Maunalua Bay) HI 96825 (tel: 808/396-7697). Local chef Roy Yamaguchi serves delicious Hawaiian Regional and Pacific Rim cuisine. Memorable lemon-grass-crusted swordfish with spicy Thai basil-peanut sauce.

Sea Lion Cafe ($) Sea Life Park, Makapuu Point HI 96795 (tel: 808/259-9911). Handy family-style cafeteria serving American, Hawaiian, and Japanese favorites. Dinner show on Friday nights.

Windward Coast

Crouching Lion Inn ($–$$) 51-666 Kamehameha Highway, Kaaawa HI 96730 (tel: 808/237-8511). A pleasant stop on the road to Laie. Lunch and dinner served in the dining room or on the *lanai* with sea views. Hawaiian-American menu; bar.

North Shore

Jameson's by the Sea ($$) 62-540 Kamehameha Highway, Haleiwa HI 96712 (tel: 808/637-4336). Renowned for its harbor and sunset views. Fresh fish and seafood a specialty, also burgers, salads, and steaks.

Kua Aina Sandwich ($) 66-214 Kamehameha Highway, Haleiwa HI 96712 (tel: 808/637-6067). Sandwiches a mile high and burgers to match. Casual and fun with a couple of outside tables, great for people-watching.

KAUAI
East Coast

Cafe Portofino ($$) Pacific Ocean Plaza, 3501 Rice Street (HI-51), Lihue HI 96766 (tel: 808/245-2121). Modern Italian restaurant close to Kalapaki Beach. All the classics from pasta to prosciutto, plus local-style *ahi* (yellowfin tuna) carpaccio.

Kapaa Fish & Chowder House ($$) 1639 Kuhio Highway, Kapaa HI 96746 (tel: 808/822-7488). Casual, outdoor dining in a nautical setting and fish every which way, from coconut shrimp to seafood pasta via a choice of sautéed or grilled local catches. (Dinner only.)

King and I Thai Cuisine ($) Waipouli Plaza, 4-901 Kuhio Highway, Kapaa HI 96746 (tel: 808/822-1642). A great Thai restaurant tucked away in a mall. Delicious Thai salads with green papaya or beef and mint. Good vegetarian dishes, three styles of curry. (Dinner only.)

A Pacific Cafe ($$$) Kauai Village, 831 Kuhio Highway, Kapaa HI 96746 (tel: 808/822-0013). One of the best restaurants in the state; Jean-Marie Josselin's Hawaiian Regional cuisine is a revelation. Signature dishes include sautéed crab cakes with a mango and ginger sauce, stir-fried lobster with eggplant and cashews. Attractive Asian-Hawaiian décor; open kitchen. Reservations a must. (Dinner only.)

Tip Top Motel, Café & Bakery ($) 3173 Akahi Street, Lihue HI 96766 (tel: 808/245-2333). Local café-bakery famous for inventing macadamia nut cookies, still sold here by the pound. Hearty breakfasts, lunches and dinners, too.

Wailua Marina ($–$$) Wailua Marine State Park, 5971 Kuhio Highway, Wailua HI 96746 (tel: 808/822-4311). Family dining by the river with seating on an open *lanai*. Seafood, plus Asian-American chicken dishes and steaks.

North Coast

Casa d'Amici ($$) 2484 Keneke Street (off Lighthouse Road), Kilauea HI 96754 (tel: 808/828-1388). Popular and pretty open-air dining room serving good Italian food from pasta to chicken, veal and fresh fish. (Dinner only; reservations advised.)

Hanalei Dolphin ($$) Hanalei Trader Building, Kuhio Highway, Hanalei HI 96714 (tel: 808/826-6113). Busy restaurant with a lovely setting right beside the Hanalei River. Features local scallops, shrimp, crabs and fresh fish, plus steak and chicken. (Dinner only.)

Hanalei Gourmet ($) Hanalei Center, Kuhio Highway, Hanalei HI 96714 (tel: 808/826-2524). Laid-back local café which doubles as a delicatessen/bar. Home-made pastries, bagels and eggs for breakfast; plus salads, sandwiches, seafood, cheese. Nightly entertainment.

Hanalei Wake-Up Cafe ($) Kuhio Highway at Aku Road, Hanalei HI 96714 (tel: 808/826-5551). Open daily at the crack of dawn (5:30) for serious breakfasts—omelettes, French toast, pancakes, hash browns. Also lunch and dinner.

La Cascata ($$$) Princeville Hotel, 5520 Ka Haku Road, Princeville HI 96722 (tel: 808/826-9644). Excellent Italian food in an elegant dining room decorated with murals and magnificent flower arrangements. Specialties include salmon with pesto, potato salad and green beans; cannelloni of roasted duck; warm mango tart and Kona coffee custard. (Dinner only.)

Tahiti Nui ($) Kuhio Highway, Hanalei HI 96714 (tel: 808/826-6277). Good food and a friendly atmosphere in a comfortable old plantation-era building. Pacific Rim/local menu; tables on the narrow veranda. Entertainment at the weekend.

Tosca ($–$$) Hanalei Center, Kuhio Highway, Hanlei HI 96714 (tel: 808/826-1222 or 808/826-2552). Jazzy café-bar serving pastas, fish, steaks and herb chicken from the *kiawe* wood oven, plus exceedingly good pizzas topped with the likes of eggplant, *shiitake* mushrooms, sun-dried tomatoes and fontina cheese. (Closed Mon.)

The South

Brennecke's ($–$$) 2100 Hoone Road, Poipu HI 96756 (tel: 808/742-7588). Casual and popular upstairs dining room overlooking the beach. Cocktails and *pupus* (hors-d'oeuvres), burgers and fish sandwiches, plus steaks, pasta, and good fresh island fish.

Gaylord's at Kilohana ($$–$$$) Kilohana Plantation, Kaumualii Highway (HI-50), Lihue HI 96766 (tel: 808/245-9593). Dining room and outside tables surrounding the grassy courtyard of a 1930s plantation house turned craft gallery. Omelettes, salads and burgers at lunch; steaks, pasta and seafood in the evening.

Grove Dining Room ($$) Waimea Plantation Cottages, 9400 Kaumualii Highway, Waimea HI 96796 (tel: 808/338-2300). Relaxed old-style dining on the *lanai* overlooking the shore through a coconut grove. Japanese- and Korean-style cuisine,

Hawaiian seafood stir-fry, and fresh seafood or steaks. (Closed Mon.)

Koloa Broiler ($–$$) Koloa Road at Poipu Road, Koloa HI 96756 (tel: 808/742-9122). Cocktails and cook-your-own barbecue from burgers, kebabs, ribs, steaks and fish or chicken. Popular, friendly and good fun.

Roy's Poipu Bar & Grill ($$) Poipu Shopping Center, 2360 Kiahuna Plantation Drive, Poipu HI 96741 (tel: 808/742-5000). Master chef Roy Yamaguchi's Kauai outpost. Inspired Hawaiian Regional cuisine: Thai stuffed chicken and oven pot roast with apple-ginger-pineapple sauce. Reservations advised.

MOLOKAI

Jojo's Cafe ($) Maunaloa HI 96770 (tel: 808/552-2803). Long bar and small tables in a simple, wooden plantation-era building decorated with period photographs. Fish and seafood with Jojo's Indian curry sauce, Korean ribs with garlicky vegetables, honey-dipped chicken. (Closed Sun.)

Kanemitsu Bakery ($) Ala Malama Street, Kaunakakai HI 96748 (tel: 808/553-5855). Downtown bakery famous for its Molokai sweet bread, also loaves flavored with apple and cinnamon, guava, pineapple and more. Salads, sandwiches, plate lunches to eat in or take out. (Closed Tue.)

Kualapuu Cook House ($) Kualapuu HI 96757 (tel: 808/567-6185). Cozy restaurant in an old plantation house. Terrific breakfasts, chilli omelettes, stir-fries, grilled sandwiches, and remarkable chocolate macadamia nut pie. Mountainous portions. (Closed Sat PM, Sun.)

Ohia Lodge ($$) Colony's Kaluakoi Hotel and Golf Club, Kepuhi Beach HI 96770 (tel: 808/552-2555). Tropical motif and picture windows opening onto the Pacific. American menu of pasta, seafood, steaks and salads. Friendly service.

MAUI
West Maui

Avalon ($$$) 844 Front Street, Lahaina HI 96761 (tel: 808/667-5559). Casual, popular brasserie with courtyard tables. Pacific Rim/Hawaiian Regional cuisine: Asian pasta with shrimp, clams and fish in an herby ginger and tomato sauce.

David Paul's Lahaina Grill ($$$) 127 Lahainaluna Road, Lahaina HI 97861 (tel: 808/667-5117). Probably the best food in Lahaina. Pacific Rim and southwestern influences yield dishes like tequila shrimp seasoned with chilli, coriander, tequila and brown sugar. Great desserts. (Dinner only.)

HOTELS AND RESTAURANTS

Lahaina Coolers ($) 180 Dickenson Street, Lahaina HI 96761 (tel: 808/661-7082). Laid-back bistro with pizzas, pastas, salads, tortillas and *pupus*. Also fresh fish, steaks and burgers.

Longhi's ($$) 888 Front Street, Lahaina HI 96761 (tel: 808/667-2288). Bustling, noisy oceanfront dining. American-Italian menu declaimed by fast-talking waiters. Live music on the weekend.

Old Lahaina Café & Luau ($$) 505 Front Street, Lahaina HI 96761 (tel: 808/661-3303). Open-air waterfront spot for breakfast, lunch and dinner. Sandwiches, plate lunches with *kalau* pork or *teriyaki* steak, seafood and Hawaiian specials. (For *luau* reservations, tel: 808/667-1998.)

Pineapple Hill ($$$) 1000 Kapalua Drive, Kapalua HI 96761 (tel: 808/669-6129). Lovely setting in an old plantation home with ocean views. Fresh fish, scallops Provençal rack of lamb, Maui lime pie, and baked papaya with Tahitian vanilla bean and coconut milk. (Dinner only. Reservations advised.)

Roy's Kahana Bar & Grill ($$–$$$) Kahana Gateway Shopping Center, 4405 Honapiilani Highway, Kahana HI 96761 (tel: 808/669-6999). Roy Yamaguchi's Hawaiian Regional and Euro-Asian cooking titillates the palate with imaginative specialties such as spinach with ricotta, ravioli of *shiitake* mushrooms, smoked and peppered duck with gingered sweet potatoes, and spicy rimfire shrimp.

Sound of the Falls ($$$) Westin Maui Hotel, 2365 Kaanapali Parkway, Lahaina HI 96761 (tel: 808/667-2525). Elegant open-air dining room with Pacific sunset views edged by pools of pink flamingos. The cuisine shows French and Asian influences: stuffed Hawaiian lobster tail, vegetable-wrapped snapper in shredded phyllo with ginger butter; Châteaubriand with black-truffle pâté. Attentive service. (Dinner only. Closed Thu and Sun.)

East Maui

Buzz's Wharf ($$–$$$) Maalaea Harbor, Maalaea HI 96753 (tel: 808/224-5426). Casual waterfront dining. Seafood specials, steaks and *teriyaki* chicken. Lunchtime fish, cajun chicken, and open beef sandwiches in the $-bracket.

Casanova ($–$$) 1188 Makawao Avenue, Makawao HI 96768 (tel: 808/572-0220). Upcountry Italian restaurant with its own delicatessen. Pizzas from the *kiawe* wood grill, home-made pasta, salads, fish, chicken and steaks. Raid the delicatessen

for *paniolo*-sized sandwiches, espressos and pastries. Entertainment Wed–Sat nights.

Kula Lodge ($$) Haleakala, Kula HI 96790 (tel: 808/878-1535). Upcountry dining room which makes a convenient lunch-time stop for trips to Haleakala. Good views and simple American menu.

Lobster Cove & Harry's Sushi ($$–$$$) 100 Wailea Ike Drive, Wailea HI 96753 (tel: 808/879-7677). Two restaurants under one roof. Lobster Cove's Pacific Rim seafood specialties include lobster cakes in a bird's nest of noodles with *wasabi* sauce.

A Pacific Cafe ($$$) Azeka Place II, 1279 S. Kihei Road, Kihei HI 96753 (tel: 808/879-0069). A Valley Island outpost for maestro of Hawaiian Regional cuisine, Jean-Marie Josselin. Grilled *opah* with banana salsa and Thai coconut curry sauce, herby goat cheese-encrusted salmon. Don't miss it. (Dinner only.)

Prince Court ($$$) Maui Prince Hotel, 5400 Makena Alanui Drive, Kihei HI 96753 (tel: 808/875-5888). Elegant restaurant with Pacific views and innovative Hawaiian Regional cuisine. Excellent fresh fish and seafood. Legendary Sunday brunches. (Dinner only except Sun.)

Seasons ($$$) Four Seasons Resort, 3900 Wailea Alanui Drive, Wailea HI 96753 (tel: 808/874-8000). Restaurant within the Four Seasons Resort hotel; romantic setting with fine food, ocean views and dancing cheek-to-cheek. Beautifully presented Pacific Rim cuisine. Memorable sautéed freshwater jumbo shrimp with minted vegetable spaghetti.

Wunderbar ($–$$) 89 Hana Highway, Paia HI 96789 (tel: 808/579-8808). A Swiss chef unleashed on Maui's finest produce. The eclectic menu includes spicy Turkish *menemen* (scrambled eggs with onions, peppers and tomatoes) for breakfast, plus burgers, sandwiches, pasta and fish. Entertainment Thu–Sat nights.

LANAI

Hotel Lanai ($$) Lanai City HI 96763 (tel: 808/565-4700). Unfussy island cooking featuring fresh fish, local venison steak, pasta, salads and sandwiches. Cozy surroundings with a big brick fireplace.

Hulupoe Court ($$$) Manele Bay Hotel, Hulopoe Bay HI 96763 (tel: 808/565-2290). Tall, elegant dining-room with sea views. Delectable contemporary Hawaiian Regional-style roasted Chinese duck with pickled ginger and plum sauce or designer pizzas and hamburgers.

The Lodge at Koele Dining Room ($$$) P.O. Box L, Lanai City HI 96763 (tel: 808/565-4580). Upcountry Hawaiian Regional cooking, stylish and delicious. Sample wild game sausage, venison carpaccio, pine nut encrusted rack of lamb and a knock-out Hawaiian Vintage Chocolate soufflé. Jackets required. There is a scaled-down menu in the less formal **Terrace Room**.

HAWAII
Hilo
Cafe Pesto ($$) 308 Kamehameha Avenue, Hilo HI 96720 (tel: 808/969-6640). Pastas, wood-fired-oven pizzas, salads, and fresh seafood served with Pacific Rim flair in a tall, airy, blue and white dining-room on the main street.

Roussel's ($$) 60 Keawe Street, Hilo HI 96720 (tel: 808/935-5111). In a gracious old bank building, Roussel's French-Creole menu makes a pleasant change. Seafood gumbo, New Orleans-style blackened *mahimahi* (dolphinfish), sandwiches.

Volcano
Kilauea Lodge ($$) Volcano HI 96785 (tel: 808/967-7366). Welcoming upcountry lodge with good food. Lots of fresh seafood, *ahi* (yellowfin tuna) with macadamia nuts and mango, rich stuffed prime rib.

The Kona Coast
Jameson's by the Sea ($$) 77-6452 Alii Drive, Kailua-Kona HI 96740 (tel: 808/329-3195). Sunsets over Magic Sands Beach and fishy décor to match the seafood menu. Baked stuffed shrimp, *opakapaka* (snapper) poached in wine, also sesame chicken and steak. (Dinner only on weekends.)

Kona Ranch House ($) 75-5653 Ololi Street, Kailua-Kona HI 96740 (tel: 808/329-7061). Inexpensive and fun family dining. Generous portions of prime rib, steaks and barbecues, heroic breakfasts.

Palm Cafe ($$–$$$) 75-5819 Alii Drive, Kailua-Kona HI 96740 (tel: 808/329-7765). Sea views, great *pupus* (hors-d'oeuvres), cocktails and a light menu downstairs at **Under the Palm**. Upstairs, a relaxed dining room specializes in Pacific Rim dishes such as snapper with mustard seed and Szechuan peppercorn crust.

Sam Choy's ($$) 73-5576 Kauhola Bay, Kailua-Kona HI 96740 (tel: 808/326-1545). The crucible of "Kona cooking," this no frills, good time restaurant serves local cuisine at its finest, from Japanese *saimin* noodle soup and steamed three-fish *laulau*

parcels wrapped in *ti* leaves to honey duck with orange sauce.

Sibu Cafe ($) Banyan Court Mall, 75-5695 Alii Drive, Kailua-Kona HI 96740 (tel: 808/329-1112). Indonesian café with courtyard tables overlooking the seawall. Salad with spicy peanut sauce, curries, stir-fries, satay and ginger beef.

Kohala
Canoe House ($$$) Mauna Lani Bay Hotel, 1 Mauna Lani Drive, Kohala HI 96743 (tel: 808/885-6622). Gorgeous beachfront setting and delicious Hawaiian Regional cuisine. Cajun spiced beef tenderloin with orange sauce, *ahi* (yellowfin tuna) in a light seaweed-*tempura* batter with soy mustard sauce. (Dinner only. Closed Tue.)

Coast Grille ($$–$$$) Hapuna Beach Prince Hotel, 62-100 Kaunaoa Drive, Kamuela HI 96743 (tel: 808/880-1111). Circular dining room with sea views—the ideal setting for sunset cocktails. Seafood specialties and an oyster bar, fresh pastas and innovative appetizers. (Dinner only.)

Dining Room ($$$) Ritz Carlton Mauna Lani, 1 North Kaniku Drive, Kohala HI 96743 (tel: 808/885-2000). One of the leading temples of Hawaiian Regional cuisine. Choice of elegant dining room or tables under the stars. Lamb carpaccio, Lanai venison with *ohelo*-berry sauce, marvelous seafood and fish. Exemplary service. (Dinner only.)

Kona Village Luau ($$–$$$) Kona Village Resort, Kaupulehu HI 96743 (tel: 808/325-5555). One of the best and most authentic *luaus* in the state held every Friday night. The enormous buffet features pork and *laulaus* (meat, fish or vegetables wrapped in taro leaves) from the *imu* (underground oven), *poi* (taro paste), salads, fresh mangoes, and much, much more, plus live entertainment.

Merriman's ($$$) Opelo Plaza, HI-19 at Opelo Road, Waimea-Kamuela HI 96743 (tel: 808/885-6822). Creative contemporary Hawaiian Regional cooking by Peter Merriman, seen at work in the open kitchen. Roasted bell peppers with Puna goat's cheese, seafood paella, Big Island beef, game in season.

Waimea Coffee & Company ($) Parker Square, HI-19, Waimea-Kamuela HI 96743 (tel: 808/885-4472). Good coffee including estate-grown pure Kona. Iced coffees and herbal teas. On the food front: fresh scones, pastries, carrot cake and, at lunchtime, soups, salads, quiches, and sandwiches.

Index

Bold figures denote the main entry of a subject

accommodations 194–199
Hawaii 198–199
Honolulu and Waikiki 76–77
Kauai 195–196
Lanai 198
Maui 197
Molokai 196
Ohau 76–77, 194–195
adventure tours 82
Ahuena Heiau 168–169
Aiea 89
airports and air services 78, **180**, 184
AJAs (Americans of Japanese Ancestry) 13, 49
Akahi Aina Hanau 174–175
Akaka Falls State Park 19, **176**
Akaka Falls (village) 176
Akatsuka Orchid Gardens 163
Ala Kahakai Trail 170
Alakai Swamp 93, 103
Alexander & Baldwin Building 61
Alexander & Baldwin Sugar Museum 140
Alexander, Samuel 43, 140
Alexander, William 100
Allerton Garden 104
aloha 10
aloha festivals 27
aloha shirts 71
Aloha Tower 56
Aloha Tower Marketplace 61, 70
ambergris 133
Anaehoomalu Beach 171
Arizona Memorial Center 67
art galleries and exhibitions
"Art Night," Lahaina 127
Contemporary Museum 57
Honolulu Academy of Arts 59
Hui No'eau Visual Arts Center 142
astronomy 159

Bad Ass Macadamia Nut Company 176
Bailey, Edward 137
Bailey House Museum 137
Baldwin, Henry 43, 140
Baldwin Beach 142
Baldwin House 127
baleen 41, 87
Bankoh Molokai Hoe 27
banks 191
banyan tree 130
Banzai Pipeline 82
Bernice Pauahi, Princess 56
bicycle tours 141, 185
"Big Island" see Hawaii
Bird, Isabella 141

birdlife 22-23
boobies 23
gamebirds 23
honeycreepers 22
iiwi 22
moa (jungle fowl) 23, 102
nene (state bird) 22-3
Newell's shearwaters 98
ooaa 22
pueo 22
waterfowl 23
Bishop, Charles Reed 56
Bishop Museum 56
Black Rock 133
boogie boards 84
botanical gardens see gardens and parks
Brick Palace 130
Brig Carthaginian II 127, 130
British royal family 66
Buddhist temples and mission buildings 63, 86, 128, 131
Buffalo Big Board Surfing Contest 89
bus services 78, 155, 185
bus tours 185
Byodo-In Temple 86

camping 188
Cape Kumukahi 162
Captain Cook Carnival 108
Captain Cook Monument 164
Captain Cook (village) 164
car rental 184–185
Chain of Craters Road 160
Chan, Charlie 57
Cherry Blossom Festival 26
Chinaman's Hat island 86
Chinatown, Honolulu 56–57, 71
Chinese New Year 26
Ching Young Village 98
Church Row 115
churches
Church of St. Raphael 104
Holy Ghost Mission Church 141
Kaahumanu Church 137
Kawaiahao Church 61, **63**
Mokuaikaua Church 169
Old Koloa Church 104
Our Lady of Sorrows 121
Palapala Hoomau Congregational Church 139
St. Andrew's Cathedral 60–61
St. Benedict's Painted Church 167
Wainee Church 131
Waioli Huiia Church 99
climate 18
coastlines 18
cockfights 13
cocoa 166
Coconut Coast 93, **94**
coffee 164–165, 166
coffee farms 166
Columbia Memorial 64
condominiums 77

Contemporary Museum 57
Cook, Captain James 35, **36–37**, 108, 164, 165
coral reefs **106–107**, 189
crafts, shopping for 71
Crater Botanical Gardens 81
Crater Rim Drive 160
Crater Rim Trail 161
credit cards 182
crime 78, 187
cruises 129, 168, 181, 184, 185
culture see people and culture

D. T. Fleming Beach 133
De Veuster, Father Damien 59, 113, **116–117**, 121
Devastation Trail 161
Diamond Head 58, 59
dinner shows 72–73
disabilities, visitors with 191
discothèques and dancing 73
diving 106, 107
Dole, James Drummond 58, 147, 148, **151**
Dole, Sanford 47, 48
Dole Cannery Square 58
Dole Plantation 82
dolphins 149, 164
drug use 187
dryland forest 148
Duke Kahanamoku 84

East-West Center 59
Edison, Thomas 129
emergencies 187
Enchanting Floral Gardens of Kula 141
Ewa 89

Falls of Clyde 59
Farmers Market, Hilo 156
Farrington Highway 89
Father Damien see De Veuster
Father Damien Museum 59
Fern Grotto 94
ferry services 184
festivals and events 26–27
Filipinos 13
film locations 93
First Night Honolulu 27
fish auction, Hilo 158
fishponds 95, 120–121, 171
Fong, Hiram 13, 88
food and drink
chocolate 166
coffee 164–165, 166
cuisines, range of 16, 74
fish and seafood 17
ices 105
luaus **16–17**, 73, 96, 128, 171
macadamia nuts 119, 157
Pacific Rim/Hawaiian

Regional cuisine 75
pineapples 48, 113, 147, **151**
plate lunches 74
poi 17
wineries 143, 163
see also restaurants
"Forbidden Island" see Niihau
forest 19, 148
Fort Elizabeth 92, **108**
Foster Botanical Garden 59
Fourth of July 27
"Friendly Isle" see Molokai

Garden of the Gods 149
"Garden Isle" see Kauai
gardens and parks 21
Akatsuka Orchid Gardens 163
Allerton Garden 104
Crater Botanical Gardens 81
Enchanting Floral Gardens of Kula 141
Foster Botanical Garden 59
Hawaii Tropical Botanical Garden 176
Hilo Tropical Gardens 156
Kapiolani Park 62
Keahua Arboretum 95
Keanae Arboretum 138
Kepaniwai Park 132, **136**
Kualoa Country Regional Park 86
Kula Botanical Gardens 141
Lawai Garden 104
Liliuokalani Gardens 156
Limahuli Garden 99
Lyon Arboretum 63
Mapulehu Glass House 121
Nani Mau Gardens 158
National Tropical Botanical Garden 104
Olu Pua Botanical Gardens 104–105
Senator Fong's Plantation and Gardens 88
Smith's Tropical Paradise 96
Wahiawa Botanic Garden 83
Waimea Falls Park 83
see also state parks
"Gathering Place" see Oahu
geology 30–31
Goat Island 86
gods and animism 34–35
golf 24–25
Greenwell Store 164
Grove Farm Homestead 94–95
Guava Kai Plantation 98

Haena State Park 99
hala (screwpine) 21
Halape Trail 161
Halawa Valley 121
Hale Kohola 133
Hale O Keawe 167

Hale O Keawe 167
Hale Pa'ahao 131
Hale Pai, Honolulu 64
Hale Pai, Lahaina 127
Haleakala 11, 18, 31, 124, **140–141**
Haleakala National Park 140–141
Haleiwa 82–83
Halemaumau 160
Halemaumau Overlook 161
Halona Blowhole 81
Hamakua Coast 176–177
Hana 139
Hana Cultural Center 139
Hanakapiai Falls 101
Hanakoa Valley 101
Hanalei 98–99
Hanalei Bay 98–99
Hanalei Center 98
Hanalei National Wildlife Refuge 98
Hanalei Scenic Lookout 98
Hanapepe 102
Hanauma Bay 81
haoles (whites) 12–13
Hapuna Beach 171
Hauola Stone 130
Hawaii 11, **152–178**
   accommodations 198–199
   restaurants 203
   sightseeing 156–178
Hawaii Experience 128
Hawaii Maritime Center 59, 61
Hawaii nei (island group) 11
Hawaii Pahinui Slack-Key Guitar Festival 27
Hawaii Pro Surfing Classic 27, 85
Hawaii Symphony Orchestra 73
Hawaii Tropical Botanical Garden 176
Hawaii Volcanoes National Park 18, **160–161**, 170
Hawaiian International Billfish Tournament 27
Hawaiian League 47
Hawaiian Open PGA Golf Tournament 26
Hawaiian Pineapple Company 48
Hawaiian Professional Championship Rodeo 27
Hawaiian Song Festival and Composing Contest 26
Hawaii's Plantation Village 89
Hawi 175
health 189–191
Hele-On bus 155
helicopter tours 92, 109, 185
Hikiau Heiau 165
hiking 191
Hilo 155, **156–158**
Hilo Macadamia Nut Festival 27
Hilo Mardi Gras 26
Hilo Tropical Gardens 156
history of the Hawaiian Islands 29–49
   annexation of Islands (1898) 48

constitutional monarchy 44
Cook, Captain James 35, **36–37**, 108, 164, 165
first inhabitants 32
geological origins 30–31
gods and animism 34–35
Great Mahele (land division) 145
immigrants 45, 48
Kamehameha I **38–39**, 59, 92, 112, 124, 130, 132, 144, 154, 168, 169, 174–75
missionaries 14, 15, 41, **42–43**
plantations 45
Polynesians 32–33, 34, 92
reciprocity with US 46–47
statehood 49
Tahitians **32–33**, 92
whaling **40–41**, 124–125
World War II 49, 67
Hoapili, Governor 137
Hokoji Lahaina Shingon Mission 131
Holy Ghost Mission Church 141
Honokaa 176
Honokaa 179
Honolua-Mokuleia Bay 132
Honolulu Academy of Arts 59
Honolulu Hale 61
Honolulu International Airport 78, 180
Honolulu Marathon 27
Honolulu and Waikiki 52, **53–79**
   accommodations 76–77
   eating out 74–75
   itineraries 52, 53
   nightlife 72–73
   practicalities 70–79
   shopping 70–71
   sightseeing 56–69
   tourist information 78–79
Honolulu Zoo 62
Hookipa Beach Park 142
Hoolulu Valley 101
horseback-riding 118, 144, 174
hotels *see* accommodations
House of the Whales 133
Hualalai 31
Hui No'eau Visual Arts Center 142
hula 14–15, 43, 119, 157
Hula O Na Keiki 27
Hulihee Palace 169
Hulopoe Beach 149
humpback whales 134–135
hurricanes 104

Iao Needle 132–133
Iao Valley State Park 132–133
iiwi 22
Iliiliopae Heiau 120, 121
International Festival of the Pacific 27
io 22
Iolani Barracks 62

Iolani Palace 61, **62**
Isaac Hale Beach Park 162
island-hopping 184

Japanese community 13
Judd, Geraint 43

Ka Lae 163
Ka Lua Na Moku Iliahi 114
Kaahumanu 42, 64
Kaahumanu Church 137
Kaanapali 133
Kaena Point State Park 89
Kahekili 124
Kahekili's Leap 149
Kahoolawe 10
Kahului 124
Kahuna Falls 176
Kailua-Kona 155, **168–169**
Kailua Pier 168
Kalakaua, King David 14, 15, **46–47**, 62, 66
Kalalau Lookout 103
Kalalau Trail 99, **101**
Kalalau Valley 101
Kalaupapa 114
Kalaupapa Lookout 119
Kalaupapa peninsula 116
Kaluakoi 112, **115**
Kaluakoi Resort and Country Club 24
Kaluanui 142
Kamakou 111
Kamakou Preserve 19, **115**
Kamalo 121
Kamehameha I **38–39**, 59, 92, 112, 124, 130, 132, 144, 154, 168, 169, 174–75
Kamehameha II 42, 93
Kamehameha III 43, 44–45, 126
Kamehameha IV 46, 66
Kamehameha V 113
Kamehameha Schools 56
Kamehameha Statue, Honolulu 61
Kamehameha Statue, Kapaau 175
Kamuela Museum 173
Kanahele, Benehakaha 109
Kanepuu 148
Kapaa-Wailua 92, **94**
Kapaau 175
Kapalua Bay Resort 133
Kapiolani 42
Kapiolani Park 62
kapu (taboo) system **33**, 42, 167
Kauai 10, **90–108**
   accommodations 195–196
   restaurants 200–201
   sightseeing 94–108
Kauai Museum 95
Kaulakahi Channel 109
Kauluapaoa Heiau 99
Kaumualii 39, 92–93
Kaunakakai 111, **115**
Kaunolu 149
Kawaiahao Church 61, **63**
Kawaikui Beach 115
Keahua Arboretum 95
Kealakekua Bay 164
Keanae Arboretum 138

Keawanui 121
Kee Beach 99
Kekela, Revd James 63
Keomuku 149
Keopuolani 39, 42, 137
Kepaniwai Park 132, **136**
Kepuhi Beach 115
Kiki o Ola 95
Kilauea Point National Wildlife Refuge 100
Kilauea (village) 100
Kilauea (volcano) 18, 31, 155, **160**
Kilauea Iki Trail 161
Kilauea Visitor Center 160
Kilohana Plantation 102
King Kamehameha Day 27
King Kamehameha's Kona Beach Hotel 169
Kipuka Puaulu 161
kites 118
Ko Olina 89
Kodak Hula Show 63
Kohala Coast 171–175
Kohala Mountains 155
Kokee Natural History Museum 103
Kokee State Park 19, **102–103**
Koloa 104
Kona Coast 164–167
Kona Coffee Festival 27
Kona Historical Society Museum 164
Kona Marina 171
Kona Village Luau 17, 171
Koolau Mountains 52
Kuakini, Governor John Adams 169
Kualapuu 112
Kualoa Country Regional Park 86
Kualoa Ranch 86
Kuan Yin Temple 63
kukui (candlenut tree) 20
Kukui Trail 108
Kula 141
Kula Botanical Gardens 141
Kure Atoll 30

La Perouse Bay 143
Lahaina 124, 125, **126–131**
Lahaina Jodo Mission 128
Lahaina-Kaanapali & Pacific Railroad 128
Lahaina Whaling Museum 131
Lahainaluna Seminary 127
Lanai 11, **146–151**
   accommodations 198
   restaurants 202–203
   sightseeing 149–151
Lanai City 148, **149**
language 28, 186
   Hawaiian 28, 186
   Pidgin 28, 186
Lapakahi State Historical Park 174
Lappert's ice-cream emporium 105
Lava Tree State Park 162
Lawai Garden 104
Lei Day 26
leis 71, **97**
leper colony 113, 114, **116–117**
Lihue 94

INDEX

Liliuokalani Gardens 156
Liliuokalani, Queen 47, 48, 66
Limahuli Gardens 99
Lindbergh, Charles A. 139
Loihi Sea Mount 31
Loko O Mokuhinia 126
London, Jack 84
lost property 187
luaus **16–17**, 73, 96, 128, 171
Lunalilo, King William 46, 63
Lydgate State Park 96
Lyman Mission House 157
Lyman Museum 157
Lyon Arboretum 63

m

macadamia nuts 119, 157
Madame Pele 35, 160
Maili 89
Makaha 89
Makaha World Surfing Championships 26, 85
Makawao **142**, 145
Makena 143
Malaekahana State Park 86
Malulani Estate Coffees of Hawaii 118
Maniniholo Dry Cave 99
Manoa Falls 19, **69**
Mapulehu Glass House 121
marine life
   coral reefs **106–107**, 189
   dolphins 149, 164
   whales 133, **134–135**
   "wholphin" 88
Mark Twain Monkeypod Tree 162
marriage licenses 65
Maui 10–11, **122–145**
   accommodations 197
   restaurants 201–202
   sightseeing 126–145
Maui Arts & Cultural Center 136
Maui (god) 34–35, 123
Maui Tropical Plantation 136–137
Mauna Kea 31, **159**
Mauna Lani 170
Mauna Loa 18, 30–31, **161**
Mauna Loa Macadamia Nut Factory and Visitor Center 157
Mauna Loa Royal Kona Coffee Mill 164–165
Mauna Loa Trail 161
Maunaloa **118**, 119
media 186
medical treatment 189, 190
mele (chants) 14–15
menehune 92, 95, **100**
Menehune Fishpond 95
Merrie Monarch festival 15, 26, **157**
Meyer, Rudolph 118
Midway Islands 30

mission buildings 42
   Hokoji Lahaina Shingon Mission 131
   Lahaina Jodo Mission 128

Lyman Mission House 157
Mission Hall, Hanalei 99
Mission Memorial Building 61
Mission Houses Museum 61, **64**
Mission Memorial Building 61
missionaries 14, 15, 41, **42–43**
moa (jungle fowl) 23, 102
Moaula Falls 120, 121
Mokihana Festival 27
Mokuaikaua Church 169
Mokuhooniki Island 121
Molokai 10, **110–121**
   accommodations 196
   restaurants 201
   sightseeing 114–121
Molokai Ka Hula Piko 27
Molokai Makahiki 26
Molokai Museum 118
Molokai Ranch Trail Rides 118
Molokai Ranch Wildlife Conservation Park 112, **119**
Molokini Excursions 128–129
Mookini Heiau 174
Mormon Temple 87
mosquitoes 189
Mount Waialeale 10, 19, 31, 90
Munro Trail 150
museums
   Alexander & Baldwin Sugar Museum 140
   Bailey House Museum 137
   Bishop Museum 56
   Brig *Carthaginian II* (whaling museum) **127**, 130
   Contemporary Museum 57
   Father Damien Museum 59
   Kamuela Museum 173
   Kauai Museum 95
   Kokee Natural History Museum 103
   Kona Historical Society Museum 164
   Lahaina Whaling Museum 131
   Lyman Museum 157
   Mission Houses Museum 61, **64**
   Molokai Museum 118
   Pacific Whaling Museum 80, **87**
   Thomas A. Jaggar Museum 161
   U.S. Army Museum of Hawaii 66–67
   U.S.S. *Bowfin* Submarine Museum and Park 68
   Waioli Mission House Museum 100
   Whalers Village Museum 133
   Wo Hing Temple **129**, 130–131
muumuu 71

n

Na Mele O Maui 27
Na Pali Coast State Park 100

Naalehu 162
Nani Mau Gardens 158
Napau Crater Trail 161
Napili Bay 133
Napoopoo Beach Park 165
Narcissus Festival 26
National Tropical Botanical Garden 104
naupaka 21, **165**
Nawiliwili Harbor 95
nene (state bird) 22–23
Newell's shearwaters 98
newspapers and magazines 186
nightlife: Honolulu and Waikiki 72–73
Niihau 10, **109**
Ninole Cove 162
North Kohala Mountains 175
Nuuanu Pali Lookout 80

o

Oahu 10, **50–58**
   accommodations 76–77, 194–195
   restaurants 199–200
   sightseeing 56–69, 80–89
Oheo Gulch 139
ohia 20
Old Courthouse, Lahaina 130
Old Koloa Church 104
Old Prison, Lahaina 131
Olu Pua Botanical Gardens 104–105
ooaa 22
opening times 191
Opaekaa Falls 96
orchids 163
Our Lady of Sorrows 121

p

Paao 33
Pacific Whaling Museum 80, **87**
Paia 142
Palaau State Park 119
Palapala Hoomau Congregational Church 139
Panaewa Rainforest Zoo 158
paniolo (cowboy) country **144–145**, 172
Papakolea Beach 163
Papohaku Beach Park 115
Parker, John Palmer 145, 154, **172–173**
Parker Ranch Historic Homes 172
Parker Ranch Visitor Center 172–173
Parker, Sam 173
parks *see* gardens and parks; state parks
Paulet, Lord George 44
Pearl Harbor 49, 53, **67**, 68
people and culture
   Filipinos and Portuguese 13, 15
   haoles (whites) 12–13
   Hawaiian culture 12
   Hawaiians 12
   hula 14–15, 43, 119, 157
   Japanese community 13

kapu (taboo) system 33, 42, 167
leis 71, 97
paniolo (cowboys) 144–145
racial mix 12–13
sovereignty movement 12
Pepeopae Bog 19
petroglyphs 150, 163, **170**
Phallic Rock 119
pharmacies 189
pidgin 28
Pihea Trail 103
Pineapple Festival 26
pineapple plantations 48, 113, 147, 151
Pioneer Inn 129
Pipiwai Trail 139
places of worship 191
plantations 45
   coffee farms 166
   Dole Plantation 82
   Guava Kai Plantation 98
   Kilohana Plantation 102
   Malulani Estate Coffees of Hawaii 118
   Maui Tropical Plantation 136–137
plantlife 20–21
   banyan tree 130
   endemic plants 21
   forest 19, 148
   kukui (candlenut tree) 20
   native plants 20, 21
   naupaka 21, **165**
   non-native plants 20–21
   ohia 20
   orchids 163
   proteas 142
   silverswords 141
poi 17
Poipu 92, **105**
police 187
Polihale State Park 105
Polihua Beach 150
Pololu Valley 175
Polynesian Cultural Center 87
Polynesians 32–33, 34, 92
Portuguese 13, 15
post offices and postal services 186, 191
Prince Kuhio Festival 26
Prince Lot *Hula* Festival 27
Princeville-Hanalei 92
"Private Island" *see* Lanai
proteas 142
Puako Petroglyph Preserve 170
public holidays 182
public transportation 185
pueo 22
Punaluu 162
Punchbowl Crater National Memorial Cemetery of the Pacific 64
Purdy, Ikua 145
Purdy's Macadamia Nut Farm 119
Puu Kukui 124, 132
Puu Loa 170
Puu O Mahuka Heiau 83
Puu Olai 143
Puu Oo 18, 160
Puu Ulaula Overlook 141
Puuhonua O Honaunau National Historical Park 167

Puuhonua O Honaunau 33, **167**
Puukohola Heiau 174
Puuopelu 172
Puupehe 149
Puuwai 109

Q

Queen Emma Summer Palace 66, 80

R

R. W. Meyer Sugar Mill 118
racial mix 12–13
Rainbow Falls 158
ranchlands 143, **144–145**, 172
restaurants 199–203
　Hawaii 203
　Honolulu and Waikiki 74–75
　Kauai 200–201
　Lanai 202–203
　Maui 201–202
　Molokai 201
　Oahu 199–200
Richards, William 43, 44
rodeos 145
Royal Coronation Bandstand 62
Royal Mausoleum 66
Russian Fort Elizabeth State Historical Park 108

S

Sacred Falls 19
Saddle Road 159
St. Andrew's Cathedral 60–61
St. Benedict's Painted Church 167
St. Joseph's Church 121
Salt Pond Beach Park 102
sandalwood 114
Sandwich Islands 36
Sandwich Islands Mission 42, 61
Sandy Beach 81
"Scottish Coast" 155
scrimshaw 87
Sea Life Park 80, **88**
self-catering 77
Senator Fong's Plantation and Gardens 88
Seven Sacred Pools 139
Shipwreck Beach 150
shopping
　Honolulu and Waikiki 70
　opening times 191
silverswords 141
skiing 159
Smith's Tropical Paradise 96
snorkeling 107, 128–129

South Point 162–163
souvenirs 70, 71
sovereignty movement 12
sperm whales 133
sports
　diving and snorkeling 106, 107, 128–129
　golf 24–25
　skiing 159
　sportfishing 178
　surfing 84–85
sportfishing 178
Spouting Horn 105
Spouting Water 55
State Capitol 60
state parks
　Akaka Falls State Park 176
　Haena State Park 99
　Haleakala National Park 140–141
　Hawaii Volcanoes National Park 18, 160–161, 170
　Iao Valley State Park 132–133
　Kaena Point State Park 89
　Kokee State Park 19, **102–103**
　Lapakahi State Historical Park 174
　Lava Tree State Park 162
　Lydgate State Park 96
　Malaekahana State Park 86
　Na Pali Coast State Park 100
　Palaau State Park 119
　Polihale State Park 105
　Puuhonua O Honaunau National Historical Park 167
　Russian Fort Elizabeth State Historical Park 108
　Waianapanapa State Park 18, **139**
Stevenson, Robert Louis 55, 64
sugar cane plantations 45
Sugar Cane Train 128
sun-protection 189
Sun Yat-sen 57
Sunrise Protea Farm 142
surfing 84–85
swampland 19

T

Tahitians 32–33, 92
Talking Island Festival 27
taxes, local 183
Tedeschi Winery 143
telephone numbers, emergency 187
telephones and faxes 186
temples
　Ahuena Heiau 168–169

Byodo-In Temple 86
Hale O Keawe 167
Iliiliopae Heiau 120, **121**
Kauluapaoa Heiau 99
Kuan Yin Temple 63
Mookini Heiau 174
Mormon Temple 87
Puu O Mahuka Heiau 83
Puukohola Heiau 174
Wo Hing Temple **129**, 130–131
Thomas A. Jaggar Museum 161
Thurston Lava Tube 161
time differences 182
tourism 49
tourist offices 192
tours 78, 79, 185
travelers' cheques 183
traveling to the Hawaiian Islands 180–181
Twain, Mark 108, 155, 162

U

Ukelele Festival 27
ukeleles 70
Ulupalakua Ranch 143
U.S. Army Museum of Hawaii 66–67
U.S.S. *Arizona* Memorial 67
U.S.S. *Bowfin* Submarine Museum and Park 68

V

vacation seasons 182
vaccinations 181
"Valley Island" *see* Maui
Vancouver, Captain George 38, 144
volcanic activity 30–31, 160–161
Volcano (village) 163
Volcano Winery 163

W

Waahila Ridge State Recreation Area 69
Wahiawa Botanic Garden 83
Waiahuakua 101
Waianae Coast 89
Waianae Mountains 52
Waianapanapa State Park 18, **139**
Waikiki *see* Honolulu and Waikiki
Waikiki Aquarium 68
Waikiki Trolley 78
Waikoloa Beach Resort 170
Wailea 143
Wailua Falls 96
Wailua River 96
Wailua Valley 96

Wailua Valley State Wayside Lookout 138–139
Wailuku 137
Waimanu Valley 177
Waimea 92, 108
Waimea Adventure Tours 82
Waimea Bay 85
Waimea Canyon 18–19, 31, 108
Waimea Ditch 95
Waimea Falls Park 73, **83**
Waimea-Kamuela 172
Waimoku Falls 139
Wainee Church 131
Waiohinu 162
Waioli Huiia Church 99
Waioli Mission House Museum 99
Waioli Tea Room 64
Waipahu 89
Waipio Valley 177
Washington Place 60
waterfalls 19
　Akaka Falls 19, **176**
　Hanakapiai Falls 101
　Kahuna Falls 176
　Manoa Falls 19, **69**
　Moaula Falls 120, **121**
　Opaekaa Falls 96
　Rainbow Falls 158
　Sacred Falls 19
　Wailua Falls 96
　Waimoku Falls 139
wedding packages 65
whale-watching 134–135
Whaler's Cove 88
Whalers Village Museum 133
whaling 40–41, 124, 133
"wholphin" 88
Wilcox, George 95
wildlife *see* birdlife and marine life
wildlife refuges
　Hanalei National Wildlife Refuge 98
　Kilauea Point National Wildlife Refuge 100
　Molokai Ranch Wildlife Conservation Park 112, **119**
wineries
　Tedeschi Winery 143
　Volcano Winery 163
Wo Hing Temple 129, 130–131
World War II 67, 109

Y

Yokohama Bay 89

Z

zoos
　Honolulu Zoo 62
　Panaewa Rainforest Zoo 158

ACKNOWLEDGMENTS

Author's Acknowledgments

The author, Emma Stanford, would like to thank the following for their help in the production of this book: Hawaiian Airlines; the U.K. office of the Hawaiian Tourist Board, Nicole Vosshall Dugan at Sheila Donnelly & Associates, Connie Wright at Avatar, Jan Loose and Lyn Utsugi.

Publisher's Acknowledgments

The Automobile Association would like to thank the following photographers, libraries and associations for their assistance in the preparation of this book.

BISHOP MUSEUM 84b (Tai Sing Loo);
BRUCE COLEMAN COLLECTION B/flap;
RONALD GRANT ARCHIVE 65a;
HAWAII STATE ARCHIVES 34b, 38b, 43, 44b, 44c, 46b, 48c;
G HOFHEIMER 74b;
THE HULTON GETTY PICTURE COLLECTION LTD 49;
THE IMAGE BANK F/Cover;
THE MANSELL COLLECTION LTD 36a, 36b, 37a, 37b;
NATURE PHOTOGRAPHERS LTD 22b (J Hancock);
NEW BEDFORD WHALING MUSEUM 40b, 41;
SPECTRUM COLOUR LIBRARY 17a, 30a, 59, 63b, 67a, 70, 71b, 144b, 145a, 176b, 179a, 181a, 187b;
E STANFORD 16b, 33, 69, 113b, 119b, 163b;
WAIMAEA VALLEY 29b;
ZEFA PICTURES Spine;

The remaining pictures were taken by **KIRK LEE AEDER** with the exception of those listed below and are held in the Association's own library (**AA PHOTO LIBRARY**)
2, 3, 6/7, 6, 10b, 11a, 11b, 13, 14b, 18a, 19a, 21b, 23a, 25b, 28a, 28b, 35b, 39, 46a, 51, 54, 55, 56a, 57b, 60, 61, 62, 63a, 64, 66, 67b, 68b, 71a, 76a, 78, 79a, 79b, 86, 87, 94a, 94b, 95, 96, 97c, 101, 103b, 105, 108, 109, 111, 114, 120, 121, 129a, 136, 137a, 137b, 138, 139, 149, 159a, 165b, 168, 170b, 179b, 180, 186a, 186b, 187a, 189, 193b (**R HOLMES**).

Contributors

Designer: Tony Truscott
Joint series editor: Josephine Perry   **Indexer:** Marie Lorimer
Copy editor: Susan Whimster   **Verifier:** Caroline Alder